D0235310

# Saddled at Sea

*Also by Josie Dew*

THE WIND IN MY WHEELS

TRAVELS IN A STRANGE STATE

A RIDE IN THE NEON SUN

THE SUN IN MY EYES

SLOW COAST HOME

# Saddled at Sea

### A 15,000-mile journey
### to New Zealand
### by Russian freighter

## JOSIE DEW

*Maps and drawings by Melanie Dew*

TIME WARNER
BOOKS

TIME WARNER BOOKS

First published in Great Britain in May 2006
by Time Warner Books

Copyright © Josie Dew 2006
Photographs copyright © Josie Dew 2006
Maps and drawings copyright © Melanie Dew 2006

The moral right of the author has been asserted.

Every effort has been made to trace the copyright holders
of work quoted in this book. Please contact the publishers
if there are any errors or omissions and these will
be put right in future editions.

All rights reserved.
No part of this publication may be reproduced, stored in a
retrieval system, or transmitted, in any form or by any means,
without the prior permission in writing of the publisher, nor be
otherwise circulated in any form of binding or cover other than
that in which it is published and without a similar condition
including this condition being imposed on the
subsequent purchaser.

A CIP catalogue record for this book
is available from the British Library.

ISBN 0 316 73262 1

Typeset in Baskerville by M Rules
Printed and bound in Great Britain by
Mackays of Chatham plc


Time Warner Books
An imprint of
Time Warner Book Group UK
Brettenham House
Lancaster Place
London WC2E 7EN

www.twbg.co.uk
www.josiedew.co.uk

For Jonnie, who died nineteen years too young

# Contents

# Acknowledgements

My biggest thank you has to go to Andrew Weir Shipping for agreeing to take both my bike and me on board the *Speybank*, and to the whole of the ship's crew for sailing me to New Zealand, not without incident. Also, very special thanks to:

Barbara Daniel (my editor, who yet again was expecting a book on New Zealand, but got one about a completely different subject instead), Simon Sheffield and Sheena-Margot Lavelle at Time Warner Book Group UK
Val Porter and Hilary Foakes
Mum and Dad
Gary Appleton and Melanie Dew
Beverley Bannister
Ian Cumming
Paul and (Dr) Angela Hallatt
Roberts Cycles: Chas, Andrew, Brian
The North Face: Keith Byrne, Éadaoin Hutchinson, Helen Samson, Tanya Bascombe, Nathalie Wheatman
Lyon Equipment Ltd: Frank Bennett
Peglers: Dave Pegler
Owen cycles: Owen, Jon, Phil, Ben
London Cycling Campaign: Rebecca Lack
Sam Dorrance at Potomac Books, Inc., Dulles, Virginia for permission to quote from *The Last of the Cape Horners* (edited by Spencer Apollonio)
Profile Books, for permission to quote from *Sea Change* by Peter Nichols

# ARCTIC
OCEAN

**North**

**2000 miles**

CANADA

75°

60°

45°

AMERIC

30°

NORTH PACIFIC
~OCEAN~

Vladivostok
(home of crew)

'tuesday'
'sunday'
date-line-of-confusion

Tropic of Cancer

15°
Hawaii

our boat
(I wish)

boobies

fat rat sea
burial

Equator

then home later

New Caledonia
'French Ammo
Dump #2'

'French Ammo
Dump #1'
Tahiti

Land
Ahoy!

overtaken
by loch Ness Tuna

Galapa
Island

spot living
torpedos

Fiji

Tonga

shark

15°

whal

Ian jumps
ship

Tropic of Capricorn

OZ

engine tries
to get mended
but
DOESN'T?

SOUTH PACIFIC
~OCEAN~

30°

(at last)
Auckland
24 December

Finish

45°

Tasmania

NEW ZEALAND

135°    150°    165°    180°    165°    150°    135°    120°    105°

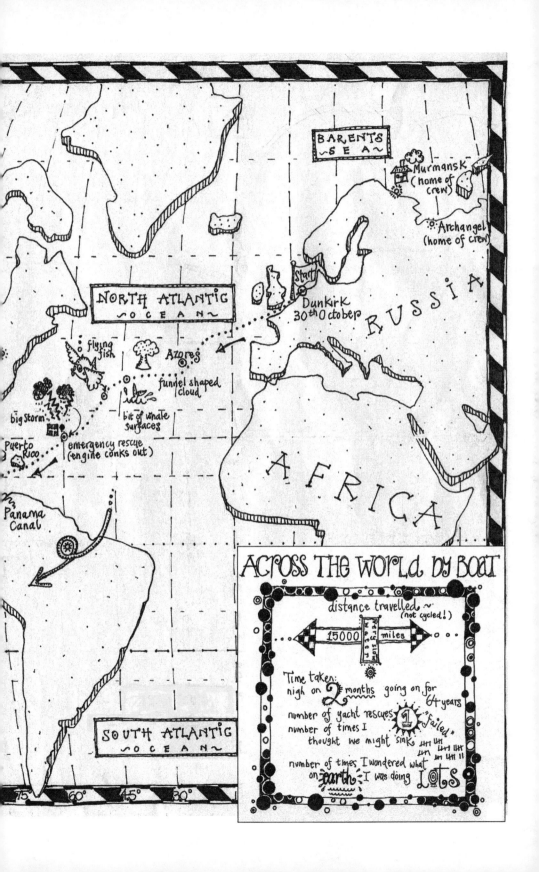

# A Backpedalling Foreword

Having just cycled a thousand miles across the blowy coastal flatlands of Holland and Germany, I was in the middle of cycling across Denmark on my way to Estonia, Latvia and Lithuania when I suddenly got the idea of cycling there via New Zealand. This may sound like a slightly illogical route to take, seeing as all I had to do to reach the Baltics was to finish riding across the tip of Denmark before sweeping swiftly across Sweden and nipping along the southern flanks of Finland to pick up the Helsinki ferry to Tallinn, but at the time it made perfect sense to me.

Ever since I've been cycling in fits and starts around the world, I have been trying to hitch a lift to distant lands on board a container ship in return for cooking or deck-scrubbing favours. Then, out of the blue in the middle of Denmark, a haphazard phone call to a shipping agency revealed that there was a non-existent chance of getting a free passage on a ship to the other side of the world.

Nothing new there, then.

Sadly, things aren't like the good old days when 'working your passage' was a viable option. Today shipping companies are all too tied up in their unions and too frightened about the tangled world of visas as well as the wild escalation of liability and the ludicrousness of people who are determined to sue, dragging a shipping company through the courts simply because they tripped over a rope on deck and broke their little toe.

So the only way to sail around the globe by very large ship these days is either by taking a cruise on one of those massively cushy floating five-star hotels (which doesn't grab my fancy or my wallet at all) or as a fare-paying passenger on one of the few freighters that allocates a handful of cabins to people who like the idea of getting nowhere fast on board an oily greasy working ship.

The idea of going to Latvia by way of New Zealand struck me in the middle of Denmark for a number of reasons. For one thing I had been trying to get to New Zealand for years but kept ending up on my bike in entirely different lands altogether – Hawaii, India, Japan, Mexico and Wales are just five that spring to mind. Maybe I need a new map. Then, while I was whipping along at a keen lick and bearing down on Esbjerg, with the smell of Swedish moose on an Arctic wind, I was summoned home to give a talk at the Edinburgh Book Festival as well as multiple points south (not easy when your head is still full of Dutch dykes and the *grønsagssuppe* smorgasbord of Danish). By the time I'd make it back to Denmark to pick up my trail to the Baltics, the weather would be closing in for a shivering Siberian wind-blasted winter, which I felt was not the most opportune time to be cycling and camping if I wanted to keep in contact with my fingertips and faculties. Also, by substituting a glorious shorts-and-shirtsleeves Kiwi summer for a northern-hemisphere winter before rolling back up in a Lithuanian direction, I might just keep up with the sun.

Then Gary the builder wanted a holiday and so I decided I would carry on where I'd left off on my slow coastal ride around the shores of England and Wales and make a start on cycling round the edges of Ireland and Scotland. In Gary's allotted two weeks off work we only managed to cycle from Rosslare to Cork (well, it was all a bit rainy and windy). I carried on for another two weeks and got as far as Killarney before I decided to put my Celtic cycle on the back burner. This was because another haphazard phone call to a shipping company (as opposed to agency) from a pay-phone in the entrance of a supermarket in Youghal had resulted in a very high chance of procuring a berth for both me and my bike on a Russian container ship to New Zealand in two months' time. It was not going to be a free passage, mind you, but by way of some high-spirited bargaining (easy to do when you can't hear a thing down the line, thanks to the rattling din of a wild flurry of Irish wheel-locked shopping trolleys screeching past your ear) it would end up costing little more than an airfare to Down Under. And instead of 26 hours of airborne, air-conditioned, air-locked, seat-belted tedium with the possibility of a serving of deep-vein thrombosis on the side, I would have five weeks, two oceans, one Panama Canal and a flotilla of South Pacific islands of excitement. Plus three two-to-three-course meals a day. Five weeks trapped on board a ship with a cargo of Russian seamen. Surely things don't come much better than that?

# 1

# *In at the Deep End*

*Dunkirk, 30 October 2003*

When I first clapped eyes on the ship that is to take me 15,000 miles across the world, my heart sank. While I didn't expect, or hope, to find anything like a gleaming white liner, the MV *Speybank* has, to my mind, something of the hard-worked look of a world-weary tub. But then if I had been battling across the oceans of the world for the past twenty-odd years, I think I would be looking a little ragged around the edges as well. I realise a smattering of rust does not mean that a ship is unseaworthy, yet I still feel slightly concerned about how we will make it across two oceans. Good thing I enjoy swimming as I believe the water can be quite invigorating at this time of year. Maybe I should investigate buying a wetsuit. There again, maybe I should just bail out now and scamper off with my tail between my legs and catch the ferry back over to Dover. I could be home and dry by tonight.

It's been a bit of a busy day so far. I was up at 4.30 a.m. to cram the last of my survival camping gear (porridge pans and the like) into my panniers before I took off on my bike on a mad dark pre-dawn dash along unnervingly icy country lanes to the station. With frozen face and fingers, I heaved my overladen steed into the big and roomy caged guard's van of a draughty slam-door train (sadly a dying breed) for a commuter-crammed shunt to Waterloo. Once disgorged, I took off for a fast last pedal through the London gridlock over Tower Bridge (lovely view!) to join a small shipment of shipping people.

These shipping people were located in the offices of Andrew Weir Shipping, the company that would be setting me a-sail and asunder with Bank Line, their round-the-world service. When I first heard the name Bank Line, I pictured ships loaded with money and full of exciting bomb-proof safes with intricate codes and automated voices alerting you to move from the head of the interminable queue to 'Caaashierrr Nuuumberrr 4, please!' But I had the wrong sort of bank in mind, as Bank Line refers more to riverbank than high street bank, which I suppose is more fitting for vessels of a watery nature.

Bank Line owns four ships: the big river-sounding *Arunbank*, *Foylebank* and *Teignbank* – and *Speybank*. Each ship takes about four months to trundle round the world, loading and discharging a mind-boggling amount of cargo at places like Tahiti, Samoa, Auckland, New Caledonia, Fiji, Vanuatu, the Solomon Islands, Papua New Guinea, Singapore and Malaysia before returning to an even more hectic session among the multi-ports of Europe via Suez.

Anyway, I had been summoned to Andrew Weir Shipping HQ at 09.00 hours to meet Sado Omer Abdi, the Somalian passenger-booking manager (I had originally spoken to her from that distant public phone hutch in the Youghal supermarket), plus the three other captives, I mean passengers, who were going to accompany me into the unknown. I was a bit apprehensive about coming face to face with three complete strangers with whom I was to be con-fined for five weeks on the ocean wave. And, what's more, having to sit with them to eat three meals a day. What if I didn't like them? In such an enclosed space within such an enforced environment, it could all get a bit tricky. Oh well, best to cross that bridge when I got to it. For now, all I knew about my fellow strangers was the little I had managed to glean from Sado: they were all quite old. And presumably, quite rich, as travelling round the world, or even halfway round the world, by container ship as a full fare-paying piece of cargo is not cheap. The only other information I managed to extricate from Sado (whom I liked a lot, by the way, not least because she had agreed to sell me a heavily discounted fare when so many of her ilk had slammed the port door in my face) was that two of the people comprised a married couple who had travelled round the world on the *Speybank* three years before. From my deductions this meant either that the *Speybank* was a cornucopia of delights, or that they were gluttons for punishment. All I knew about the third person was that he was a man.

I found the offices of Andrew Weir Shipping sitting among the rather intimidating (for someone whose clothing was already splattered in bike oil) and swanky location of Royal Mint Court. Things didn't start off on a great footing, because the security man in the Buckingham Palace-like sentry box presumed I was one of those kamikaze lycra-nut cycle couriers (which I used to be – albeit a very sensible traffic-light-stopping one, of course), to be treated brusquely and at arm's length. Not without difficulty, I managed to convince him that I wasn't an oily scumbag or a terrorist and that I had an appointment in Dexter House that required my taking my bike into the building as it was packed to the rafters not with POBs ('packages on board', for those of you who are not couriers) or WMDs but with my various gaffer-taped worldly possessions. There followed a lot of walkie-talkie talk before I was permitted to proceed with caution towards another walkie-talkie security man in Dexter House who would vet my bike for explosives or shiny floor-soiling oil, or whatever it was that might get up their noses.

Fortunately, at this stage in the ponderous procedures my parents intercepted me. They had been to visit some friends overnight in London and had said they would try to get an early start to meet me in Mint Court so that they could bid their farewells and make sure I was really going (I was supposed to have gone about two to three weeks earlier but the boat had been delayed). They engaged the security man in some lively banter and, as they looked a lot more respectable than their dishevelled Goretex-clad daughter, they soon managed to put him at ease. My bike was wheeled into the spotless foyer and Mum and Dad acted as very effective bicycle guard-dogs on the ground floor while I went shooting up the building in mirrored lifts.

The moment I walked into the reception of Andrew Weir Shipping and came face to face with Sado and a small gathering of boat-passenger type people, I felt severely underdressed. Sado, who unlike me was dressed like a woman, introduced me to a very well-spoken man, as tall as a door, with a shiny pate and a friendly face. This was Ian Cumming, whom I gauged to be hovering somewhere in the hinterland of his sixties. He was immaculately turned out in blazer and tie, gold cufflinks, flashy gold Omega watch and polished shoes. All a bit daunting for a scruff-bag like me. Although he was almost twice my size, I had this innate feeling as he firmly shook my hand that I was going to like him.

Alongside Ian stood another tall man holding a Hackett's bag and a copy of the *Financial Times* tucked under his arm. Apart from his props and his impeccably clean brown brogues, he looked like he had just stepped out of the ominous gas-lit, fog-filled streets of a Dickensian London, cloaked as he was in a dashing Sherlock Holmes-type cape. Or he could have stridden straight off the moors following a spot of grouse shooting. His name was Michael Melville and I soon gathered he was a friend of Ian's, come for a free lunch and a day out to Dunkirk and back to check out the *Speybank* and to get a taster of what this cargo ship travel lark was all about.

Sitting in the cushy seats of reception was a medium-to-elderly couple called Llewellyn and Eleanor – him in tie and jacket, her in fancy frock. When talking to Ian, I had noticed them out of the corner of my eye sitting full back in the sumptuousness of the sofa with legs crossed, giving me the once-over. And as I shuttled across to say hello, togged out head to toe in my North Face wet-weather repelling garb with a black Cordura Ultimate3 L Plus Ortlieb handlebar bag slung recklessly across my shoulder, I could see them thinking: *Good God! What have we got here?*

Fortunately there was no time for small talk as Sado, suddenly realising that time was running away, ushered us in a great fluster of excitement downstairs to pile into the waiting van that was to take us to Folkestone to catch the Shuttle to Calais. Among a small shipment of phenomenally hefty suitcases belonging to the others, my bike was wedged into the back. Multiple eyebrows were raised at the amount of weighty panniers I had unhitched from the various racks.

'You surely can't cycle with *that* many bags?' said Dermot, our multi-earringed and ponytailed Irish driver.

'I can,' I said, 'but slowly – unless I'm going downhill.'

There was just time for a bracing bout of hugs with Mum and Dad. Mum looked quite worried.

'How long do you think you'll be away, Jose?' she asked, not for the first time.

'I don't know,' I said, 'but don't worry, I'll be fine. As long as we don't sink!'

Mum grimaced, gave me another quick hug, and then we were off, scything a path through an ocean of traffic heading south on the A2.

As I hadn't been in a vehicle for weeks (I'm a bit allergic to cars – I like my fresh air) I sat up near the front with Dermot, who generously opened the window a little bit for me, like people do for a dog. Dermot was a good laugh and he told me all about Dublin and his music (he was a musician) and his girlfriend (an artist who lived in a studio). I thought what a shame it was that he wasn't coming on the boat too, because I felt he was more my sort than the shiny-shoed brigade in the back. Every now and then I caught snippets of conversation that drifted up to the front. One of them was telling a story about some man who was driving an Aston Martin at full pelt down the motorway and was pulled over by the police. When he was asked for his name, the driver replied, 'Bond.' 'I wouldn't try getting funny with me, sir' replied the constable, but when he saw the driver's licence with the name Bond on it, he let him off. This tale was greeted with a hoot of laughter from the back. Dermot glanced at me and said, 'I t'ink we must have missed the funny part!'

Llewellyn and Eleanor seemed to be doing most of the talking – though a lot more him than her. Somewhere near Ashford, I overheard Llewellyn going on about the annoyance of sloppy speech. 'You must have noticed,' he said to Ian and Mr Hackett's Bag Man, 'how these days everyone – well, not *every*one – seems to add all these completely superfluous words to their conversation, like "basically" and "yer know" and "like" and "absolutely" and "know what I mean". If yer know wot I mean! It's only something that's come about in recent years. It's mostly young people who say these things, *yer know!*' More laughter.

Dermot, who had overheard this too, glanced at me again, and pulling a face, raised his eyes. I returned the look, while steadily getting more worried about just what I was letting myself in for, not to mention opening my mouth.

But for most of the trip Llewellyn was telling the other two about his and Eleanor's experience three years earlier when they sailed round the world on the *Speybank*. It seemed that, along with hitting huge rolling seas that shouldn't have been there soon after leaving Europe, they had fallen out with almost all the other passengers (mostly American) on board. It got so bad they even had to sit at different tables at meal times as they couldn't bear to look at, let alone talk to, each other. 'We called it the Voyage from Hell!' said Eleanor. 'It was character forming, if nothing else.'

Sounds lovely.

During the long journey south, Dermot pulled off at a service station for his charges to take a toilet and leg-stretching break. While the shiny-shoed brigade disappeared into the cafeteria for morning coffee, I found a little sheltered nook outside to sit in a burst of watery sunshine and began to fill up the first few pages of my fat-leaved notebook. At one point I looked up to see a young mum with a lower back tattoo and a pushchair ask the time of a semi-comatose teen with a nose ring and pit-bull eyes. He just shrugged, tucked his hands in his armpits and slouched lower on the bonnet of the black Fiesta where he was sitting. The young mum sloped off, looking far from impressed.

I had never been in the Channel Tunnel before and I wasn't quite sure what to expect, apart from maybe feeling stuck in a sealed tube beneath an awful lot of water. As it turned out, it felt like being stuck in a sealed tube beneath an awful lot of water. The tube was actually like a very long silvery, artificially lit, horizontal-shifting lift. People were instructed to remain seated in their vehicles and to shut all windows (presumably to keep any water out), which only added to the sense of claustrophobia. I couldn't help thinking how easy it must be for the tunnel to spring a leak. After all, most things leak if you stick them under water for long enough. Like . . . well, inflatable camping mats (I've had a lot of flooded tents in the past). And look at whales; even they have to come up for air from time to time and to blow out several bucket-loads of water that seem to have percolated in. So in this vein, I feel it's an oversight on the part of the Channel Tunnel operators not to issue each occupant with a snorkelling mask and an oxygen tank and a set of water wings. I always believe it's best to be prepared for the worst in this world.

About twenty minutes passed and then, before I knew it, we had popped out the other side. Just like that. We had left an island nation, entered another country, and had no sign of sea. How uninteresting is that? I think I'll take the boat next time. Tends to be a more bracing experience.

Now we had to get from Calais to Dunkirk. What would have taken a good morning's cycle, with lots of stops in *boulangeries* and patisseries and market places and cemeteries and *centre villes*, took a white transit van on the autoroute a very unexhilarating half an hour at most. We ploughed bonnet first into the most unbecomingly industrial part of Dunkirk – all odoriferous and sinister metal and chemical manufacturing plants and factories and flaring oil refineries spewing scary amounts of lung-killing substances into the air. And then we were in the slagheap section of the port, rearing up over a bridge and a slop of filthy water. I looked down upon what I thought was the corpse of a container vessel waiting to be broken up for scrap metal in the ship-breaking knacker's yard. But then I heard Dermot declare, 'There we are, ladies and gents – home sweet home for the next five weeks!'

I thought he was having us on, but then to my alarm I espied the big, painted letters spelling SPEYBANK daubed in white across the hull's blackened rust-bled aft. All ships suffer from surface rust, but to someone who was about to launch into the unknown on their first-ever crossing of the world's two largest oceans, it was not a particularly reassuring sight.

Five minutes later we had all piled out on to Port Est and were standing alongside the hulk of the hull. This was so huge it appeared to block out half the visible world. The rest of the ship towered over our heads, leaving us shivering in its cold, wintry shadow. 'It's deteriorated a lot in three years,' I heard Llewellyn remark to Ian.

With a strange mix of intense uncertainty and bristling excitement, I gazed up and down the 174-metre length of the *Speybank*, trying not to read too much into the rust streaks that scrambled up the walls of the hull like ivy. Almost as transfixing as my new home was the frenzied activity of the straddle-carriers – the massive and awkwardly ungainly vehicles that hurtled up and down the quay like demented insects, straddling and then locking and lifting the huge rectangular containers to the various ships tethered to the quay.

The *Speybank*'s purser, David Ball, a small round man with a squinched face encased in a carpeting of greyish facial hair, appeared on the scene. He shook everyone's hands, except mine. Maybe my shoes weren't shiny enough. And then he said some words of greeting, most of which were drowned out by the crashing clamour of the rushing straddle-carriers and the rumble of the reverberating engines and the container-clamping hullabaloo of the hingeing cranes.

I presumed that we would all have to carry our own bags up the grimy, skew-whiff greasy gangway. But oh no. When he saw me hefting my bike out of the van and shouldering it towards this slippery obstacle of escalation, David stopped me in my tracks. Apparently the procedure was for all baggage to be caught in a very large net (like one might a buffalo) and hoisted by crane to the upper echelons of the ship. I was a little dubious about entrusting my precious wheels to such forms of possibly hull-whacking elevation (one has to treat the tender region of one's bottom bracket with all due respect, you know). On top of that, I had two very easy-to-smash wing mirrors protruding half a mile from either brake hood. But then I thought, if I can't entrust the Russian crew with the relatively simple operation of capturing an inert bicycle in a net and winching it to safety, then what the devil am I doing thinking I can trust them to sail me to New Zealand without sinking? Such little faith would not bode well for either a smooth crossing or my blood pressure. So there and then I abandoned to the wind any preconceptions I might have had about the safe hoistings of netted bicycles and, without further dally, relinquished my treasured steed to a very good-looking Russian in a white boilersuit.

And so on to the *Speybank* we climbed and up the layers of stairs we clambered. These stairs were enclosed in a bare and basic stairwell of the crew's living quarters – quarters that sat like a big white block of flats, known as the 'superstructure', situated towards the back of the ship. I worked my way up to the fifth level (as instructed by Purser David) and various Russians bade me good day as they trotted up and down the stairs.

By this stage Purser David had disappeared on to the fourth floor to show Ian to his cabin. Llewellyn and Eleanor knew where to go to find theirs because they had already spent four long months on the *Speybank*. Obviously not ones for variation, they had requested the same cabin as before, one called 'Honiara' (could that by any chance be the capital of the Solomon Islands?), which was situated just along from the captain's at the front of the superstructure, over-looking the bow. I kept going, down to the bottom of a short and narrow fore-aft corridor past a door marked 'Private – captain's store'. Stores of what, one wonders? Toilet rolls? Secret food supplies? Clean underpants? Inflatable dolls?

I located my cabin on the portside wing opposite a door that led into a lounge area and bar (useful if I want to drown my sorrows in drink). It was adjacent to a heavy door that required you to lose half your shoulder as a battering ram in order to open it and which led out to the outside fire escape-like steps that ran up to the bridge and down past a suspended lifeboat and on to the main deck and poop. I was pleased about this. I always like to be located close to a handy evacuation point. Tends to help in those moments when you think you're going under.

My cabin seems to be called 'Rabaul', which I believe is the chief town and port of the island of New Britain in Papua New Guinea. Head-hunting land. Lends my cabin a rather exotic edge, don't you think? So I feel good about this too, as it would be a bit disappointing to find myself sailing the seven seas ensconced in a room called Basingstoke.

Whatever it's called, it's a lot bigger than I expected. For some reason I was imagining not much more than a ropy old hammock strung up in a dark corner, but maybe I've spent too much time in the past wandering through the darkened creaking depths of eighteenth-century battleships. This is all very different. I have a cabin that is more like two cabins. For some lucky reason I've been issued with a double cabin instead of a single (two for the price of one!). Perhaps so few people want to travel on this particular ship that there is a surplus of empty cabins. Whatever the reason, Sado has boosted me up a notch from a lonesome single to a . . . well, lonesome double.

I have two rooms in which to swing cats – or in my case, bicycles. One of these rooms contains two bunks, a fixed cupboard and set of sliding-runner drawers with fasteners. Wedged in a corner sits a handily compact vacuum toilet-cum-shower unit, with just enough room to swing a loofah. A sticker stuck to the wall over the toilet informs the user in no uncertain terms that:

ONLY THE PRODUCT OF BODILY FUNCTIONS AND TOILET TISSUE TO BE FLUSHED DOWN THESE TOILETS (NO DETERGENTS, PAPER TOWELS, ETC).

Well, in that case I shall take particular care not to dispose of any etceteras down my vacuum. Etceteras have got me into a spot of trouble in the past and I'd rather not go down that road again, if you don't mind.

Set into the wall at the far end of my bunkroom is a rectangular porthole thickly smeared with salty, sooty gunk. All I can see out of it is dirty-grey murk. The porthole is secured with a hefty metal butterfly bolt. Despite straining my wrist to try to open it, and nearly turning apoplectic in the process, I fail. Never mind, I've got plenty of time on my hands to devise a means to prise it open. At least the porthole in the other room functions and it's currently supplying me with a plentiful dose of all-pervasive chemically blown power station 'fresh' air. The view from this window is of a mountainous slagheap. Beyond rises an industrial plant's forest of belching chimneys.

The 'day room', as I believe Purser David referred to it, is a bit bigger than my sleeping quarters. It measures about two-and-a-bit strides by four. Big strides too, like John Cleese's, but in a small way as I don't have half as many fathoms to my leg length. In this room there is a heavy chair and a heavy low, long table, to both of which I've wedged and tethered my steed in the name of high-seas sturdiness. There's also a heavy hard couch (piled high at the moment with a mountain of avalanching panniers) and a fixed desk with drawers containing a shortwave radio and a small blue hairdryer (useful for taming Atlantic storm-soaked manes – not that I'm imagining we're going to have anything other than sun-drenched mill ponds to cross, of course). On the sideboard, plonked on special cross-hatch non-slip mats, sit a kettle and a bowl of fruit, the contents of which I seem to have devoured already. There is also a small fridge (containing a carton of long-life milk, so far untouched), on top of which perches a TV and video. How very upmarket. I don't remember seeing such luxuries in the crew's quarters of the *Victory*. It's going to feel a bit hard going back to my tent after this.

Not long after dumping our kit in our cabins, us fresh-out-of-the-Tunnel mob were ushered downstairs for a late lunch. The crew had long since eaten, so it was just us lot and a table covered with a white tablecloth, a basket of sliced white bread, a few slabs of plated cold meat, a row of bottled condiments, and two bowls of salad. One bowl contained coleslaw; the other was mostly shredded red cabbage and onions. Not being a meat person, I had salad. Quite a lot of it, actually, as the others weren't too taken by all that cabbage.

Ian wanted a glass of wine. In fact he was very anxious about being able to obtain a regular supply of wine for the voyage. 'I get through half a bottle a day,' he told me. 'It's my medicine.' When he asked me what my favourite tipple is and discovered that I don't drink, he said, 'What a very dull life you must lead!'

'I try to make up for it in other ways,' I said.

As for Llewellyn, he kept correcting my nautical terms. 'Not *boat*!' he said, looking heavenwards, 'Ship'. 'Not *back*!' he said, 'Aft'. 'Not *floor*!' he said, 'Deck'. Well, it does take a while to get into the swing of things. And anyway, all the others have had their own boats in the past so are *au fait* with sailing lingo.

After lunch I explored a few floors . . . sorry, decks. My major concern was to find what means there are for exercising on board this boat. Whoops, ship. Way down in the bowels of the vessel near the engines I was surprised to find a gymnasium – though gymnasium is perhaps a little too grand a word for it. The room was windowless and airless and lit by a few swinging striplights, one of which was broken and buzzed annoyingly like an army of angrily trapped hornets. The grubby walls and floor were littered with oily rags, cigarette butts, mugs containing thick and congealed remnants of coffee, empty beer bottles, crunched-up cigarette packets, all of which lent the room more the makings of a mausoleum than a gymnasium.

Over in the corner I found a punctured basketball, which I tried to lob through a basketball loop. Third time lucky. Then I picked up a bald ping-pong paddle bat and attempted to rap-tap a ping-ponging ball up and down on its surface, but because the ball was dented it kept zinging off at unpredictable angles. Next I launched myself on to the exercise bike and, for a few humdinging moments, cycled like a person possessed until I noticed the crank was bent. Not good news for dicky knees. Then I hung myself off a high solitary bar of horizontal metal suspended at a rakish angle from the wall and did a few feeble pull-ups until my arms went shaky. So I hung off it by my legs instead while casting an upside-down eye over the Mr Universe barbells held together by gaffer tape and bits of wire. I decided in the name of life-preservation to leave them be. And that was my thorough workout, hit on its head in a jiffy.

Further towards the engine room, I found another one of those heavy, lever-operated doors like you get in submarines, labelled with the word 'swimming pool'. Well, what a discovery! As I nego-tiated the muscle-wrenching levering of the lever, I excitedly anticipated a scene of aquamarine water glinting in the tropical sunshine of a large kidney-shaped pool, surrounded by gleaming white loungers just asking to be flopped upon in a heavenly sun-worshipping manner of gay abandon. Either that or I was about to release the seal of a forbidden hatch that would allow half the Channel to come flooding in.

Reality was a very different kettle of fish. For what greeted me, once I'd relocated my dislocated shoulder back into its joint (those submarine doors are a bugger for opening), was a bluish-green tank, about the size of your average greenhouse, but completely devoid of water. It was walled in on two sides upon which someone had painted a mural of an octopus and shark. The empty fag packets and booze bottles had worked their way into here too, so that the whole area had more in common with an illicit behind-the-bike-shed scene (though thankfully minus the used condoms – I'd be a bit worried if I found those as well) than with a place of clean-living recreation. Tucked away in the corner, past a scary-looking toilet with a door that didn't close, was a wooden entrance to a sauna. I was sorely tempted to take a peek inside but I lost my nerve lest I found a Russian sailor reclining in a wholesome state of nakedness and demanding that I flagellate him with a painful tuffet of birch twigs. I mean, how could one say no?

Climbing back up the stairs I bumped into Purser David and asked him if the swimming pool ever saw water. 'It doesn't tend to get filled until we reach the Caribbean,' he said. 'We could fill it up earlier, if you want, but as it's seawater you might die of hypothermia – the Atlantic can get rather cold in winter.'

Just at that moment one of the doors banged on the next level up and a man in jeans and scuffed white trainers came trotting down the stairs. He looked fiftyish, short, a little broad in beam and with more beard than hair. His voice, if not his looks, won me over in a trice: Highland Scottish, enchantingly kilted in lilts.

'Hi there!' he said, pumping my hand in hearty greeting. 'I'm Chris Tran, nice tae meet ye!'

Chris, it turned out, was the elusive fifth passenger that Sado had briefly mentioned but she hadn't been sure if he was coming or not. He'd been lurking around Dunkirk for about a week, apparently kicking his heels and bored out of his mind, waiting for the tardy *Speybank* to make its grandiose appearance.

Next point for exploration was the bridge. Up here I found Ian and Hackett's Bag Man and Llewellyn and Eleanor milling with an air of authority about the decidedly dated-looking Russian equipment. All the big, jackpot machine-like handles and heavy old-style telephone receivers and clumpy switches and dials and a general lack of computers and the faded Russian-script labels bore a resemblance to the control panels of battleship bridges that you see in black-and-white movies of the First World War. Hackett's Bag Man kept strolling around, hands clasped behind back, slowly repeating the phrase, 'Well, well, well. You're going to have a marvellous time!' From that I read: *Bloody glad I'm not coming with you chaps! This ship's a joke!* Then Dermot appeared and said, 'Got to go, mate,' and whisked Hackett's Bag Man off to the van to channel him back to England through the tunnel.

Gazing out of the front windows of the bridge, I became transfixed by the intricate and highly skilled loading of the ship's cargo. It wasn't just the expertise of the Russians manning the on-board container-dangling cranes that was so mesmerising (though that was quite captivating enough in itself), but the size of the five hatches and holds and the contents that were being dispatched into them: spanking new trucks, crawler tractors, diggers, 4 × 4s. It was all so enthralling that I had to climb up to the top deck that sits on top of the bridge (known as the monkey deck) to have a proper look and hang over the sides to see just what was going on.

The *Speybank* and her sister ships ply something of a unique trade for vessels flying the Red Ensign, because they are not just container ships; they are multi-purpose vessels. They even have a ro-ro ramp, clamped like an afterthought to the starboard stern. This, along with the eleven purpose-built deep tanks suitable for the carriage of more than 6,000 tonnes of vegetable oils, and the five hatches for conventional, dry-bulk and 'unitised' cargo, plus the facilities for refrigerated containers and the lifting ability for up to 80 tonnes, which is just the job for fitting into the space on deck what's called 'project' cargo (trawlers, yachts, bungalows, refinery equipment, oil-drilling rigs, wind generators and so on, not to mention the towers of containers), means that these ships are all incredibly flexible. They are able to load anything and everything, including vehicles of every description (trucks, buses, tractors, railway carriages, tanks, Herculean earth movers with wheels the size of houses), plus an enormous range of construction materials such as steel in all conceivable shapes and forms, sawn timber, pipes, logs, cable reels, wire rope and rubber.

I never realised what a logistical nightmare and finely honed and detailed process this cargo-ship conveying business is. I'd always thought you just shoved a few things into a container, humped it on board and off you went. But it's slightly more complicated than that, at least for the Bank Line voyages, and involves never-ending storage challenges amidst its 'multi-port rotations', as it seems to be known. On top of that, there may be more or less of something than expected, it may not be available on arrival, the weather may intervene and turn complex schedules pear-shaped, or, in the case of project cargo for instance, it may be a completely different size to the original specifications. In this trade there must be an awful lot of heads being banged against hulls.

The southbound cargo varies hugely from the northbound. This is because the outward trade from Europe to the South Pacific is characterised by mind-boggling diversity since these tropical islands are so geographically remote. While they generally have pot-loads of natural resources, they have mostly been unable to develop any substantial manufacturing bases. So they remain reliant upon imports not only for capital goods but also for many of their daily necessities. The typical cargo on a southbound run includes vehicles of all sorts, building materials, salt, malt and other basic foodstuffs for baking and brewing, supermarket and trade-store supplies, fertilisers, insecticides, pesticides (watch out all you butterflies and bees!), agricultural commodities, industrial consumables and European luxuries ranging from high-quality malt whiskies and champagne to cheese, pâté and perfume.

Northbound cargo is a whole different box of tricks. One of the staple exports from Papua New Guinea and the South Pacific is copra – coconut flesh. The copra is extracted by hand in a very labour-intensive process, dried in the sun or by hot air and then in Europe the coconut oil is extracted from it. Carried along with all that copra are natural rubber and palm oil and cocoa and coffee and charcoal and tea and spices and tuna and timber and logs. And, after calling at Singapore, a good bit of machinery too for good measure.

When you think of all that sea and weather and distant lands, most boats must have pretty interesting lives (apart from maybe those ones that tend to loll around in fancy marinas doing very little for most of the year). The *Speybank* seems to be no exception. It is one of sixteen identical ships built in Turku in Finland in 1983 as icebreaking freighters for the Russian Navy in the Barents Sea and was originally called *Okha* after the city, a boom town for the oil industry, on the northern tip of Sakhalin Island. (The name Okha comes from the local dialect and means 'bad water', which doesn't sound like a particularly auspicious name for a ship – just as well it's turned into a riverbank.) Bank Line acquired their four ships from three Russian companies in 1995 and extensively refurbished and converted them for service in the South Pacific.

The ships were designed for the Arctic trade and although they have since had their icebreaker bows replaced (if not a lot of the dated Russian military hardware), they still retain many of the inherent features and idiosyncrasies that you might expect to find on bitterly cold-weather ships, such as seas of insulation, a totally enclosed bridge (most ships have open wings) and an intriguing heating system with a mind of its own. Oh, and a sauna and an indoor shed-sized swimming pool.

As for the Russian crew – most of whom hail from either Archangel, Murmansk or Vladivostok – they all transferred with the ships so now it's mostly only the senior officers who are British. In the *Speybank*'s case, the captain, chief engineer, purser and third officer are British. There are a couple of young Irish cadets on board too. All the rest of the twenty-eight-strong crew are Russian.

I could quite happily have spent the rest of the day watching all the port's frenetic activity from the eyrie of the monkey deck. But at four o'clock I was summoned to the muster point of the saloon bar by Purser David to be drilled in emergency procedures with the other passengers. I found it all quite complicated as I'm never very good at remembering sequences of numbers. Apparently, if we hear a continuous ringing of the alarm bells supplemented by four long blasts on the ship's whistle, repeated as required, then that means emergency stations and a clean pair of underpants. But if we hear seven or more short blasts and one long blast (or was that one short blast followed by seven long blasts?) on the ship's whistle and alarm bells, repeated as required, then that means water wings to the ready and take to lifeboat stations. However, we aren't allowed to abandon ship until we have verbal instruction from the Master of Ceremonies – or whatever the other name is for captain.

This left me slightly worried and with one or two questions up my sleeve. I mean, what if the captain has already jumped overboard? Or what if, in his haste, he slips on a banana skin, tumbles down some steps, bangs into a trapdoor which swallows him whole, leaving the remaining crew mystified by his absence? Are we then to hang around nervously twiddling our thumbs waiting as the ship goes down beneath us, or are we permitted to take our life into our own hands by trying out a high-five flying dive followed by a spot of panicky breaststroke?

I posed these thoughts to Purser David. There was an awful silence for a moment as the gathered heads of purser and passengers turned to stare at me. I gave a meek little grimace-smile back. I was then ordered to walk the plank. Actually I wasn't. My punishment was even worse. I was simply ignored.

As soon as we had been dismissed from our muster point, I stomped off in an offended sulk back up to the monkey deck, thinking: *Silly name, there aren't any monkeys up here anyway.* But then maybe it did once have monkeys, a whole howling jungle of them, swinging on their Tarzan twines as they crossed the Barents Sea. Well, you never know. The world's full of surprises.

I didn't have the hump for long, though, because the views from the monkey deck in the dark were just too good to dwell on lesser matters. Things were crashing and banging with containers dangling and hanging and spotlights were swivelling and stevedores shouting. Although the *Speybank*'s gross tonnage is barely 20,000 tonnes (a lot of the big freighters are 80,000 tonnes or more), it still looked like a massive toppled skyscraper stretched out before my eyes. And with all those cranes and hulking great holes of dark holds into which containers and men and machines disappeared, it was a night-time construction site on the grandest of scales.

Chris came up to join me and he seemed about as excited as me with the action-jammed scene. As we gripped the railings, up in the front stalls of the monkey deck, he told me a little about himself and how he had come about joining the *Speybank*.

At the beginning of January at the beginning of this year, he woke up to find it blowing another Scottish gale again. Rain hammered the windows. It was horribly dark and cold. He thought: There's got to be a better place than this in winter. So, there and then, he decided he would emigrate to New Zealand, despite never having been there in his life. His brother, George, lives there though. Has done for quite a few years. George is 62 – exactly ten years older than Chris. On that stormy January morning, Chris decided he would pack in his job as a physics teacher in a local school (he started out life as an electrical engineer – worked for quite a while as a television sound engineer for the BBC) and rent out his house. A big truck dumped a 40-foot container in his garden. He spent months boxing up the contents of his life, which seems to have included an awful lot of aerials and radio equipment – he's a radio ham nut, much like my sister-in-law Mel's 'Golf Four Bravo Echo November' dad had been. Chris even bought a pallet truck to lift his crates around hydraulically. He is divorced but has a long-term (ten years) partner, Pippa, a South African with a jewellery and basket-making business. She took a while to take on board Chris's shockingly sudden brain-storming plan. Seems quite keen now, though. She's going to fly out to Auckland in December. They're going to get married in New Zealand in July and Chris wants a Maori woman to sing at the wedding.

'I'm generally quite a calm person,' Chris told me, 'but I'm totally bored of Dunkirk – or *Dull*-kirk, as my daughter calls it! I'm so angry about the delay. I just want to get going. We're already over two weeks later than the original departure dates. All the bookings I've made in New Zealand – like the ferry crossing I've got reserved across the Cook Strait – are getting totally messed up. At this rate, Pippa's going to be in Auckland before me. And it's going to give me hardly any time to find a house to rent in Upper Hutt before I start teaching. I feel like shouting at the ship to get a bloody move on!'

Hmm. Not a happy man.

At five-thirty Chris said, 'I guess we'd better go doon. There's supposed to be pre-dinner drinks in the bar.'

Oh no! I'd rather stay up here. I'm never very good at bar-drink mingling. I always feel too confined. But I went down anyway. I'd better look like I'm playing the part on my first day. I didn't fancy doing any more plank-walking.

By the time I made it into the bar, Chris had changed out of his jeans into more trouser-like trousers and put on a shirt. I was still in cycling kit (my wardrobe – pannier – repertoire is a little limited, you know, and anyway, I thought this was meant to be a 'working ship' and that you didn't have to get all togged up in your glad rags). But I had at least made an effort to wash the oily grime off my hands. So that was something. Ian was looking even more dashingly flash in the gold cufflink department than earlier on. Llewellyn was in immaculately pressed trousers, shirt, jacket and tie. His black shoes were so spit-polish shiny that they dazzled like a sun-reflected mirror. As for Eleanor, well, blow me – a very elaborately embellished frock and tottery heels. Dripping in jewellery too.

Both she and Llewellyn were nursing tall glasses of spirits and sitting with legs delicately crossed on the bouncy cushioned bar stools, facing each other, looking very at home. At one point I even noticed them playing a momentary game of footsie. How very shocking!

They were making convivial conversation with the captain, Chris Baines, a big strapping bloke in his fifties from Preston. I was a bit scared of him at first. He has the physique and hard scrummed-up face of a rugby prop forward. But when I made him laugh he had a very disarming smile so I warmed to him pretty fast after that. He stood propped up behind the bar beside Phil Clegg, the chief engineer, a relatively taciturn Yorkshireman in big glasses. Shoring up the end of the bar, throwing back the drink in convivial mood, stood Purser David. All three of them wore their officers' starched naval whites, shoulders decorated in gold epaulettes. The captain naturally possessed the higher echelons of stripes. After all, he had been at sea a long time, joining Bank Line straight from school in 1971. He was promoted to master in 1989.

Llewellyn and Eleanor seemed to be acting all a bit familiar with our white-clad top-dogs, but then I discovered they had already spent four months with them, as the *Speybank*'s crew is more or less identical to the one they had travelled with on the Voyage from Hell. This was purely coincidence, as the four Bank Line ships have a rota of crew. The crew we've got tend to flip back and forth between the *Speybank* and the *Arunbank*, or sometimes the *Teignbank*, working an average of three to four months at sea with two months off back home. This works out as about two trips a year.

Tea, or 'dinner' as it's called, was at six o'clock sharp. I don't like to miss out on food if I can help it, so at the allotted hour, if not a minute before, I descended at speed the eight flights of steps (each deck is separated by two flights, or fourteen steps) to the officers' mess with Radio Ham Man in my slipstream. Ian followed ten minutes later. It wasn't until half past six that Llewellyn and Eleanor hove into view. As she moved from the door to the table, Eleanor appeared hampered by her heels. She walked like someone navigating a freshly mopped floor.

Three longish tables fill the officers' mess. The one furthest from the door and closest to the galley is the top-brass table for the captain and slightly lesser epaulettes. The captain sat at the head, Chief Phil to his right, Purser David to his left. Sitting at various positions round the rest of the table were Vitali Agudalin (second engineer), Grigori Akulov (third engineer) and Alex – aka Sasha – Nepomnyashchikh (second officer). Not a name to run off the tongue with ease. A space was also set at the table for Alexi Khil, the chief officer, who was currently on duty on the bridge. I only know these tongue-challenging names because I found them pinned to the wall on the 'Emergency & Boat Stations' ('Don't panic! Don't panic!') leaflet and diligently copied them into my notebook. Now I'm trying to learn them. I like to know who's who.

Sitting at the table nearest the door were more crew dressed in white. At the head sat the third mate, Alex Fogarty, from Dover. He's got a head of hair cropped to stubble and can't be much more than his early twenties. Flanking him on either side were the two young Irish cadets, Steven Molloy and David White. The remaining two I keep bumping into on the stairs: Valeri Ananin (fourth engineer) and Benjamin Evgrafov (electrical officer). They both seem like good fun because we've already had a silly misunderstanding time together holding doors open for each other.

That leaves my table. Eleanor sat at the top with Llewellyn to her left and Ham Man to her right. I slotted in next to Ham Man with Ian sitting opposite, dazzling me with his gold watch, cufflinks and signet ring. I have to say the dining process was much swankier than I was expecting. I thought it would be more canteen-like, as on a cross-Channel ferry with sliding trays and flap-up shrivelled-sandwich and sausage display cabinets. Oh, and someone in the corner being sick. But, instead of Formica tables covered in sticky patches and crumbs, there were starched white tablecloths, admittedly with the odd stain, but impressive none-the-less. We've even all got a big white napkin rolled up in a silver napkin ring. I can't say I've had the occasion to use a napkin for a very long time. I usually use my sleeve. I noticed Eleanor dabbing the corner of her mouth with the corner of her napkin. Like the Queen.

Apart from helping ourselves to a big stainless silver bowl of salad on the sideboard, we were served by one of the two stewardesses, the very fluttery, strikingly flame-headed and charismatic Elena Golubtsova. Llewellyn kept looking at her breasts, which were harnessed up high in a white bra, its delicately lacy top visible through the open buttons of her blouse. Helping out in the galley with Valeri Evglevskiy (chief cook) – who looks like a Spanish matador – and Andrey Uss (second cook) – who looks like a Sumo wrestler – was the other incredibly attractive stewardess, Natasha Kochmar – dark haired and sultry with big sad eyes. She looks like she's just stepped straight out of a Tolstoy tragedy.

An imitation-leather-bound menu perched on each table offering us the choice of two starters ('soup of the day' – green pea – or 'chilled tomato juice'), two mains ('roast Tom turkey with chipolata sauce', or 'trout Cleopatra' – there seems to be a worrying amount of people in our food) with 'Duchesse potatoes' (not more!) and 'broccoli spears' (sounds dangerous), a 'Pear Belle Hélène' pudding (this is getting silly) and 'French bread, cheeseboard'. Needless to say, I ate a horse. Ian was happy because he had managed to acquire a bottle of wine. All the others partook of some wine too. They looked at me as if I was missing out on something.

Before the arrival of Llewellyn and Eleanor, I had discovered from Ian that he is sixty-four and has been divorced for some twenty-three years. I think he's more or less retired now but he is some sort of business consultant. The business card he handed me reveals that he was also a 'Director, Non Executive' of a wine merchants. No wonder he likes his wine. The top of the card is embossed with lots of 'By Appointment to Her Majesty the Queen . . .' insignia. It seems that Ian lives alone in a Scottish castle in Ayrshire. Has done since the 'seventies. He says he's Scottish, yet he sounds like Prince Charles, though a bit more yoikish. 'My father was a Scot, my mother came from Yorkshire,' he told me, 'so I'm as mean as they come!' He mentioned a daughter, in her thirties, married to an Aussie. They live near Sydney and Ian is on his way to visit them – the long way round. Like Ham Man and me, this is his first time on a freighter.

Llewellyn and Eleanor, on the other hand, have had quite a bit of practice. For the past two decades they have spent several months a year travelling the world by either cargo ship or cruise. Being something of an old veteran in this department, Llewellyn told us how before September 11th most passengers were American.

'So we've got Osama bin Laden to thank, then!' quipped Ian.

It didn't take me long to surmise that Ian is not too keen on Americans. Later on the talk touched on mobile phones. Llewellyn commented that the Americans weren't so keen on technology as the Brits, as there was no 'texting' facility on their phones. 'That's because Americans can't write!' said Ian. He then explained that he found Americans very hard to get on with.

'Well, I'm half of one,' I said. 'So this isn't boding particularly well!'

'Ah, but I do have *some* American friends,' replied Ian defensively.

Before we had to clear the decks at seven for Natasha and Elena to clear the tables, the only biographical snippet I picked up from Llewellyn was that he is seventy-eight, though he looks more like seventy. He's fine-featured and sports a thick shock of wavy white hair atop a rather enchantingly mischievous face. When he smiles, you catch a flash of a partially gold front tooth. A garrulous Welshman, he's spent the past twenty-eight years living in Shetland with Eleanor, his second wife. Eleanor is sixty-four and originally from Cheshire. They are only going halfway around the world on the *Speybank* this time, disembarking in Auckland (as we all are) to have a two-month holiday touring New Zealand. They are then going to spend forty-five days sailing home on board the *Aurora*, the $200 million, 76,000-tonne flagship of P&O Cruises, which I remember reading has been jinxed ever since Princess Anne attempted to name her about two years ago – the champagne bottle, instead of breaking across the bow, fell unceremoniously into the water. I believe seafarers know few worse omens.

It's now nearly eleven o'clock at night and I'm sitting in my cabin at my desk, writing this scrawl. Things are still crashing around outside and I keep jumping up to stick my head out of the porthole to see what's going on, being careful to check that a rogue container isn't swinging wildly from a crane about to garrotte me. The ship's rails, incidentally, are full of massive dents, which evidently bear witness to previous container bashings. No one seems to know how long we are going to be stuck in Dunkirk. Hopefully we'll be allowed off the ship tomorrow, because I want to go and explore the docks and the famous battle beach.

Right, that's it. I think I'll go to bed now.

# 2

# God Save the Cranes

*Dunkirk, 31 October*

Not a good night for sleep. I think I am suffering from lack of cycling. Although my head was tired my body was wide awake, wondering where my usual fifty-mile-a-day bike ride had gone. So I got up at 5.30, went down to the gym and pounded on the wonked exercise bike for an hour until my mind went numb from boredom and I had produced enough sweat to fill . . . well, the swimming pool. Cycling on a static machine in an airless mausoleum does not produce quite the same endorphin-popping vigour as cycling over hill and dale.

At 7.30 I undid all the good I had done by eating enough break-fast to sink a ship. Ian looked a bit sheepish because he had already managed to block his vacuum toilet. But he soon got over it and said, apropos of nothing, 'You know what they say about the Harold Wilson government – that it was run like the Columbus expedition: when they set out they didn't know where they were going; when they got there they didn't know where they were; and when they got home they didn't know where they had been. And they did it all on other people's money!' We all looked at Ian as if he was mad. Which perhaps he is.

There is an undercurrent of suppressed excitement this

morning. Rumour has it that we are off tonight. In the light of this I wasted no time in skedaddling down the gangway to try to spend the day in a must-walk-as-far-as-I-can-for-as-long-as-I-can pent-up sort of frenzy. Oh dear, I can already feel the confined space and lack of boundless freedom getting to me. And we haven't even left yet.

As I navigated a hazardous path through the stacked walls of containers of Port Est, a curdled grey sky draped across the oil refinery chimney tops and rooftops of Dunkirk. A spitty rain and a sharp wintry wind frisked their way through my layers of clothing. To get my blood circulating, I started to run, out past great swirling waves of graffiti and more docks and derelict buildings and a vast warehouse called 'BOIS DES TROIS PORTS – BOIS TROPI-CAUX'.

Dunkirk was virtually bombed to pieces in the Second World War. Fortunately, a few nice old buildings remain. To get an aerial view of the port and town I climbed up to the top of the big fourteenth-century square tower that was originally attached to St Eloi church. One of the things I love about France is all the chiming clock towers and this fine belfry is no exception as it has forty-eight head-clanging bells. The heaviest bell weighs seven tonnes and is called Jean Bart, having apparently been named after one of the *Simpsons* characters. As I looked out over the rainy scene of jumbled rooftops I thought, funny how the English, unable to keep their hands to themselves, used to own Dunkirk. That is, until 1662 when Charles II, he of the Declaration of Indulgence (whatever all that's about – eating lots?), wanted a few more bob in his pocket and sold it to Louis XIV. How very generous.

From the top of the belfry I got my bearings over Dunkirk and made a beeline for the beach – the beach which in 1940 was the scene of Operation Dynamo, the evacuation of 335,000 Allied troops by warships, requisitioned civilian ships and a whole host of smaller boats, all under constant attack from the air. Today, though, the beach, with its stretched miles of hard washed-out sand, is a very different scene, dotted with dog-walkers and cockle diggers and joggers. There are sand-yachts too, racing at rushing speeds in jiving zig-zags along the beach, some even capsizing on to their sides. Lining the town end of the beach sits a rank of not exactly traditional eateries serving perhaps not the finest of French fare, all parading far from evocative *français* names: Pub McEwans, L'Irish, Glaces à L'Américaine, Ma Patata, Costa Café and Le Milk Bar.

With a good few miles under my belt, I made it back to boat base-camp in time for dinner. Ham Man had a very long face.

'What's wrong?' I asked him. 'Are you suffering from lack of antennae? You don't look very happy.'

'Och, have ye no hearrrd? We cannae leave noo 'til tomorrow afternoon!'

I can't say the news came as too much of a crushing blow to me. In fact I was quite pleased. Gave me a chance to have another big walk back up the blowy beach and to explore a bit more town. Ham Man was so dispirited that he only spent about ten minutes shovelling food into his mouth before disappearing back upstairs to his cabin. That left me with Ian, as Llewellyn and Eleanor were still in the bar.

'I don't think Chris is too happy being stationary,' I said. 'He's desperate to get going.'

Ian latched on to the word 'stationary' by flying off on one of his tangents to tell me a little story about how one day his daughter (who, he says, inherited his off-the-wall sense of humour) went into a department store in which she often shopped. But this time she couldn't find the stationery department. So she found a shop assistant and said, 'What's happened to the stationery department?' 'It's moved,' replied the assistant. 'The stationery department's moved? But that's impossible!' exclaimed Ian's daughter. The assistant didn't get the joke. I admit there was a momentary pause of silence while I waited for the coin to drop. Then I got it.

Elena was in plate-servicing attendance again tonight, looking as radiant-haired and translucently pale of face as she did yester-day. When the others appeared, Llewellyn was all a bit flirty with her. Eleanor just smiled meekly throughout. So far, Eleanor, who seems quite blanched and wisp-like, hasn't done much talking. But then she doesn't really have a chance, because Llewellyn doesn't often pause for breath. And whenever Eleanor does pipe up, Llewellyn tends to talk right over her. I feel he needs a good slapping. Despite all this, it is obvious that he loves her very much. They move around the ship like two people rolled into one, scarcely ever leaving each other's sight. And I have noticed that when they stand together looking out of the windows of the bridge, Llewellyn often has his arm around Eleanor or is stroking her hand. When he isn't being patronising or didactic, or just a complete pain in the arse, he can be quite tender. And it is in these moments that he has a twinkle in his eye and calls her 'Elliana'.

*Dunkirk (still), 1 November*

Having a snoop around the bridge, I came across a book sitting on the chart table. It was entitled 'Movement Book – Steering Gear Tests'. It was open on the page cryptically bulleted as:

  a. Main Steering Gear
  b. Auxiliary Steering Gear
  f. Rudder Angle Indicators
  i. Full Movement of the Rudder Verified

No, it didn't mean very much to me either. But although I have yet to ascertain whether the *Speybank* possesses such a thing as an engine (after all, we have so far gone nowhere), at least we have a rudder. So that's good.

Close to the Movement Book I noticed the 'Bridge Order Book'. This was open on the page dated '26/10/03' and I read:

LAST PORT: Hull. TOWARDS ANTWERP.

. . . Give all traffic a wide berth avoiding any possible close quarters, situations and always following the Rules of the Road.

　　　　　　　　　　Standing Orders, Chris Baines, Master

Sounds much like what I try to do when cycling.

It rained hard last night and it was still at it this morning. While the others stayed on board I walked back into town, stopping to look at the cathedral, its inside walls pockmarked with bullet holes. Then I sauntered through some back streets, passing a bar called 'Le Picardy'. Scribed across the window were the words: PUB NO PROBLEM. This left me a little baffled. Was it, I wondered, a pub with no problems, simply possessing a sunny disposition about its carefree premises? Or did it mean that it forbade entrance to any clientele with a hang-up or in need of therapy? There again, could it have been saying that no, it wasn't a pub – it was a *problem*? It's a job to know whether this meant it was a 'problem area' with perhaps dodgy squat toilets, or whether it was simply a problem like a sulky teenager or an insoluble sudoku. I needed a little dash of punctuation to help me out.

Back down on the beach I walked and walked. The rain fell fiercely in short-lived showers, and the wind was like a dog – just waiting to bite you. As the morning progressed into early afternoon, the sun jostled for position with the armies of big black clouds sweeping at speed across the sky. The battle was at last won by the sun, and I enjoyed walking into its dazzling rays as it arched its way towards the west.

As I re-entered the town end of the beach, I spotted a cyclist in the distance leaning their bike against the rear of one of the concrete benches on the prom near an eatery called 'La Chlorophyll' (which presumably serves nothing but *à la carte* menus of photosynthesis). Although I was still a long way off from the cyclist, who was little more than a miniature stick person, there was something about the way they moved and the pannier-like bulge on the back of their *vélo* that innately told me that up ahead lay not a cycling *madame* with a cycle-load of *charcuterie*, but a heavy-duty cycle-tourer. I walked in their direction, thinking I would just do a fly-by, but as I got close I saw that the cyclist, dressed in a blue fleece and baggy fawny-buff shorts over a pair of black lycra cycling tights, was cooking up a bit of tucker on his Trangia stove. And I thought, that's just the sort of thing I would do if I were touring: find a bench on the beach in the sun and eat some food.

Drawn irresistibly towards a laden bicycle, I took the opportunity of going to say hello. The next thing I knew I was being blamed for sending Rory James on the longest cycle of his life after reading one of my books. In the summer of 2001, after nine months of planning, Rory left Stoke-on-Trent with four other blokes he had met on the internet to travel 13,000 miles through twenty-two countries and arrive in Singapore a mere ten months later. But Rory's knee conked out in places so he was forced to catch lifts and buses from time to time. He was now on his way home after a short trip to Düsseldorf for a friend's party. In January he was planning on going back to Singapore to collect the bike he'd left there before cycling down through Indonesia to Australia. He was feeling a bit dubious about Indonesia, because he recently went on a backpacking recce there with a girl he met and he hadn't much liked what he saw.

'It's a very unlawful country,' he said. Then he told me how they were on a bus that crashed into a man on a motorbike. Rory thought the rider was killed. 'But the bus driver didn't want to stop and get out because he thought he would be set upon by the mob of angry bystanders who saw the whole thing happen. So when he started driving away they started hurling rocks through the windows. It was quite a nasty experience.'

Before Rory left for Singapore he was working as an engineer for Caterpillar. One of his latest long-range plans was to cycle to the South Pole.

'No one has ever done it before,' he said. 'I've invented a bike on paper which I think will cope with the Antarctic conditions.' Then, with a sudden inspirational fancy, he said, 'Would you be interested in coming with me? How are you with the cold?'

'Not very good,' I said. 'I even feel a bit shivery when I pass through the chilled meat section of the supermarket.'

So that hit that subject on the head like a lump of collapsing glacier.

After offering me a chunk of halva (sticky Middle Eastern sweet made of sesame flour and honey that, once in your teeth, is highly effective at locking your jaw), Rory said, 'I love travelling by bike because don't you find it makes you turn all sort of feral? Now when I drop food I'll eat it straight off the ground. I don't worry any more about hygiene and cleanliness.'

I agreed and told him that when I'm cycling and camping my fingernails are always dirty and my hands are always oily and I'm always dropping bits of food on the ground, which I then pick up (can't have food that you've just carted over a mountain going to waste) and put in my mouth, only to find that I've got a small stick or spoonful of gravel in there as well.

'Since I took up cycling,' Rory said, 'I've stopped biting my nails. It's calmed me down a lot.'

Walking back to the *Speybank* I bumped into a very forlorn-looking Ham Man.

'I would nae hurry,' he said. 'We cannae leave till tonight now. Ye know, I think all this delay is making me go slowly mad. First we were going to leave three weeks ago. Then we were going to leave last week. Then we were going to leave two days ago. Then we were going to leave yesterday. Then we were going to leave this afternoon. Now we're not leaving until tonight – if we go at all! I mean Jee-suss Chrrrrist!'

I spent the rest of the afternoon having a very enjoyable time photographing graffiti and twisted metal scraps and walls of ruinous warehouses and smashed-up car corpses in the derelict wastelands of the docks. The low angling sun made a maze of stretched shadows and deep kaleidoscopic colours. Everywhere lay extensive hews of surfaces sprayed with chaotic swirls of slogans, many in English. One richly rust-encrusted door was covered in a sun-glinting, silver-sprayed and almost hieroglyphi-

cally written word, repeated hundreds of times like punitive school
lines: ALONE ALONE ALONE ALONE . . . Then, spreading itself
across a wall beneath a smashed-window bastion of warehouse, I
peered through my viewfinder at the arcanely majestic scrawl of:
GOD SAVE THE CRANES. At my feet lay a fallen metal girder
sloshed with a dentistry-sounding MOUTHWASH 03.

From the scrambled screed of the wasteland I moved closer
back towards the ship to take pictures of corners and angles of
the piled-high containers all named with the various exotica of
an ocean-spanning life: KLINE; HANJIN; HYUNDAI; P&O;
TIPHOOK; MAERSK SEALAND; HAPAAG LLOYD; HAMBURG
SUD. Between the *Speybank* and the rail tracks and the overpass, vast ponds of puddles reflected in a fiery sun-setting sky
chunks of ships and bridges and streetlamps as well as streams of
cables from the overhead pantograph and snakings of container-
perched trains. I was busy taking yet more pictures of these
inverted scenes when I noticed a group of Russian crew leaning
over the side of the *Speybank*. They watched me intently, some
joking, some grinning wolfishly, some looking genuinely worried
for my welfare.

'It's all right,' I shouted up to them. 'I'm just taking some photographs of some very nice puddles!'

They shouted something back but it was a job to know what they
said.

At dinner Ian asked me what I had been doing all day.

'Mostly wandering around taking pictures of graffiti,' I said.

This prompted him to tell me how a friend of his had once
passed a wall sprayed with the words: 'The Italians make the best
lovers'. To this, someone had scrawled underneath: 'Yes, but the
Japanese make them smaller and faster'.

Llewellyn then told us rather proudly how he more or less
won the Battle of Britain single-handedly (he was a fighter pilot in
the war). When he exhausted that subject he suddenly fired me with
an out-of-the-blue question: 'Do you know where the longest single
span stone bridge is in the world?'

'Bosnia-Herzegovina,' I said, because frankly I haven't a clue.

'No, very wrong!' said a scholarly finger-shaking Llewellyn. 'Pontypridd, Wales. And which river does it cross?'

'It's either the River Rhondda or the River Taff,' I replied. 'I only know this because there's a very nice Sustrans cycle trail that runs up the Taff from Cardiff. Apart from the bit, that is, where a man dropped his trousers on me near Rhydyfelin.'

But Llewellyn didn't want to know. He was more interested in telling Ian and me (Ham Man hasn't hit it off with Llewellyn so has gone upstairs) how he started out life working in his family-owned bakery near Pontypridd. Along with being a baker he had also been a banker, an RAF pilot, the apparent inventor of fibre optics and, for forty years, an air-traffic controller. For thirty-six years Eleanor had also been an air-traffic controller. 'The finest in the country,' declared Llewellyn rather grandly.

They had met each other when working as air-traffic controllers and spent years sitting side by side.

'Together we've saved thousands of lives,' added Llewellyn, plumping up his wings. 'You won't know this but the official figure for near-air collisions is one per cent of the true figure. That's why we don't fly.'

Ian does fly. That's why he didn't want to hear any more doom-making statistics so he took himself off upstairs. Llewellyn then launched into a very long-winded story about his air-traffic control-ling days. I got a bit lost, but the gist of it was that Llewellyn once wrote a report on a very near air collision he witnessed on another air-traffic controller's screen. His bosses ripped it up and told him to keep quiet. Llewellyn didn't keep quiet.

After falling out with his bosses Llewellyn walked out on his job. Months later he and Eleanor moved to another air-traffic control place to work together again. Before long Llewellyn handed in another file of a near miss he had witnessed. Once more his bosses denied such an event had ever happened. But this time Llewellyn had the tapes to prove it, so it was reported to the authorities.

\*

There's been an amazing revelation. An engine has been found! So we leave tonight, albeit not for our original first planned stop of distant Tahiti but for Le Havre, where we have to offload and load another ocean of cargo.

Ham Man and I were the only ones to brave the monkey deck as we slid slowly out into the Channel. It was blowing a hooligan up there. Hardly surprising, I suppose, as we are heading into a Force 9 gale. Purser David warned us to expect a rocky ride and to secure everything in our cabins, including our sliding drawers, which apparently are predisposed to doing a lot of violent sliding given half a chance.

The *Speybank* slunk out into the night, the industrial French coastline ablaze with port lights and the eerie blue hydrocarbon flames leaping into the shimmying blackness of the sky. Unfortunately we were downwind of the titanic colossi of power stations. The air blew thick with the acrid reek of chemicals. There then came a moment of high angst when we were nearly rammed broadside by a couple of semi-submerged nuclear submarines with busy flashing lights and conning towers extended. But then Ham Man and I realised that these submarines were nothing more than a harmless posse of marker buoys and farewell beacons all wildly waving their heads. What a stroke of relief! Just as well we weren't steering.

Everything had suddenly turned very funny. Now that he'd finally waved good riddance to Dullkirk, Ham Man was in fine euphoric form.

'I cannae believe we're off at last!' he said.

I could nae believe that he was grinning. Getting going had entirely transformed his face and demeanour. I also could not believe how underdressed he was. It was knobblingly cold up there, the stinging November wind so strong you could feel it rearranging your cheeks. I was togged up head to toe in multiple layers and full Goretex garb, plus gloves, neck tube, hat and hood. Ham Man, on the other hand, was clad merely in jeans and fleece. To give him credit, he did have a tartan scarf, so that was something. Still,

I was concerned. He looked very cold, with his head screwed into his shoulders.

'Chris,' I said, 'where's your jacket?'

'I have nae brrrought one,' he replied. 'I'm banking on warmer weather.'

'But we're crossing the Atlantic in winter.'

'Aye,' he said. 'But it should nae take long.'

Ha! I thought. Ha!

As I was effectively one large slab of plastic, Ham Man positioned me directly in front of him to act as his windbreak. He draped his arms over my shoulders and clutched his hands in front of my chest and stood there giving me one big continuous spoon-standing hug. Bloody men. Us girls always have to bear the sacrificial biscuit. But I didn't really mind. At least his body felt a bit warmer against my back. And anyway, dressed as I was, he would never be able to work an exploratory hand down into my clothing because I was like Fort Knox – all chinks and clefts and apertures effectually sealed with bombproof zips and Velcro. So we remained in this locked position as the *Speybank* continued spelunking westwards into the waves.

*Le Havre, 2 November*

It took seventeen long hours to do 170 miles. That means, if I can shunt my un-arithmetical brain into gear, we were only travelling at about 10 knots even though the *Speybank* is supposed to have a 'service speed' of 17.5 knots. Ian, who marched about the bridge like an army colonel taking bearings with his handheld GPS, told me that we had done the leg from Dunkirk on only one engine. There hadn't been any point in going any faster because it was so busy at Le Havre, chock-a-dock with ships waiting to unload, that we wouldn't have been allocated a berth any quicker anyway. So we queued up in the port's outer anchorage with a large and mixed fleet of other container ships swinging at anchor for hours and hours and hours.

Meanwhile, as all the others around me were coming down with flu, I found myself suffering from cycling cold turkey. It's nearly three whole days since I've ridden my bike and my moods are swinging wildly between fidgety and crotchety and manically neurotic. I am liable to be seen erratically jumping on to the railings to launch into a frenetic hour of step-ups until I can no longer see straight, followed by a rapid succession of pull-ups and press-ups off every pull-up-able and press-up-able surface or obstacle I pass. The other passengers, not to mention the Russian crew (especially Mr Alex Sasha second officer Nepomnyashchikh), look at me as if I'm four ball-bearings short of the cups of a Campagnolo Nuovo Record bottom bracket with Dura Ace lockring and Specialised S1 spindle. But don't they realise this is normal behaviour for someone deprived of their wheels?

A riveting dinner was had tonight. I learnt that Llewellyn has no tonsils or appendix. He then told Ham Man that he invented fibre optics. Ian and I already knew this, of course, because he had given us a sneak preview into his past life. Eleanor sat so straight throughout you'd think she'd been electrocuted.

At last, amidst much hull-reverberating chain-churnings, the anchor was raised and a pilot taken on board to see us through the port locks to the docks. Ham Man and I stood outside on the monkey deck in the dark and the cold and the wind watching all the lock-opening operations. I've noticed that when Ham Man is looking at something intently he keeps his mouth open. Further study has diagnosed that the hinge on his lower jaw appears to be loose.

Whenever I scarpered down the steps to see what was happening on the bridge (darkened to allow the crew on duty to see outside), I found the captain standing with legs apart at the bridge window, hands clasped behind back, looking grave with a face like cut granite. The French pilot looked equally stern of face. He occasionally asked the helmsman for a heading correction (in a language of degrees) or a small turn. Each order was then repeated by the helmsman. I was glad to note that the helmsman, Zhenya Sotnikov, looked deeply lost in concentration. Too bad if we were to wipe out a lock gate, or worse, run full steam ahead into some potently explosive oil refinery, as it looks like Le Havre is all flaring chimney.

Huddled together in a far corner stood Llewellyn and Eleanor. Gadget-loving Ian, on the other hand, was anything but huddled – striding up and down the bridge conducting operations with his GPS cradled in his palm. 'I'm a control freak!' he said, as if we hadn't noticed.

*Le Havre, 3 November*

What a gigantically industrious place! But then I suppose it should be, seeing as it is France's second largest port after Marseilles. I've passed through Le Havre many times with my bike fresh off or on to a cross-Channel ferry, and *le centre ville* always seems rather nice and French and quaint, despite being another one of those places largely destroyed in 1944. I can't say that I've felt much inclined to spend time poking about the port and environs, not with the swathe of power stations and oil refineries and chemical and engineering and car-assembly plants, bang in the middle of which we seem to be berthed. Despite the lively weather (sheeting rain and chaotic wind) the view of the port from the monkey deck is an amazing sight – a dauntingly infinite scene of industry.

As for the containers, I have never seen such a colourfully vast expanse – football stadium after football stadium of huge blue, green, grey, red and rust metal monsters piled one on top of each other until they reach several storeys high. Darting among them unceasingly are the giant straddle-carriers, the driver up high in his glass cab with his computer screen telling him what to straddle and where to straddle it and at which crane or dock to dump it. They all make very peculiar whistling and buzzing and bleeping noises (the straddle-carriers that is, not the drivers) which Ham Man says sounds like an army of bagpipes. Odd bagpipes, if you ask me, but then maybe he is missing Scotland, and if you miss Scotland, maybe you miss bagpipes, and if you miss bagpipes, maybe you begin to hear them calling to you in the most unlikely things. Like straddle-carriers.

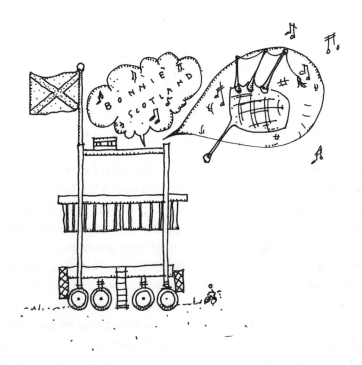

Another hour spent pounding and shredding my hamstrings into nothing much more than strings of ham on the lopsided exercise bike did little to rid me of an overdose of itchiness – an itchiness that is bound to grow as it seems we might be marooned in Le Havre a while because of the weather. It is so diabolically wet that it's preventing *Ita-est*, the barge that has tethered itself alongside the *Speybank*, from offloading its enormous and easily ruined cargo of flour (600 tonnes of it, all in dusty great sacks), which is destined for Tahiti. It's Tahiti's month's supply and goes solely into making French bread and patisserie. Tahiti could quite easily import flour from other places but it is very particular about its flour. It has to be French flour, otherwise it is not proper French patisserie.

With nothing better to do, I kept hanging over the sopping wet side of the monkey deck for an aerial view of the barge. I love barges – they are such peaceful and sensible cargo-carrying pack-horses, far better than all those stampeding double-trailer trucks. I like their rusty bikes too, strapped to the cabin-house roofs. Every time I see a barge it reminds me of cycling along the banks of the Rhine and the Seine. The north bank of the Seine estuary is where Le Havre is moored. It's such an enjoyable pastime, gazing down on this flour barge and the husband-and-wife team scrambling about the long and narrow side-decks and to think that when they're done and dusted, they can barge right up the mighty Seine all the way to Paris.

The rain might not have been very conducive for weather-sensitive cargo, but it didn't stop anything else from being loaded: more shiny trucks and chassis, diggers, tractors, 4×4s, earthmoving equipment, police cars for Tahiti, and an airport's aircraft-step lorry. There was rumour of a whole bungalow being lifted on board too, but I never saw it. They must have sneaked it in the moment I went below to tackle my vacuum toilet. What I didn't miss was the delicate and potentially disastrous loading (one man narrowly missed being flattened) of two privately owned vessels to the *Speybank*'s aft deck: a large money-oozing motor launch, and an even larger catamaran called *Greenland. Greenland* – a chilly sounding boat heading for a sultry South Pacific.

Lots more high-rise heaps of containers were lowered and hoisted in and out of the seemingly bottomless holds. It was early morning and I was up on the bridge talking to Alexi Khil, the dark-haired and gentle-mannered chief officer who does the 4 a.m. to 8 a.m. watch as well as the 4 p.m. to 8 p.m. one. After telling me about winters in Russia (flipping cold!) and how he had spent some time in China supervising ship-building at some kerplunk-ingly leviathan ship-building plant, he unravelled the mystery about TEU. I told him that I had spotted several lists and documents on the bridge on which I kept seeing the mystifying letters 'TEU' pop up. Like: 'Reefer Container Plugs: 40 TEU'. Could it, I wondered, be short for 'Teutonic' so that 'Reefer Container Plugs: 40 TEU' was just another way of saying there were forty German-like stowaway reefers plugging up the containers? Or could 'TEU' be an acronym for Tightly Enclosed Urinals? (In that case, with so many men on board, it is good to know we have forty.) Or, seeing as the *Spermbank*, I mean *Speybank*, has only four women among twenty-nine men on board, could 'TEU' simply be shorthand for the ship's football team: Testosterone United?

But no, no and no. Or, as Alexi said in Russian, 'Nyeht, nyeht and nyeht.' I was wrong on all three counts. TEU stands for the comparatively mundane-sounding 'Transport Equivalent Unit'. A ship's container capacity is measured in TEU. For example, the *Spermbank*'s is 600 TEU, which doesn't sound like a very high sperm count if you ask me. I prefer to think of them in millions. Anyway, $1 \times \text{TEU} = 1 \times 20$-foot container with a width and height of 8.5 feet, and $2 \times \text{TEU} = 1 \times 40$-foot container. And that's really about the long and short of it all. What a terrible disappointment.

By the way, I don't think I've told you yet that the *Spermbank* is registered in Douglas, Isle of Man. How fitting that a ship of men should be recorded in its official eligibility in a male-named town on a manly-sounding island.

At midday an alarm bell rang a short, sharp but resonating ear-clanging trill. This alerted all on board that it was time for lunch. When at sea, the alarm bell is sounded in unison with a blast on what is daintily called the ship's whistle. Calling it a whistle strikes me as a rather euphemistic name for it. Kettles whistle. So do builders and small boys in short trousers wheeling their delivery bikes up cobblestone streets in olde worlde Hovis bread adverts. At least I always imagine they do. Small bread boys, that is, because builders invariably whistle.

But this ship's whistle is anything but a whistle. It is more a deaf-ening skull-cracking foghorn. I have learnt that it is not a good idea to stand on the monkey deck at midday. This is because the megaphone-type loudhailer is attached to the masthead above the deck and should you be lolling about beneath it in a state of dazy-headed reverie when the high noon hour arrives, the shattering blast is so shockingly explosive that it can make you jump clean out of your skin. And jumping clean out of your skin when standing outside on a ship a hundred or more feet above the sea is not a good idea. Could make you jump clean overboard.

Ham Man and I were the first down to lunch. As we ate ('her-ring in tomato sauce with broad beans and Garfield potatoes') I mentioned to him that the thing I found the hardest about meal-times on this ship was having to eat off a plate and use a knife and fork again. Ham Man stopped eating and looked at me a little oddly. So I elaborated by telling him that at home I eat all my meals out of a saucepan using nothing more than a spoon. I think this is one of the detrimental side effects of having spent three-quarters of my life pottering about the world on my bike. When you cycle and camp, you very soon start to throw out any super-fluous equipment rather than having to haul it all over endless mountain passes. Bare essentials are what you want. So, out goes the plate. Out goes the bowl. Out go the fighting irons. You can eat anything with a spoon, but you can't eat soup with a knife, or a bowl of cereal with a fork. And when you cycle all day you are hungry all day. There's no time to be wasted chasing around piles of peas on your plate with an impractically pronged utensil. You need to shovel with speed.

After lunch it was still blowing merry hell but at least the rain had stopped. The sun even came out, though it didn't look like it would last, as a big black cloudbank was rampaging in from the west. Grabbing the opportunity of a brief lull in the weather, Ham Man and I sought permission to leave the ship for a wander. We had big plans for traipsing all the way into Le Havre to spend the last of our euros on some edible treats.

But we didn't get very far. Walking through the port of Le Havre is not quite like going for a pleasant saunter in the countryside. It is interminably vast and spectacularly dicey in so far as weaving a path among the furious fleets of gargantuan straddle-carriers and container-loaded articulated trucks is concerned. As we didn't fancy getting mown down among the many bulldozing death traps, we darted in zig-zagging ground-hugging SAS style across the enemy ground of the docks until we reached the relative safety of the outer fenced-in perimeters of the prisoner-of-port camp. Here we found a piece of no-man's-land wasteland where we walked around in circles. As we walked, we talked, and Ham Man told me he didn't like Llewellyn and thought he was very rude to me. (This morning at breakfast Llewellyn said that if I continued eating the cycling proportion amounts I was eating I soon wouldn't be able to fit through the messroom door.) I said I didn't mind. I could take it.

'Aye, but he seems to have it in for ye, Jose. He keeps pootin' ye doon.'

Ham Man said that if anyone had to watch their weight while on this sedentary voyage it was him. 'I weigh 89 kilos,' he said. 'And I want tae stay that way.'

Ham Man had turned all dispirited again because of our lack of progress. As in Dunkirk, no one knows for how long we will be docked in Le Havre. If the rain holds off for a day, then at least the flour can be loaded. The flour is holding up a lot of the other cargo too, which can't be loaded until the flour is on board so that the various giant hatch covers can be closed for more containers and large lumps of things to sit on top. Ham Man said that all this delay was just wasting his time and that he could have gone to a radio ham convention that had been held last weekend in Manchester. He'd been keen to attend because he was supposed to have been awarded with lashings of cups and prizes for doing so well at a radio ham competition.

'What happens at these competitions?' I asked.

'Well, the one I did well in was a forty-eight-hour marathon of making as many transmissions as ye can. It can get very tiring. It was easier tae do when I was in my twenties. But it's okay if ye can keep DVT at bay.'

By the time we made it back to the ship we found a bit of a hulla-baloo going on, with half the French army on board. They had been instructed by their chiefs in command that the *Speybank* was to take them to New Caledonia (distant South Pacific islands annexed by France in 1853). This was news to the captain, so he sent them all packing. But later I found a couple of the soldiers bil-leted in the two single cabins beside me. This is quite exciting. They look rather splendid in their khaki berets. They have also topped up the *Spermbank* count. So now it is four girls swilling among a sea of thirty-one men.

The two Frenchmen, Mickael Sailly (dark, muscular and a little too good-looking for comfort) and Xavier Leportier (wiry, mous-tachioed and not a lot to write home about), brought a little luggage on board with them: twelve containers stashed with ammunition and high explosives. Suddenly I'm treading very cau-tiously. It would be a shame to set anything off. All the ammo is bound for Tahiti and Nouméa (capital of New Caledonia). Ian, who speaks fluent French, said that he'd had a word with Xavier who told him all the shots and shells are for target practice. Ten thousand miles sounds like a long way to go to fire at some targets, if you ask me. Can't they just lie prostrate on their stomachs and aim at a few bull's-eyes set up in some back gardens in France? Frankly, I suspect that there's a dodgy undercover operation going on, just so that the French army can make a lot of scary bangs on some distant atoll in the South Pacific.

I'm beginning to get a little bit worried about just exactly what this ship is carrying. Apart from the large amount of sperm, that is. Stalking about the bridge this afternoon, Ham Man and I came across the 'Dangerous Goods List'. Seems that along with the twelve fat containers full of military hardware, we are also sitting on top of 43 tonnes of 'dangerous goods'. This list includes such 'Environmentally Hazardous Substances' as '13 cartons of explosives, aerosols, tars, adhesives, corrosives, flammable liquids, hydrocarbons, liquids N.O.S, acetone, turpentine, xylenes, ammonia solution, phosphoric acid, sodium hydroxide, hydrochloric acid'.

Sounds positively delightful.

*Le Havre, 4 November*

More rain. More manic static cycling. More Llewellyn telling me not to eat so much. Then the sun comes out. Sacks of flour everywhere. A flurry of floury people.

What a surprisingly mesmerising pastime it is to stand high up on the monkey deck, leaning over the railings, watching sack after sack after tonne after tonne being hoisted airborne by crane from the barge in strapped-together sack-loads before being lowered into the dark shadowy pits of the hold, where a forest of outstretched arms await their arrival. Almost as good is watching a big bashed-up container ship called *Anja* slide into a nearby dock and unload its huge hollow hold crammed full with rocks and boulders the size of bungalows. The onboard crane has a clawed grasping hand (an orange-peel grab, as it's called in builder's lingo) like one of those money-feeding seafront games that can never latch on to the cuddly-toy booty. Only this crane's one is much bigger. The rocks are fed on to the backs of a continuous taskforce of prodigious earthmovers that charge off across a waste ground to a distant land-reclamation site. And then they charge back again. Some of the drivers have started to wave to me.

Just as I was launching pell-mell into my monkey deck step-ups, Llewellyn and Eleanor appeared. Llewellyn was in jeans, socks and sandals and a blue shirt with a 'Speybank Round the World' emblem on the top left-hand pocket. Eleanor was topped in a blue sweatshirt adorned with the word SHETLAND and a motif of a Viking ship.

Llewellyn walked over to me and said, 'You're an exercise maniac, you are. Keep that up and your legs will fall off.' Eleanor just looked a bit pointy faced.

Then Llewellyn bleeped his Casio digital watch into the stop-watch mode, caught Eleanor's eye, pushed another bleeping button and they were off, striding at a keen lick in circular weavings up and down and round the monkey deck. Llewellyn had told me earlier that he and Eleanor walk two miles a day at home at a continuously brisk pace. 'If you stop and start and don't walk at a fairly fast speed then you might as well not walk at all,' he told me. 'Ambling along doesn't do much for the old ticker. Last time on the *Speybank* we tried to walk up here most days.'

It's not easy walking on the monkey deck. It's not big and it's crammed full of obstacles to crash into and trip you up and break your leg; like raised ridges, masthead ladders, large-mounted bin-nacles, growling engine vents, satellite dish things and something else very large that is plastered with hazardous signs warning you to keep well away to prevent radiation poisoning and dying a long and horrible death. Positioned on either side of the deck there are two gigantic round-beamed spotlights mounted on hulking great pedestals. Ham Man and I love these lights. They look just like the sort of searchlights you see tin-pot helmeted German guards manning on top of watch-towers in *The Great Escape*. We keep grabbing hold of the spotlights' handrails and pretend to swivel them as if sweeping the high barbed-wired perimeter fenc-ing of a night-covered prisoner-of-war camp. Searching for Steve McQueen. Even if he did escape in daylight. It's all a bit worrying, really. But then you've got to amuse yourself somehow. You can't stare at rocks and sacks of flour all day long. Actually you can. And I do.

The monkey deck is the only deck on the ship where you can walk for 'lee-sher', as the Americans would say. Saying that, we passengers are allowed to walk on the narrow just-above-sea-level side decks that stretch the length of the ship on either side of the hugely heaped fortress of containers. But not without permission from the bridge, and not when the *Speybank* is in port being loaded, and not in anything more than calm and gentle seas. It looks like a very easy place to die, either by being crushed by a toppling container or by falling into one of the many dark and bottomless hatches and holes.

Things suddenly started happening tonight. With all the flour finally loaded and the last of the containers dropped into place, we were off. I looked at my watch: 20.16. It took two hours to clear the locks and the port. I spent most of the time up on the monkey deck with Ham Man, but occasionally I climbed down the steps to the bridge to warm up my fingers and toes. A French pilot was on board again to navigate the ship through a maritime minefield. He was amazed by the archaic Russian equipment still in use on the bridge. '*C'est folklorique!*' he cried, throwing up his arms in that shocked theatrical style that characterises many a gesticulating and excitable Frenchman.

At least we can be thankful that the *Speybank*'s budget has stretched so far as to allow radar. On my way back outside I stopped to have a look at it. The blipping screen was a drift of green and rose-coloured confetti of passing and anchored ships. I love the bridge at night. It's all so dark. The only light comes from the instruments and the screens and panels and switches and buttons of the strange creaking and bleeping and blurping-sounding equipment.

As we skulked out into the Channel, the *Speybank* moved at a moderate speed, barely trembling with the exertion. We passed a varied and scattered armada of container vessels riding glumly at anchor, all awaiting new orders for a slot at the dock. They were lit up like fabled castles of floating fairylands. I was pleased about this. Too bad if they were all unlit and we crashed into one and sank. Sinking in cold dirty dark water in the Channel a mere stone's throw from, say, Bognor, or Shanklin, doesn't have quite the same romantic ring to it as sinking off, say, Rarotonga or Bora Bora in the South Pacific. Not that I want to sink anywhere, of course. It's just that if we have to sink I would rather sink somewhere a bit more exciting and preferably in warm blue water near a white sandy beach. It would be better for my circulation (I do suffer from the cold) and I could even try out my desert island penknife survival skills. That's presuming I make it to the island and don't get eaten by sharks en route. What a spot of rotten luck that would be.

# 3

# All at Sea

*Nearly in a bit of the Bay of Biscay, 5 November*

I stood up on the monkey deck in the dark for a long time last night. The wind blew bracing and briny. Ham Man had long gone as the cold had got to him. He'd kept insisting I stand right in front of him, but there's only so much a girl can take as a manhandled windbreak.

Not long out of Le Havre, and before any signals were swallowed by the distance of the ship from the shore, I made my first-ever calls on a mobile phone. I think my reluctance in embracing this form of conversational technology might have something to do with having been severely traumatised when, in 1995, while cycling around Japan, I read in the *Japan Times* (paper motto: 'All the news without fear or favour') of the first reported death caused by a mobile phone: a man in Korea was walking along the street busy chatting on his phone when he walked into a tree, crashed to the ground and died. But I've since been on the therapeutic couch for some deep-rooted mobile phone counselling and it seems I'm now okay and have overcome my fear of the condition known as mobile-induced premature arboreal death syndrome – or MI PADS, as I believe it's known in medical circles.

Miraculously, despite my mobile-ringing backwardness, I some-how managed to push the right buttons without either the whole thing blowing up in my hand, or sending the ring-tone module into a dementedly continual techno-version of *Greensleeves*. Before I knew it, I had Dad in my ear telling me to be careful and not to talk to any strange men. Mum said that as I wouldn't be around for a while to offer any puncture-mending services, she had been to see Owen (local bike shop man) to have anti-puncture green slime put in her tyres. Then she said that my roof at home was overrun with mice. I said that I'd set Gary on to them. When I spoke to Gary he told me he had spent most of the day cutting rafters. Or to be more precise, oak rafter couples with a few undersquinted abutments on the side. I would have been quite happy if he'd left it at that but, being a chippy, he felt predisposed to tell me that he had also been busy producing a nice end to the lamb's tongues stopped chamfers on his large crown posts. And he had been making some side halved and bridled butt joints using two-edge pegs and four-face pegs. It all felt a bit surreal to be hearing about the finer detail of his lesser known chamfers (whatever *they* were – best not to ask) while standing on top of a big ship heading deeper out into the night and the open ocean. It also felt a bit odd not knowing when I would speak to Gary again, let alone see him. He said I sounded very excited. And I was. But I was also quite excitedly scared. I took this as a good sign because, as the French writer Albert Camus once said, 'What gives travel value is fear.'

After a short night filled with a restless tumbril of dreams, I was back up on the monkey deck by dawn. The wide Atlantic had opened up, the great grey cylindrical waves lifting and dropping the bows. Somewhere around here we cross over the edge of the continental shelf, the outer edge of the slab of continental crust that, like all continental shelves, forms the true boundary of a continent. As we've poked our way out of the Channel into the Atlantic, the continental shelf has dropped a mere 100 metres or so. But when we drift over this undersea cliff edge, the floor of the ocean will begin a sharp dive in a relatively short distance, plunging to an abyssal depth of over 4,000 metres. Blinkin' 'eck! That's 13,000 vertical feet, or over two miles from the bottom of our insubstantial steel hull down to the blackness of the ocean floor. If I think too hard about this boundless chasm that is about to fall away beneath us, and what monstrous creatures with unworldly-sized suckers and eyeballs as big as baseballs might be swilling around down there (giant squid spring unappetisingly to mind), I feel a definite dose of giddiness coming on.

As usual, chief officer Alexi was manning the bridge on the early morning shift. He looked exhausted. But then so did most of the crew. This is hardly surprising; Europe is the most taxing part of the trip, as there is virtually no let-up for the crew for two or more weeks. The pilotages in and out of the many ports – Hamburg, Hull, Antwerp, Dunkirk and Le Havre – are all long and the work is relentless and tiring. No matter how many times they might have done it, the toil takes its toll on the crew. Because of this busyness, none of the Bank Line fleet tends to carry any passengers around Europe. They usually join the ship at the last port and get off again at the first, and any passengers' cabins are often stripped and used by shore gangs brought aboard to carry out essential repairs and maintenance. Us lot only joined in Dunkirk because the *Speybank* was supposed to be giving Le Havre a miss this time around. At least that's what Sado had told us in London. Still, it's good to be kept on your toes.

When I climbed up to the monkey deck this morning, a tumult of wind hit me in the face like a fist. But as I like being outside, I held my ground by tethering myself to the heavy bench on this uppermost deck. And there I spent all morning in the cold and vigorous wind, swaddled in practically every piece of clothing I possessed to stay warm, including three pairs of socks. No one else appeared at all. I read my book, Bruce Chatwin's *Anatomy of Restlessness*, which I found in the onboard library. Bruce keeps coming out with quite deep but interesting stuff. He thinks we are all travellers by birth. 'Prolonged settlement has a vertical axis of some ten thousand years,' he writes, 'a drop in the ocean of evolutionary time. We are travellers from birth. Our mad obsession with technological progress is a response to barriers in the way of our geographical progress.' (Bloody mobile phones – but at least they move with you.) He says, 'The few "primitive" peoples in the forgotten corners of the earth understand this simple fact [that we are all travellers from birth] about our nature better than we do. They are perpetually mobile. The golden-brown babies of the Kalahari Bushmen hunters never cry and are among the most contented babies in the world. They also grow up to be the gentlest people. They are happy with their lot, which they consider ideal, and anyone who talks of "a murderous hunting instinct innate in man" displays his wanton ignorance.' To demonstrate how much we should all be on the move instead of staying plonked in our houses all our lives, Bruce quotes Robert Burton, author of *The Anatomy of Melancholy*: 'The heavens themselves run continually round, the sun riseth and sets, stars and planets keep their constant motions, the air is still tossed by the winds, the waters ebb and flow . . . to teach us that we should ever be in motion.'

In between all this heady stuff I learnt a few apposite words and phrases from my Russian phrase book that I thought might come in useful to fire at a Russian on board should I find myself in a tight corner of the poop: *Pahzhahloostah gdyeh vahkzahl* ? ('Where's the railway station please?'); *Kahgdah yah vahs vstryehchoo?* ('What time shall I meet you?'); *Vighdyeetyeh! dvyehr' ahtkritah* ('Come in! The door's open'); *Polniy pahzhahloostah* ('Fill her up, please'); *Ehtah sleeshkahm vyehleeko. Mahglee bi vi yehkhaht' yehdlyehnnyehyeh?* ('It's too big. Could you drive more slowly please?')

But mostly I just stared at the sea.

At 11.40 my aimless musings were shattered by the sudden sounding of the ship's whistle, which, as I've already said, is not a whistle but a shockingly socking great horn. The initial body-booming resonance gave me such a fright that I very nearly measured my length falling backwards off the bench in a state of advanced cardiac arrest. But I soon settled down again when I realised there was no urgent need to abandon ship quite yet. Always at this time of day, when you are inside, an announcement can be heard on the ship's tannoy system. This time it emanated from the voices of the two officers changing over duty on the bridge, third mate Alex Fogarty and Mr Alex Sasha second officer Nepomnyashchikh. Third mate Alex announced the announcement in English: 'Your attention please! Your attention please! The ship's fire alarms will now be tested!' There then followed the same announcement, but in Russian, as announced by Mr Nepomnyashchikh. It sounded something like this: '*Pahzhahloostah! Pahzhahloosta! Yehst' oo vahs soop s kooreetsay? Vizhaveetyeh meeleetsiyoo. Pahmoytyeh golahvoo ee sdyehlightyeh ooklahdkoo pahzhahloostah.*'

Actually, it only sounded vaguely like this because what that lot of mumbo-jumbo means is: 'Please! Please! Have you any chicken soup? Call the police. I'd like a shampoo and set, please.' That's because I've just learnt that in my phrase book. I thought it might come in handy one day.

At noon on the nose I was ready for the horn's boom-bawling call to lunch and had my hands clapped tight over my ears. Down below in the officers' mess we now have seven on our table, as the French army has boosted our numbers. Mickael, the one who sets my heart a-flutter, has taken a seat next to me, which makes it a bit hard to concentrate on anything. His leg touched mine under the table today, which sent me into quite a quiver. Xavier sits opposite, next to Ian, looking very upright and angular. His face reminds me of a mixture between a ferret and a Ford Anglia with pointy front wings and a cut-back rear screen. For some reason I was thinking he would look very good in drag, strutting about like a peacock in red killer-spiked heels. But that was probably the last thing on his mind at the moment: he had taken one mouthful of his salad – a cottage cheese dollop on a slice of pineapple with three fanned slices of tinned peaches – when he turned whey-faced and rapidly disappeared upstairs. Our first victim to seasickness, perhaps? I was a bit concerned for his welfare but Mickael merely turned to me with a little chuckle and said, 'I sink eeze no feel good!'

Mickael and I then had a comically getting-nowhere-fast con-versation thanks to his lack of English and my lack of anything but elementary French. But I did manage to ascertain that he was married with a sixteen-month-old daughter called Eva. What a blow!

Ham Man was the next casualty to beat a hasty retreat upstairs. I was quite surprised at how well I was still feeling. Despite the sea growing in size I felt as right as rain and was still eating an arm and a leg. After Ian excused himself from the table – not to be ill but to go and play with his charts and dividers and GPS – that left me and Llewellyn and Eleanor. Once out of earshot, Llewellyn remarked upon Ian's rounded back and hunched shoulders. 'He ought to do something about his posture or else he's going to be very sorry.'

Ian is definitely no Mr Alexander Technique but then, being so thin and long, it can't be easy keeping such a gangly stretch of back straight. But Ian's wasn't the only back Llewellyn had his corrective sights on.

'And you need to improve your posture too, young lady,' he said in lordly fashion. 'With all that hunching over your handlebars and writing and eating *so* much, you should make amends while you're still young enough to change. Back straight, bust out.'

I gave him a steely glare and thought: *If you don't shut up, Llewellyn, there won't be so much a bust out as a bust-up.* Meanwhile, Eleanor gazed on, expressionless.

Llewellyn then told me that in the name of knee preservation I shouldn't pound up and down so much in an exercising frenzy. Knees can have their fragile moments, he said, and told me how he had injured his in the war. I thought he was going to say something exciting like how he was dodging shells and machine-gun fire and single-handedly winning the Battle of Britain when, shot down over enemy territory, he got a hail of bullets in the knee. Instead he said, 'I was climbing into the cockpit of my aircraft when I caught my leg on something, fell forward and wrenched my knee. I had to fly for two hours in agony. I damaged the cartilage. Had to have it removed.'

That led on to the subject of flying and one of Llewellyn's long-winded but confusingly interesting stories of self-heroism and it went something like this. A decade or two ago, Llewellyn was invited to sit behind the pilot and co-pilot in the cockpit of a private jet full of the high-flying dignitaries of Manchester. It was a day flight and the honourable guests were all in the cabin sipping champagne and supping smoked salmon. Or whatever you're supposed to do with champagne and salmon in a sipping and supping fashion. The idea was to fly out to the Bay of Biscay and back. (Ah, what a topical theme! We're sitting ducks in it now.) If I've got this right, there were two signalling types of signal stations from which they had to get their signals (bear with me if I'm getting a bit technical with my signals). One of these signal stations was near Manchester and had a name like Burton Wood or Birnam Wood ('do come to Dunsinane'). The other was situated at Birkenhead on the Wirral. The captain misread the signal of one of these signal stations because it was apparently very similar to the signal of a signal station off Portugal. So it was this signal station off Portugal that the captain confused it with, which made him think he was off the balmy hot Iberian coast and not the drizzly cold Wirral. Or vice versa. Llewellyn just happened to be peering over the captain's shoulder and noticed that they were flying due east when they should be heading due north. Or due north when they should be heading due east. It was all getting terribly complicated because Llewellyn was demonstrating this story to me by moving the jars of mustard and horseradish around the table like pieces in a chess game and I kept getting distracted when, in between these moves, Llewellyn would idly play around with a silver napkin ring that he kept suggestively slotting over the top of a tomato ketchup bottle – an action that was rewarded by a slapped hand from Eleanor.

But back to the jar of mustard, which I believe was the jet. When Llewellyn drew the captain's attention to this decidedly serious blunder (no one else in the cockpit had noticed his mistake) the captain said, 'What shall I do?' – which isn't exactly a comment that inspires confidence in anyone whose life is in the hands of someone controlling the destiny of their flight. The upshot of this rather longwinded tale was that Llewellyn put the captain straight before the mustard ran out of fuel and fell into the ocean of the tablecloth.

Back in my horizon-scanning position up high on the monkey deck, I noticed how the grubby-coloured sea showed itself as a messy mass of enormous and ever-moving swells picked out here and there by tumbling cusps of off-white skeins of spray. A deep-grey stain of cold November sky continued to lie like a blanket above us, as it had in the Channel. As the hours went by, the wind became big and bullying, hitting the *Speybank* portside on. The ship was really beginning to dip and dive and roll as it plunged into the oncoming waves, sending masses of water boiling across the main deck. Vast sheets of spray piled over the bows and the solid block of stacked containers. Even my face and waterproofs received salty wet soakings of spray carried far and high by the wind. The severe pitching and jouncing movement of the ship made it impossible to stand or move around the deck without a hand gripping a railing. Sometimes, in between moves, when I had to dare to let go completely, it felt all too easy to be catapulted over the side. Every so often a rogue wave would slam violently into the hull, sending an alarmingly jarring shock ricocheting throughout the entire vessel. As if we had sailed into concrete. The ship would momentarily sag and stagger through the trough, slewing from side to side.

The only ship I saw all day was a long low-lying container vessel that appeared out of the murk, passing surprisingly close. Along the length of its hull spread the word *HANJIN*. I found it impossible to look at this ship without wondering where it was going and where it had been and what cargo it was carrying and who the crew were and what they were doing and what they were thinking. And whom they had left behind. I know the life on board these working ships is anything but easy, but there's still something rousingly romantic about a life at sea.

One of the books I'm reading at the moment is called *The Last of the Cape Horners*. It's edited by the interesting-sounding veteran sailor Spencer Apollonio and is all about firsthand accounts from the final days of the commercial tall ships, those magnificent multi-masted ocean-going cargo-carrying beauties known as square-riggers that voyaged every year around the world, out from Europe and then home again around Cape Horn (that devilishly southern-most rock of the Andes) or Africa's Cape of Good Hope, deep loaded with the grain of Australia. They sailed without engines or mechanical power, without electronics, even without Ian and his suitcase of wizardry gadgets and globally positioning equipment. Fantastic as it may seem today (after all it's not *that* long ago – even Mum was in this world when all this was still going on), they sailed without any contact with the world for the hundred days or more that were usual for their voyages. The distances they covered as they circumnavigated the world were immense – 25,000 to 30,000 miles, only once touching land, racing on their ways solely by wind and sails. These Cape Horners, or windjammers as they were also known, a few of which sailed on even into the 1950s (though their hey-day was several decades before), were not built for speed like the fast and famous clipper ships of the mid-nineteenth century – the California gold-rush clippers or the English colonial or tea-clippers like the *Cutty Sark* (currently residing in Greenwich). Instead, many of the windjammers were built more like warehouses, to harbour vast amounts of stores, and as they fought to survive against the ever-expanding competition of steam, they reduced their crews and increased their cargoes at the least possible cost.

Most of the tales in the book are by men, but one is by a woman, Betty Jacobsen, a Norwegian by birth, who spent the first five years of her life at sea in her father's ships. Then in 1933, after working in New York for a while, she sailed as an apprentice in the *Parma*, a square-rigger built in Glasgow in 1902 and broken up in 1936. It was on this trip that the *Parma* took only eighty-three days to sail from Australia to England, the fastest sailing ship voyage since the First World War. You'd think that there would be a definite degree of romanticism experiencing a voyage like this. But Betty didn't think so. 'I do not see anything very romantic in all this, nor anything adventurous either,' she wrote. 'It is very discouraging, and I am inclined to look upon this life as one of the least glamorous pursuits of hard labor known to man. The sea is always the same and there is not much beauty to be seen in the sails when they are wet and cold and gray, and you are wet and cold and gray, and they fight you with a malignant ferocity when you go aloft to take them in.'

Apart from going down to eat or change the film in my camera or to be vacuum toileted, I spent all day up on the monkey deck being thrashed about by the anarchic wind. I loved it up there, even when it started raining. Unlike Betty, I wasn't working and I was cocooned in modern storm-repellent kit. All I had to do was zip all hoods up high and disappear tortoise-like further into my protective shell of Goretex. No one else showed up at all. But then, amazingly, none of the other passengers seems to possess any wet-weather garb. It's all fancy frocks and shiny shoes. Still, at least they all seem perfectly content inside. Ham Man appears to spend most of the time asleep. Ian, still dressed in dazzling gold cufflinks and pressed stripy office shirt, goes to and fro with furrowed brow between the bridge and his cabin taking plottings and bearings. His cabin is like a mini bridge in itself – the table concealed beneath measuring instruments and a full set of charts covering the Atlantic and Pacific. His desk is a veritable humming hive of computers and gadgets and things that go bleep. This phenomenal helm of personal technology looks far more high tech than the *Speybank*'s.

As for Llewellyn and Eleanor, they, like Ham Man, seem to do quite a bit of sleeping too, at least in the afternoon. Otherwise they spend the majority of the time in their cabin reading, watching videos or, at least in Llewellyn's case, getting all curmudgeonly with a new laptop he bought just before they came away. Apparently I'm the only passenger who hasn't got a computer on board. Everyone's rather amazed that I'm supposed to be writing a book but haven't got a laptop with me. But I prefer staring at seas to screens. And anyway, I've got my ragged-edged notebook-diary, which is far more adaptable than a laptop. It stuffs in a pocket, doesn't need charging and is always conducive to a doodle or two. Doesn't crash on me either. Only my bike does that.

I find that, unlike the others, I want to spend as little time in my cabin as possible. Things are so wild and exciting up on deck I don't want to miss a minute. This afternoon I espied a few big black-wing-tipped torpedoes dropping out of the sky. They were gannets, falling like living arrowheads into the sea.

As daylight diminished, the seas increased into vast ship-dropping troughs. The growing wind became so abrasive and strong it ripped to shreds the tennis-court sized blue cover shrouding the *Greenland* catamaran. As sheeting rain strafed the deck I finally decided to retreat to my cabin, where I found the sliding drawers in the small cupboard and under the bunk crashing in and out in time to the juddering rolls of the ship. The drawers' securing bolts were obviously not secure enough so I rigged up elaborate drawer-ramming devices involving heavy panniers, gaffer tape and tightly stretched bungees. Later on I lay on my bunk wedged against the bunk's preventer board and tried to sleep. Not an easy thing to accomplish when your body is being jolted about your bunk from one shoulder blade to the other in time with the ship's violently rowelling jerks and shudders. So instead I lay listening to the howling wind and the rhythmic banging of a nearby door.

*The Atlantic, 6 November*

At one point during the night the *Speybank* slammed with such force into what must have been a particularly unfriendly wave that the strength of the reverberating shudder shoved aside the three deadweight panniers I had trussed together in front of my under-bunk drawer. The drawer then shot out at speed, catapulting its contents (my lifejacket) into the other room. I tried not to take this as an ominous sign of things to come.

This morning there was still a vicious maelstrom pounding the ship. As if the weather wasn't enough of an eye-opener in itself, I was surprised to come across the captain walking around inside in short blue shorts and flamboyant Hawaiian-print shirt. I wondered whether this was maybe a time-honoured seafarer's tradition of combating the tempestuous elements that thrummed beyond the doors; if it's horrible out, dress sunny within.

The good news is that, despite the deteriorating weather, we're still floating. What's more, I haven't been sick yet. Also, despite, or because of, all the shuddering judders that appear to stop the *Speybank* dead in its tracks, the ship's clocks went back an hour last night. So we must be getting somewhere.

There's been no sign of the Frenchmen today. Nor Ham Man for that matter. (*Mal de mer,* I feel, is taking its toll.) Llewellyn is all mopey because he's got a bad throat and cold (like many others on board). Every time I see him he keeps groaning. But that's men for you – make a hypochondriacal mountain out of a mole-hill. I've noticed, though, that his near-deathbed poorliness doesn't seem to have stopped him from downing a load of drinks at the bar. Doesn't seem to have put him off food either. Eleanor's also not feeling too hot. But at least she's not complaining. At one point at breakfast Llewellyn turned to Eleanor and said, 'How're yer doin', kid?' Eleanor looked at him with one of those looks that sheep give you when they suddenly stick their heads through a hedge as you're cycling past; ruminatively unimpressed. This amusingly blank expression was helped by the fact that Eleanor was carefully chewing an unhurried mouthful of scrambled egg and toast at the time.

I don't think I've told you yet that there's a very large picture of the Queen on the messroom's wall near the galley. She's standing in such a position that her eyes keep watching me. I find this off-putting. It strikes me as rather out of place having a picture of the Queen on board a ship mostly full of Russians. I think it would be far more appropriate to have one of a babushka or an onion dome or a Cossack's hat. I think I might have a word with the captain.

I've now given up trying to wreck my knees on the bent-cranked exercise bike. For one thing the ship is rolling so much that it feels more akin to riding a bucking bronco than a bike. At this rate, I'm not so much going to ruin my knee as break my back. And as for the incessantly buzzing and crackly noise of the broken striplight, well, it's driving me nothing short of insane. So it's up to the monkey deck for my exercise fix.

But I've even had to abandon that idea today as the *Speybank*'s been getting such a right old clobbering from the weather. The yowling wind has thrown up a hugely disorderly spume-whipped sea full of deep depressions and unpredictable potholes into which the lurching ship falls like a reeling drunk. Every now and then we plough head on into an oncoming roller, which somehow sends us flying off the top into the centre of another, a great spray cannonading upward. It's completely impossible to walk even two steps on the monkey deck without feeling you're about to be sent crashing into the railings or rudely jettisoned over the side. Even the heavily rooted garden-like bench has been sent for a burton by being hurled about thirty feet into the base of the funnel. The only way I could remain up on the top without being blown overboard was to lie wedged in a cranny, semi-prostrate on the spray-wet deck, with my back and head pressed against my scrunched-up backpack. And there I remained, hour after hour, hypnotised by watching the dipping and diving horizon rise and fall below and between and over the horizontal bars of the deck's side railings. Sometimes, when the ship plunged into a particularly deep valley of water, the horizon disappeared altogether.

*The Atlantic, 7 November*

More confusion: the ship's clocks went back by another hour last night. But whatever the time is supposed to be, one thing is for certain – it was virtually impossible to get any sleep again. With the *Speybank* smashing its way into such a hugely shambolic sea, my body got shunted and flung around my bunk as if on a big-dipper. I felt quite battered and bruised this morning.

But this is nothing compared with the unnerving sensation that men experienced when sailing their vast ships in the Roaring Forties (that 'exhilarating' zone of the southern hemisphere between 40 and 50 degrees latitude characterised by savage west winds and towering seas) around Cape Horn. I've just been reading about the young seaman Ray Wilmore as he described being on board the *John Ena,* a four-masted square-rigger, at the beginning of the twentieth century when voyaging in the thick of the Forties. The seas and winds were so huge that he couldn't believe any ship could live through it. Life inside the bunkhouse was a scene of uncomfortable chaos. The room was awash with around half a foot of water slapping back and forth against the bunks, and the men who weren't trying to sleep were fighting a battle with trying to bail it out. 'But every sea higher than the door board lets in more gallons of water.' The men were bitterly cold and everything in the bunkhouse was constantly wet. When they turned in for a battered-about few winks of sleep, they didn't even bother peeling off their sopping wet clothes. The only dripping things worth removing were boots and oilskins. So as not to fall out of their bunks in the near-knockout blows the ship received as it fell at an angle down one mountainous wave into another, the men wedged themselves into their wet wooden bunks, building up the outer edge of their soggy donkey's breakfasts (cheap mattresses of cloth stuffed with straw) by bundling up old canvas into bulky sacks that they crammed under the mattress along with anything else they could lay their hands on, such as old clothes or fat coils of rope. By doing this,

> . . . we fit down into a V between the mattress and the sidewalls and can't be rolled out. Even at that, we frequently have to brace ourselves against the upright stanchions to stay in. Frankly, the bunks are about the least inviting spots on the ship. If we could stand up in a corner, and could learn to sleep standing up, that would be more comfortable than lying on our soggy donkey's breakfasts covered with wet, smelly blankets. What a mess!

By breakfast things had marginally improved. The sea was still big and the horizon still lumpy with a spanking breeze abeam, but the lashing rain of the night had given way to welcome bursts of sunshine. Fighting with the punching side wind, I dragged the bench back into position on the monkey deck, gave the oily wet seat a cursory wipe with my sleeve, and lashed it down with rope before resuming my semi-slumped sea-scanning position. After a while I had to sit up straight and shuffle along the bench, because Ham Man appeared and wanted to sit down. He was feeling a fair bit better and had even brought one of his toys up on deck to play with: a digital thermometer. After flipping up its aerial and measuring the air temperature (a nippy 6°C) he said, 'What shall we measure now?'

I looked around, scanning the options, and said, 'How about our armpit temperature?'

There followed (at least for me, togged up as I was in multi-layers) much excitable unzipping of zips and rip-tearing of Velcro and hoiking and shuffling about deep into the recesses of clothing. Finally I found my armpit. By concentrating very hard on internal core heat, I was able to score a surprisingly toasty 36.5°C. Ham Man, on the other hand, could only peak at a measly 35.9.

'Goodness!' I said to Ham Man with exaggerated exclamation. 'Isn't it amazing what fun you can have with your armpits? In the middle of the Atlantic, too.'

Next on the morning's agenda of entertainment was to sit scanning the crashing seas with our mini binoculars for any signs of shipwreck victims, hull-ramming whales or German U-boats that don't yet know the war is over. But after an hour, nothing had made itself apparent down the barrel of our binoculars. Apart from sea and sky. How very disappointing. Then, at approximately 11.00 hours, I spotted a distant yacht. What excitement! This was the first vessel I'd seen since that *HANJIN* monster nearly careered into us.

'I can't see anyone on board,' I said to Ham Man as I monitored its progress through my binoculars. 'Maybe it's just phantomly sailing itself. It looks a bit like that boat in *Dead Calm* where everyone on board's been murdered. Shall I send you over the side in one of the lifeboats to go and investigate?'

Ham Man didn't think this was a good idea at all. In fact he didn't seem at all concerned about the whereabouts of the non-existent crew, but only because he was sure that this boat was one of the yachts that had recently left France on the single-handed race to Brazil. It looked tiny and very insignificant and not just because it was a fair way away. Staring at it through my magnified tunnel, I felt really quite in awe. How the devil, I wondered, does anyone manage to sail something so far by themselves? If it felt like

I was being tumbled about all over the shop on this massive floating block of flats, then what would it feel like in something that looked from here to be so insignificantly dinky?

Peering at this yacht bouncing around in the waves reminded me of a book I've brought with me called *Sea Change*. In it the author, Peter Nichols, a very likeable-sounding man, describes his journey sailing alone across the Atlantic in an engineless and twenty-seven-foot long wooden sailing boat called *Toad*. *Toad* had been built in Devon in 1939 as a little weekender day cruiser for gentle nosing about the rivers and estuaries of southwest England. Half a century later Peter Nichols bought the boat for $6000 in the Virgin Islands, where he took three years to rebuild it. He then spent quite a bit of time sailing it about the Caribbean and Mediterranean. But when his marriage ended he had to sell his much-loved *Toad*, as it was the only thing that he and his wife owned. So he set out from England to sail to America, where he planned to sell the boat. In the middle of the Atlantic, *Toad* sprung a leak.

Our companionable distant racing yacht appeared to be not so much leaking as overtaking us. It was flying along as fast as a witch. This seemed highly unfair, for I like to think that in the Law of Physics of the Theoretical World of Buoyancy, he who is bigger by far travels far faster. I had forgotten that I was not on board a sylph-like knife of fibreglass and titanium cutting through the water like an arrow, but instead frothing and flamming along like an obese and geriatric walrus in an old battered wardrobe. And though our much heralded 'service speed' was supposed to be a mildly exhilarating 17.5 knots, we had yet to hit much over thirteen. Maybe if I stopped eating so much, we could pep up our pace.

The captain appeared up on the monkey deck. He asked how we were doing.

'Very well, thank you,' I said. 'We've been having a busy morning measuring our armpit temperatures and contemplating the speed of passing yachts.'

The captain looked at me a little askance before turning his attention towards the sea and explaining something about how the chop and swell was much bigger than normal, thanks to the turmoil a not-so-distant hurricane had left in its wake. Ham Man and he had a bit of talk about various blowy weather conditions which led on to the ship's communication systems which led on to Ham Man asking the captain if he could strap to the railings a telescopic Kevlar fishing rod he had in his suitcase to form an aerial for his radio hamming purposes. The captain said that should be okay as long as his radio signals didn't start confusing the ship's ones. I jumped on the bandwagon by asking the captain if I could move the exercise bike up on to the prow for a spot of breezy fresh air pedalling. I was joking, of course, but the captain at first thought I was serious. He looked as if he was seriously regretting ever taking me on board. But then he laughed and said he was getting some very strange requests from passengers this time around.

After a bit more chat the captain said he had better get going and took himself off to another part of the monkey deck to peer into a big vent-box thing. Then he stood beetle-browed and hands on hips staring up at the navigation lights and telecommunication mast. Frowning gave his forehead a netted look. He seemed quite troubled by something. Not a promising expression to see on a captain.

'Maybe something's been blown away over night,' I said *sotto voce* to Ham Man.

'Like what?' he murmured back.

'I don't know, maybe a light or a lifeboat or a "where-the-bloody-hell-are-you?" search and rescue global navigation unit.'

'I think you'd better ask him.'

'I think I'd better not,' I said. 'I think I've already overstepped my mark.'

At this point I noticed the sudden and unexpected appearance of a sparrow-sized bird, which I think could have been a rare lesser spotted storm petrel. It fluttered for a moment over a bank of containers, but by the time Ham Man swivelled round to try to follow the point of my finger, it had gone.

\*

Alone on the monkey deck I've been pondering on the unpeopled yacht we've seen and start thinking about the *Mary Celeste*, the hundred-foot long part schooner-rigged, part square-rigged brigantine that in 1872 was found sailing aimlessly in the Atlantic, her crew strangely and inexplicably missing. The ship had apparently sailed more than 300 nautical miles without a hand at the wheel. Countless theories based on the few known facts (some of which have turned legendary, such as the half-eaten meals and mugs of lukewarm tea found on the galley table and the strong aroma of fresh tobacco smoke lingering in the captain's cabin) were bandied about, speculating on just what could have happened. Had the *Mary Celeste* been severely shaken by a seaquake (an earthquake at sea) or hit by a sudden storm of a particularly violent and terrifying kind? Were the crew victims of a crime or had they abandoned ship for no apparent reason? Had there been a mutiny or murder or had every person on board been snatched from the deck by a devilfish or a giant man-eating octopus with suckers the size of Swansea? Or had they simply been abducted by aliens when the ship sailed over the lost city of Atlantis or fallen to the strange forces thought to exist in the Bermuda Triangle? No one has ever known. This unresolved mystery gives me a little edge of excitement, further enhanced by being adrift in the Atlantic right now. Actually, thinking about it, I haven't seen anyone for quite some time. Maybe I'm the only one left. Maybe, as I sit here writing a seesawing scrawl that is pitching a yawing path across the page of my diary, there is some horribly huge creature, the likes of which have never before been witnessed, slowly smothering and devouring the crew and passengers one by one, deck by deck. Maybe, before I even have time to finish this wavering sentence, I'll be overcome by the shocking sight of an advancing army of hawser-thick tentacles sliding up over the sides of the monkey deck on an unremitting mission to annihilate all living life from their slippery grasp. Maybe . . . aaaarrrghhhhhh . . .

At lunch Llewellyn regaled (or, in Ian's and Ham Man's case, bored) us all with more near-air collision horror stories from his air-traffic controlling days. Hearing such gloomy tales did at least make me feel relieved to be afloat on the relative safety of a Russian rust-bucket in the middle of a heaped Atlantic with a cargo of high explosives and the possibility of being abducted by extraterrestrial beings.

After Ham Man and Ian had left the table (Ham Man to go back to bed, Ian to globally position himself or read more bearings) Llewellyn told me how he had started to write a book when he was last voyaging round the world on the *Speybank* during his much fabled Voyage from Hell trip.

'What's the book about?' I asked, imagining a nail-biting tome of near-air disasters, with maybe a healthy flotsam of sinking ships and awkward passengers for good measure.

'It's called *An Attempt to Reconcile Mathematics and Science with Time and Consciousness.*'

'Sounds riveting,' I said as my eyes glazed over.

Llewellyn, clearly deducing that I was in need of some mathematically scientific enlightening, later dropped off his manuscript to my cabin for my perusal. I wasn't so sure this was a good idea. After all, I feel much more at home reading about a sinking *Toad* than about quantum leaps and (as I was alarmed to read in Llewellyn's first paragraph) 'algorithms and turing machines'. 'Algorithms,' he explained in his text, 'are calculating procedures, whereas turing machines are a piece of abstract mathematics and not a physical object.' Well, I'm glad he cleared that up before I started looking for them in the cupboard under the stairs.

The first few pages passed way over my head but by page eight I briefly woke up at the mention of REM (Rapid Eye Movement) and the recording of dreams. In 1949, when Llewellyn was a student studying literature at the 'University of Wales College of Education', he read a book by J.W. Dunne called *An Experiment with Time.* Llewellyn explained that 'in the 1920's [Dunne], an educated Edwardian gentleman and talented engineer who lived in Paris and designed and flew his own aeroplanes before the First World War, stumbled accidentally on a peculiar discovery: a proportion of all dreams are of actual events that will take place in the future'. Llewellyn called this 'remembering the future'. He said that although he was highly sceptical and found Dunne's reasoning extremely difficult to follow, he 'nevertheless decided to try the "experiment" of recording my dreams'.

So the first night after waking from a dream, Llewellyn jotted down a few words on a bedside pad before falling asleep again. In the morning he read what he had written and 'though I had no memory of the dream itself, I had written:

Black Panther
Leaps wall
Killed.'

Although this sounds like the makings of a rather dramatic haiku to me, to Llewellyn it meant nothing more than 'a lot of old rubbish'. But then this is where things get really exciting because after he had washed and shaved and headed off to the university dining hall, he called into the library reading-room to scan the morning papers ('as was my wont'). He was particularly interested in the *Daily Express* as it featured his favourite cartoon character, 'Jeff Hawke, pilot of the future'. But before he had a chance to flip the paper over to the back cover, his attention was caught by a headline (a very mealy-mouthed one at that) on the front page:

Black Panther Escapes from Zoo
Leaps over the wall
And killed by a passing car.

When Llewellyn read this, he said, 'the hairs on the back of my neck stood up'. From then on he was a smitten advocate for Dunne's writings and convinced that it was possible to dream of events that would take place in the future.

I spent the rest of the afternoon slumped in a heap on the heavily rolling monkey deck trying not to dream of any futures or pasts, but just reaping the giddy delights of the present. My cold-turkey lack of cycling seems to be getting fairly well compensated for by the novelty of travelling so slowly in such a watery world. Lying

wedged in my monkey deck nook I can see nothing but the swaying sea and oscillating sky and the gentle gliding curvature of the
earth. Everything feels so wide and roomy, with horizons as wide as
the world. I'm amazing myself how long I can stare at all this and
not get in the slightest bit bored. The others say that if they didn't
have their computers and gadgets with them they would go off
their rockers. I find this all quite strange, but then maybe, in a sort
of paradoxically navel-gazing way, having spent so much of my life
on my bike has put me in good stead for this inactive burst at sea.
When I cycle, my mind seems to lapse into a different level of consciousness, like a kind of meditatively unpressurised (and mostly
unproductive) breezy whirring of thought. And that's how I feel
now with all this mesmerising rocking around and cogitative staring at sea. Like on a bike, it's all very slow and all very calming.

At one point I spotted Ian, still in his office shirt, hanging over
the side. At first I thought he was being seasick, but then I saw he
was simply adopting his usual posture of looking fixedly into the
screen of his GPS. I went down a deck and joined him to see
whether we were still going in the direction we were supposed to
be going. Ian, who had donned his Captain Cumming cap, said,
'More or less.' Then, after pushing a few more buttons, he told me
we were doing 14 knots and were 370 miles and 36 hours away
from the Azores. That's about a week in cycle-touring terms.

Once past the Azores we supposedly hit the Doldrums (the
zone of ocean between the northeast and southeast trade winds
characterised by calms, heat, sudden storms, drenching rains and
bafflingly unpredictable winds) and then it's full steam into the
Caribbean (in hurricane season) and the hot and steamy equatorial weather of the Panama Canal and Pacific. First stop comes
in the shape of palm tree-swaying Tahiti. Heavens, what a trying
life.

I've been doing more thinking about the *Mary Celeste* because
rummaging around below decks in the book cupboard I came
across *After the Storm* ('True Stories of Disaster and Recovery
at Sea') by the maritime historian and top sailing man John
Rousmaniere. In his book there is a chapter on 'Derelicts' that

includes a chunk about the *Mary Celeste*. It seems that, although this ship has inspired more speculation than any other seafaring mystery, it is far from being alone as one of history's enigmatic drifting derelicts known as 'ghost ships'. Between 1846 and 1850, 680 British sailing ships were abandoned by their crews and left to sink, burn, or drift for thousands of miles. Sometimes these ships could drift for years without sinking, crashing into another ship or running aground. The *Fannie E. Wolston* holds the nineteenth-century longevity record for phantom ships: after her crew abandoned her in October 1891 she drifted for 859 days (nearly two-and-a-half years!) and seven thousand miles. The problem of these derelict vessels straying across shipping lanes day and night has lessened, but it has not disappeared. During a four-and-a-half-year period in the 1990s, 116 ghost ships were reported in the North Atlantic. The 1990s is but a mere drop in the ocean of time away, which means there is probably a whole phantom fleet of ghost ships still floating about out here. Jeepers! What a daunting thought! 'I say, Captain, old boy? Would you mind just stopping the boat a minute? I think I'd like to get off now, please.'

Major excitement late afternoon was a rainbow that nearly landed on the deck. With a fierce burst of extended sun, the sea, which had transmuted from dirty dishwater to the black-green sheen of a mallard's head, suddenly flooded with a brilliant emerald that appeared to consume the entire surface of the ocean. Later on came the sunset – streaky lines of blood-red light spilt along the split of horizon and folding sky.

*The Atlantic, 8 November*

Big storm and mad wind all night. Everything crashing and banging and pell-mell in motion. Ham Man's fishing-rod aerial snapped and shattered in the thrashing gale. He's taken it off to his cabin for major modifications. There's been no sign of the Frenchmen at meals for days. I believe they are still alive, but only just. Everyone else was present at breakfast. I've now taken to bringing down various utensils from my cycle-camping kitchen (mini chopping board, sharp knife and vegetable peeler) to enable me to peel and chop additions of fruit (apples, bananas and grapefruit segments) into my bowl of porridge. The others refer to this breakfast-enlarging procedure as my 'cabaret act'.

Ian was a bit subdued at first because he's blocked his vacuum toilet again. These vacuum toilets are sensitive things because, as the captain explained in his introductory letter to us, 'this system is very particular and can be blocked by as little as a cigarette end or facial tissue and our staff are neither trained plumbers nor paid like them'. I said to Ian maybe it would be easier simply to go in a bucket and hurl the lot over the side.

For part of the time that I've been spending strapped down in the wind on the monkey deck scanning the sea and sky with my binoculars for half-submerged icebergs, phantom ships or enemy aircraft, the other passengers have spent hours busy emailing. In an annex off the bar sits an old dinosaur of a computer on which we are allowed to send free emails. Because I've never sent an email in my life (I'm a bit backwards – I like my feathered quill and nice solid pad of touchy-feely paper), I've put off doing anything about learning for as long as possible. But as Mum and Dad bought an email telephone (very technologically uncharacteristic behaviour for them) before I went away specially so that they could know whether I was still in one piece, I thought today that I'd best make an effort to try to learn. So Ian gave me a lesson and a short time later I was hearing all about the mice extravaganza going on in my roof. There was word from Gary, too. The riveting news was that he had just made a mortice gauge out of a log he had found in the woodpile. It had also been the hottest November day at home on record.

It's a Force 8 today, known on the Beaufort scale as a 'fresh gale'. The sea is a mass of lumpy and unruly spume-flying waves that send the ship rocking and jarring and slamming and pitching in hugely awkward yawing rolls. At lunch the tablecloths had been wetted to prevent the plates slipping and sliding and smashing. But it's not so bad that we've had to raise our fiddles (the wooden sliding flaps that line the edges of the table). If the eating areas weren't so close to sea level but positioned five flights high we would need more like fences than fiddles to keep food and crockery from capsizing and toppling. It's like clinging to a wide-arcing pendulum up there.

It was at lunch that Ian expressed his distaste for the ship food, saying that he ate better when he was at school. But then he did go to Charterhouse. Being an ex-wine merchant and organiser of top-class Scottish restaurant competitions, he's also got very high standards. I said I thought the food was top-notch, considering that we're bobbing about in the middle of the Atlantic. Ian then slightly diverted the subject to say that he had never eaten a decent meal in America. 'And it seems the only salad dressing the Americans have ever heard of is Thousand Island,' he said.

With five generations of dead relatives lying in a cemetery in the middle of the Prairies, I felt called upon to stand up for the land of the Surf 'n' Turf. I also said that, with all those All-U-Can-Eats, America was a refuelling culinary delight for cyclists. 'The bagels are good, too.'

'That's if you happen to like bagels,' replied Ian, 'but I'm not a Jew. There again, the best meal I ate in America was an Indian I had in New York. But then I'm not an Indian! All I can say is that the nation that invented the Surf 'n' Turf has got to be in serious serial decline!'

I'm not quite sure if it was coincidence in all this rough-and-tumble sea, or whether it was preparing for the imminent and likely eventuality that we might sink, but we had a lifeboat drill today. This rather farcical charade involved becoming engaged in a momentary power struggle with my lifejacket (I could swear the unruly straggle of straps were out to throttle me) and donning a hard blue hat as heavy as a Victorian deep-sea diver's helmet (too bad if I went over the side topped in this – I would sink like a sack of bricks). After making haste to the passenger muster station, conveniently located in the bar, we all had to clamber down the outside steps to one of two lifeboats. Most modern container ships these days have what are called 'freefall' lifeboats. These are space-capsule type vessels that sit poised at forty-five degrees on shoots at the ship's stern. At a split moment's notice, these large bright orange lozenges rocket into the sea like something guided by Mission Control in Houston. Not so on the *Speybank*, where, to the uninitiated and slightly panicky eye, the two pods appear to be rather too firmly wedged into the cradle of their hoists. I worry about them being lowered into a raving chop of a sea with anything like fast and efficient ease. Oh well, best not to dwell on the prospects of drowning until that fateful moment arrives.

Back in position on the monkey deck this afternoon I saw a weird funnel cloud stretching the beam of its goblet wide across the sky, its long diagonal tail spiralling down to the horizon. Suddenly the air seems to be warming up. I no longer have to wear gloves or two pairs of socks. I even spotted one of the Russian crew walking up to the bow bare-chested with the top of his boilersuit tied around his waist. I ask you! Anyone would think it was the height of summer the way he was carrying on. But then he might have just emerged from the engine room and it is about a thousand degrees down there. The second engineer, Vitali Agudalin, who looks like a young Boris Johnson with a foppish swab of thick blond hair, offered to give me a guided tour of the engine room. But no sooner had I clambered down into its sweating and deafeningly thrumming depths than I began to feel decidedly wobbly of stomach. So I beat a hasty retreat. I don't know how anyone manages to work down there in those conditions. I take my deep-sea diver's helmet off to the lot of them.

Apart from the more senior officers, I'm quite surprised how few of the Russian crew I see. I pass the time of day with the odd one or two I meet on the stairs, and every now and then I spot an oily-looking apparition in overalls drifting along the lower side decks or vanishing behind an ominously groaning stronghold of creaking containers. But apart from that, they are noticeably thin on the ground and seem to simply disappear into the rust-work. This is because they are all either very busy or very asleep. The captain solved a portion of this disappearing act conundrum by informing me that around one third of the ship's crew are watchkeepers, doing half their work while I am asleep, and sleeping while I am awake. Or in Ham Man's case, they are doing half their work while he is sleeping, and sleeping while he is still sleeping.

Today was the day, though, when I saw more Russian crew than normal because it was one of the crewmen's birthday. Ship tradition has it that he whose birthday it is buys everyone else a drink. Which doesn't sound like a very good sort of birthday to me. So we all assembled at the appointed hour (17.30) in the bar department. It was here that Valeri Ananin, the fourth engineer (and Vinnie Jones look-alike), latched on to me. He told me he was from Archangel and had two 'childrens'. Both boys. The twenty-year-old was at university while the fifteen-year-old was a speed ice-skater racer. When on ship leave, Valeri is not one to sit back and put his feet up. The last time he had a couple of months off he went to Vladivostok, bought a cheap Japanese Nissan truck, and drove it over 10,000 kilometres to Moscow through dust storms and snow storms and roads that disappeared completely beneath mires of mud. He trotted off to his cabin to fetch his fat pile of photos to show me.

'I have many danger in parts,' he told me. 'Many criminal. Also many vodka! All Russian drink vodka! Every shop sell hundred different vodka. From very special vodka to vodka out of oil can!'

At dinner Llewellyn got on to the subject of royalty. 'Although I'm not a royalist,' he said, fixing me with a queenly disapproving glare, 'I think the younger generation need to look up to something to respect.'

Ham Man woke up at this point (he is always falling asleep) and said that although he wasn't a royalist either, he had a suitcase full of corny royal objects he was taking to New Zealand to sell for profit. Llewellyn ignored this comment and said how he felt the youngsters of today have it too cushy. He then branched off on to some story about how in the war he'd had to go to sea with 200 men sharing two basins and four toilets between them. 'Now that's character forming!' he said.

By pudding course (tutti frutti sundae) conversation had swivelled to the subject of Llewellyn and Eleanor's family. We were all very surprised when I asked them how many grandchildren they had and they didn't know. They sat there for a moment, quietly conferring like on a Radio 4 *Round Britain Quiz* team ('hands on the buzzers'), counting up various possibilities on their fingers, before they felt assured enough to call out the answer: 'Ten!'

'Have you never counted them up before?' I asked, slightly incredulous.

'We never see them,' said Llewellyn. 'Haven't done for years and years. There's even some we haven't *ever* seen but then that's because we don't see our children.'

I was about to ask why not, when Ham Man turned and gave me a look that said: *Don't go there, Jose.* Which is probably a good thing because I do tend to have this rather unfortunate habit of asking completely the wrong questions at completely the wrong time.

Walking back upstairs with me, Ham Man said, 'Something's gone on there. I bet I can bank on ye tae find oot!'

I didn't have to try very hard because later that evening, as I sat at the email machine reading about how Gary had just made a plumb bob reel from a piece of laburnum he had found in the coal shed, Llewellyn poked his head round the door before sauntering over towards me. After shunting aside a jigsaw of the *Titanic,* he half sat on the edge of the desk, smoothing out his trouser legs as he did so. He then launched straight into telling me that he and Eleanor had been married since 1971 and that they have had one daughter together who lives in Kent. He also has two sons and two daughters from his previous marriage but he might only see them once in a blue moon. It seems he's fallen out with all of them.

The door opened and Eleanor stuck her head round the corner. 'Ah, *there* you are,' she said in a voice that made me feel as if I had been caught doing something sinful. Ten seconds later Llewellyn was gone.

I turned my attention back to the computer screen. 'Here is Mum with her first ever email,' wrote Mum, testing the cyberspace waters. 'I wrote you a letter a short time ago . . . left it for a few moments and it completely disappeared! So here goes again.' Even more of a revelation than discovering that Mum was getting to grips with email was hearing how 'next week I am getting a dishwasher. I've had enough of washing up by hand!'

I was still two-finger typing when Ian and Purser David came into the bar. 'I don't normally like drinking after dinner,' Ian mumbled to me on the quiet while David was pouring the drinks, 'but I'm just being sociable!'

Despite his daily half-bottle of wine, Ian drinks hardly anything compared with Purser David and Chief Phil, who tend to spend a fair bit of time drinking together.

He and Ham Man have been estimating how many units of alcohol David and Phil can drink. Ham Man said the government's recommendations advise a weekly maximum of twenty-one units for men, where a unit is equivalent to the amount of alcohol in half a pint of normal-strength beer or lager, a small glass of wine or a pub measure of spirits. 'It's usually recommended that units should be spread across the week, with men drinking no more than four units on any one day,' said Ham Man, sounding as if he was on the Statistical Board of Dire Drinking Directives. I said I didn't really care how much anyone drank as long as they didn't decide to take the helm at the time and ram us on to a rock – not with twelve containers of high explosives on board. It could make a horrible mess and would be a terrible waste of a bike.

# 4

# *Always Saturday*

*The Atlantic, 9 November*

The sea is completely different today; all ruffled with disorderly swells and wavelets and whitecaps that keep colliding and collapsing into each other from every direction in a state of muddled confusion. The horizon is about eight or nine miles away at the moment but it never seems to get any closer. When I hang over the edge and look directly down into the screwy churn of the wake, it feels like we're barely moving. But despite this, the lumbering *Speybank* is managing to cover around 400 nautical miles a day – a nautical mile, as 'Captain Cumming' (Ian) keeps reminding me, being 265 yards longer than a statute mile. So every day we're chugging along the equivalent from London to Edinburgh. Or about six days' cycle.

Most mornings so far I've been managing a frenzied pre-breakfast splurting of unleashed energy around the leg-breaking obstacles of the monkey deck. Sometimes, when the ship is violently tipping and diving like an uncontrollable see-saw, walking feels akin to fighting up a mountainous incline one moment, only to be catapulted headlong down a precipitous ravine the next. I follow this entertaining activity by a rigorous burst of step-ups on the railings to get myself panting. I find I need to pant heavily every day or else I don't feel normal. It's a spin-off of not cycling.

This need to pant is making me filthy. Everything I touch on the ship is so sticky and oily and greasy and grime-salted that my clothes and hands and face look as if I have just dragged myself backwards out of a chimney. All the other passengers, apart from perhaps Ham Man, seem to remain relatively shiny and clean. I got even dirtier this morning because along with David, the Irish cadet, I was enlisted to help Ham Man resurrect his reconditioned fishing rod into an aerial. While we were being instructed to hold this here and tie that there, David told me how he and Steven (the other cadet) had spent every day since Le Havre having a horrible time scrubbing and scraping out the chemically reeking below-deck tanks that in a couple of months' time will be filled with RBD (refined/bleached/deodorised) palm oil. It's a complicated business, transporting this gloop, because it has to be carried under a nitrogen blanket. This means taking daily readings of the oxygen level in the tank and topping up the nitrogen so that the oxygen is maintained at less than two per cent. Otherwise, the whole lot goes to pot.

By mid-morning I was flopped on the deck outside the bridge wings learning some more useful phrases of Russian (*Pahzhahloostah gdyeh bleezhighshahyah stahntsiyah myehtro?* – 'Where's the nearest underground station, please?') that I felt could prove indispensable should we lose our way mid-Atlantic. I was interrupted from my *pahzhahloostah* incantations when the third officer, Alex Fogarty, emerged from the bridge. Alex is known as Young Alex – he's in his early twenties – to differentiate him from chief officer Alexi and second officer Alex.

Attached to the railings just outside the bridge wing door is a small white box with a dainty roof and little louvred door upon which are the words: 'METEOROLOGICAL OFFICE – IMPORTANT – HANG TO WINDWARD BEFORE READING'. This is another one of those commands that can send me into a state of advanced multi-choice confusion. Could it mean that you've got to

A puddle-reflected *Speybank* – an upside-down boat to take me to an upside-down land. Dunkirk, France

Last feet on land for a long time. Le Havre, France

The *Speybank* in all its glory.
Papeete, Tahiti, French Polynesia

View from my cabin porthole.
Dunkirk, France

Unloading containers. Papeete, Tahiti

Crunched up cars and metal and yet more reflecting puddles. The photogenic wastelands of Dunkirk port, France

Trucks, tractors and aircraft steps
in hold

Loading hold with 600 tonnes of
French flour for Tahiti

Man on hold

Men in hold

Clinging to a rusty rung over a black hole.
On board the *Speybank*

Berthed behind a huge
gleaming pile of a ship.
Le Havre, France

A hat and a hook.
On board the *Speybank*

Phoar! Who's been
in there? Chemical
alley on board

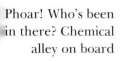

Large loads and power stations.
Le Havre, France

This should feed us for a month!

Morning ablutions on deck

Cranes and containers

hip's bulb ploughing the seas

Sploosh! Getting a feel for the Atlantic

Togged up to tackle
he elements

Mr Alex Sasha second officer
Nepomnyashchikh on the bridge

The shape of the sea

Mid-Atlantic sky

hang yourself to windward (with all the uncomfortable time-consuming, not to mention health and safety, complications that involves) before you read the louvred door, or could it mean something more sinister involving slip knots and gallows? I had previously solved this little dilemma by simply opening the box's door. Inside I found a couple of long test tubes containing a 'wet' thermometer and a 'dry' thermometer complete with complicated dials and gauges for measuring various temperatures of air and humidity. It was these that Young Alex had come to read.

As he went about his measuring procedures, Alex told me that although he comes from a seafaring family ('My old man was a chief engineer for years, though he now flies out to survey oil rigs off places like Nigeria'), he spent years after leaving school 'just dossing around', working as a cashier in Tesco, then on a factory line before spending a couple of months with a bunch of students in Morocco. 'We spent the whole time dossing around in a hippy commune outside Marrakesh,' said Alex.

He paused to scuff a hand through his buzz-cut. 'My old man was trying to get me to do a proper career for years,' he said. 'So I finally decided to do what he wanted and now I love it. This is my fourth time around the world. My mates back home in Dover think what I do is really exciting, but it's a bit of a weird life spending so much time at sea. It's really hard trying to keep any girlfriends interested, too. They hang around for a bit and then they give up and go off with someone else.'

Lunch today was a choice of either a pasty or macaroni cheese. Ian said he couldn't think of anything worse. I asked him what sort of food he ate at home for lunch.

'Well, I might have some ciabatta bread with parma ham and salad, or a bowl of fresh pasta with seafood, or a piece of wild salmon, or roast peppers with feta cheese and pitta. All with quality wine, of course! I do like a good lunch. Especially as I don't eat breakfast.'

'But you eat breakfast here,' I said.

'Yes, but that's because of the thought of what there is for lunch!'

I'm not quite sure how, but what Ian ate or didn't eat got Llewellyn on to the subject of pregnancy. One moment I was visualising Ian in his Scottish castle dishing up a nice bit of Notting Hill fare, and the next I was being asked by Llewellyn whether I would like to be pregnant. What here? Now? On this very *Spermbank*? No thanks. Not when I've got a plate of congealed macaroni cheese in front of me. Ian then chipped in with something I hadn't heard since I was at school.

'You know what they say about virginity? One prick and it's burst!'

'But we're not talking about virginity,' said Llewellyn brusquely before raising his eyes heavenwards to Eleanor.

Ham Man missed this enthralling conversation because, now that his fishing rod was up and running, he was otherwise engaged with hamming on his radio. When I sauntered past his cabin I heard a lot of chanting of his call sign going on: 'Zero Lima One Charlie Tango. Zero Lima One Charlie Tango . . .'

Later, after he'd had a conversation with a Japanese man in Osaka (*'Ah so, desu-ka?'*) as well as a chat with a trucker storming along a Pennsylvanian Interstate in his artic towards Pittsburgh, Ham Man came bursting into my cabin armed with his extra long and extra tough screwdriver, which he carried in his suitcase among fishing-rod aerial adaptors and the many Royal Family-adorned baubles and trinkets that he was planning to flog in New Zealand. I had spotted this useful tool that morning when we were erecting his rod. So I'd asked him if I could borrow it to prise open my stuck porthole.

Following a momentary tussle with the argumentative seal, it cracked open. Now I can lie in my bunk listening to the wash of the breaking waves thrashing and fizzling against the hull. Unfortunately, it means I can also hear the shattering crash as the nightly kitchen crew tip crate loads of empty bottles over the side into the sea. Surprisingly, hurling bottles into the ocean is all quite above board for the ship's legitimate rubbish disposal. When I asked Purser David about what happened to all the *Speybank*'s rubbish, he told me there is an incinerator on board to burn plastics etc., but as long as the ship is a certain distance away from shore, it's perfectly permissible to dump cardboard, wood, food waste and bottles over the side. The other day Valeri, the Vinnie Jones fourth engineer who trucked his way across Russia, came up on to the monkey deck to drink a bottle of beer. He'd also brought me a bottle of orange juice and we chatted about this and that, like the amount of vodka Russians drink, and what a lot of money Russians could make shipping trucks from Japan to Vladivostok. Valeri then said, 'This life at sea very hard for men. No woman for four month! So we must drink very many beer for helping unhappy heart!' With that he lobbed his empty bottle into the sea. He told me to do the same with my bottle. But I couldn't bring myself to do it. It just felt wrong. So I told Valeri that as I didn't want to risk giving concussion to a passing turtle, I would put it in my cabin instead for safe keeping.

Newsflash! We passed 100 miles south of the Azores today. Just thought you'd like to know, in case you're wondering if we were still struggling to clear the Channel.

*The Atlantic, 10 November*

The heat is pouring in through my portholes. As the rest of the ship is now air-conditioned, Purser David has told me to keep my cabin door closed so that my real-life air doesn't mingle with the artificial air and confuse the system. Outside, the disc of blue-grey sea that for the past few days has quivered and collapsed beneath a dome of mottled grey sky has deepened into an incredibly dark azure blue. The foaming and sea-slapping fallout from the bursting bow waves that peel away down the sides of the ship is an effervescent lather of marbled turquoise froth. As is the seething wash. Watching the exploding colour and the friskiness of the spuming counter-waves is so astonishing that I can stare at it all for hours.

Mid-morning we were suddenly hit by a ferocious burst of squally rain. But then just as suddenly everything turned blue again. The noise of the shrieking wind up on the monkey deck was so screech-ingly loud that when Ian climbed up to take his daily bearings, we couldn't talk to each other without shouting. After several attempts I managed to decipher his wind-whisked words. He said he had been working out with his instruments that dropping off half a knot, as we had done, could set us back by fifteen hours.

'Oh good,' I said. 'All the more time to stare at the waves.'

Ian frowned and looked rather worried.

For lunch I've started having the floating-in-fat Russian soup that the chief cook Valeri Evglevskiy and second cook Andrey Uss throw together every day to satisfy the hearty appetites of the Russian crew. Afloat among lots of potatoes and cabbage it seems to contain a bit of everything. As long as I navigate around the unidentifiable bits of scrappy meat and shinbones, it's really very tasty.

I was on my second or possibly my third bowlful when Llewellyn said, 'I suggest you watch the amount you eat, because you look to me as you're putting on weight.'

'Good,' I said. 'And I don't care. I'm building myself up for tackling New Zealand.'

'Well, you should care,' he said, 'or else before we know where we are you'll be asking "does my bum look big in this?"'

'Llewellyn,' I said, 'sod off.'

Ian, who claims to be a self-confessed 'fattist', said to me as we were walking back upstairs, 'Don't listen to Llewellyn. He's an obnoxious cad!'

At twenty to four this afternoon I went up to the bridge to see where we were on the grand scale of things. Mr Alex Sasha second officer Nepomnyashchikh was on duty and he showed me on the charts that we were 31° 30′ N, 35° 48′ W, and 2783 nautical miles from Panama on a heading of 244°.

In other words, a blinking long way from anywhere.

Mr Alex Sasha second officer Nepomnyashchikh is a small and very rotund man who smokes like a chimney. He comes from Vladivostok and the cruel Siberian winds that howl down across the icy Sea of Okhotsk seem to have set his face with a rigid intensity. I found him a bit intimidating at first and would tend to tread water rather cautiously whenever I was in his presence. But I'm warming to him fast now because when I say something nonsensical (like trying to pronounce Nepomnyashchikh in a fetching Russian accent) the hard frozen features that appear set in a timeless permafrost suddenly thaw into a disarmingly becoming smile. He even put his arm round me this afternoon when I was wrestling with his dividers in the dimness of the chart room.

We passed over a sea mountain today. It rose to a giddy height of 4000 metres. That's a thousand metres higher than the summit of Haleakala Volcano on the Hawaiian island of Maui. It took me one-and-a-half days to cycle up the House of the Sun (as it's known in local tongue) and when I reached the top it felt like not a lot else could get much higher. But here we are soaring over the top of something that's even bigger. Sometimes I think how interesting it would be just to pull the plug. I've come away with a map of the sea floor showing a fantastic submarine landscape loaded with fanciful names. I see from this map that leaving the Channel after passing over the continental shelf we glided above the Porcupine Abyssal Plain. We then breezed over the Horseshoe Seamounts that lie west of Spain and southeast of the Charlie-Gibbs Fracture Zone. Next we skirted the Azores, which appear on this map like snow-capped peaks, before entering the Pico Fracture Zone of the Mid-Atlantic Ridge. This ridge is a range of underwater mountains that almost girdles the globe, stretching the length of the Atlantic Ocean from the Arctic to Antarctica, and is the largest relief feature on the earth's surface. We are now in the North Atlantic section of this mid-oceanic ridge, crossing a range of mountains up to two-and-a-half miles high and almost a thousand miles wide. It's a strange feeling to think about the weird and unseen world that lies in the hidden pitch-black depths beneath us. If we were sailing over a transparent ocean I could hang over the railings as if peering out of a plane and look down upon an ocean crust of hills and valleys, plains and plateaus, rifts and trenches, mountains and canyons. And I'd see sharks patrolling the waters like marine Rottweilers, and whales floating like airships, and fish travelling in flocks like birds.

*The Atlantic, 11 November*

Like the rest of the Russian crew, the two stewardesses, Natasha and Elena, work eleven or more hours a day, seven days a week. Along with helping in the galley and serving the food, they also have to do most of the laundry and wash and polish and hoover the inside of the ship, including our cabins. Natasha, who looks both sad and exhausted, has been allotted to clean my cabin every day along with the Frenchmen's and Ham Man's. To try to save her a bit of work I've told her to give my cabin a miss and that I can give it a quick whisk round with the vacuum cleaner once a week. As it is, it's quite hard moving, let alone cleaning, in my cabin because, unlike the other passengers, I haven't got enough clothes to fill the washing machine so I wash everything out by hand in my small basin before hanging it out to dry on a chaotic tangle of gar-rotting bungees that I hook criss-cross from one side of the room to the other. Even my bike has got a gaggle of socks and knickers pegged to the hooped brake cables and draped across the handle-bars and top-tube.

The nature-spotting excitement this morning was seeing a flying fish, the diving flop of tail of either a killer or pilot whale and a big bird with a silvery white undercarriage that swooped and skimmed inches away from the tops of the furling waves. I even saw some rubbish drift past: a lump of polystyrene and a large wooden box that looked like a coffin. To add to the scene there were clouds of every variety today, including vast puffy cauliflowers stacking peri-lously high overhead and sinister streaky ones looking as if they were up to no good, prowling the horizon like sharks.

Then, at 3.46 p.m. precisely, a container ship passed a mile away to starboard. It's the first ship I've seen since the overtaking yacht. And when I think about it, I haven't seen an aeroplane since leav-ing the coast of France. It's lovely to look at a sky that isn't cross-hatched with vapour trails.

Ian came to sit beside me on the monkey deck. He asked me about my long-range plans.

'I haven't really got any,' I said, 'apart from cycling around New Zealand and then maybe trying to cycle home from there – by either riding up through South America to Alaska or over to Australia and back through Asia.'

'When are you supposed to be home?'

'No particular time,' I said. 'It just depends how long my money and knees hold out.'

'What about Gary? When are you going to see him again?'

'I don't know, but I'm going to try and talk him into coming out to New Zealand.'

'Does he often come out and meet you?' asked Ian.

'No,' I said. 'The only countries we've ever cycled in together, apart from England, are Wales and France. Apart from that, he's never really been abroad before.'

'Goodness me!' said Ian.

'He says that travelling any further south of Alton – where he's lived all his life – and he's out of his comfort zone.'

Ian looked genuinely concerned, which was quite amusing. Smoothing back his mad-professor windblown wings of hair above his ears, he said, 'How long do you think you'll stay in New Zealand?'

'I'm not sure. Anything up to nine months, which is how long my visa is valid for.'

Ian looked a bit puzzled. 'I thought if you're British you don't need a visa.'

'You do if you haven't got an onward-going ticket out of the country. And because I didn't want to fork out for an air ticket to take me somewhere that I didn't want to go to before I was ready to get there, it took me a lot of visits to New Zealand House to persuade the consulate people to give me one of their maximum-stay visitor visas.'

Ian was quiet for a moment and then he said, 'I could never do what you do – travel without an itinerary or end goal. It would drive me mad. That's one of the reasons I'm finding this journey so frustrating. We're so delayed that my schedule is already messed up. I need to be in control!'

As he got up to go Ian turned and said, 'By the way, I don't think you'll need long in New Zealand – there's not a lot to see. A few years ago I drove around it in two weeks, which was quite long enough!'

Later on I sat propped up outside the bridge wing door writing in my oil-stained and wind-ripped notebook. Before long, Mr Alex Sasha second officer Nepomnyashchikh stepped outside to have a fag. He leant against the railings, cupped a windbreaking hand to give life to his light, and then, contemplating me, said, 'Whata writing you do?'

'My diary.'

He took a long deep draw on his cigarette while observing me in his stern and unfathomable manner. As it didn't look like he was going to say anything this side of Thursday (it was now Tuesday) I said, 'Do you write a diary Mr second officer Nep-pom-knee-ash-key?' The sides of his mouth quivered with a hint of a smile at my spectacular mispronunciation of his name.

'Nor,' he said, raising his shoulders into a prolonged shrug. 'Why-I-wanta-writer-diary? Every day same.'

'But it's not always the same,' I said. 'The weather changes, the sea changes, you see different things, you have different thoughts.'

'Nor, never,' he said. 'I gettup, I gota-work, I eata chicken soup lunch, I work, I eata dinner. I sleep. Always same!'

Back up on the monkey deck I was lost in another dazy-headed sea-staring session when second engineer Vitali Agudalin came and plonked himself on the bench beside me. He had just come up from the engine room, or the pit, as he called it. He undid the top of his grimy white Andrew Weir Shipping overalls and wriggled out of them until they dropped to his waist. He was bare-chested and carried the beginnings of a spare tyre or two about his waist. He looked hot. His glistening face was red and spikes of damp blond hair were plastered to his forehead. His lumpy bumped-about nose bore all the results and remnants of his past life as a boxer. He's now been working as a ship engineer for seven years. For all the Russian crew, the money is good compared with a job back home. They earn on average US$10,000 a year compared with a wage of US$100 a month if they were to stay and work in Russia.

'But all this looking into my glass ball,' said Vitali a trifle enigmatically, 'is very hard work. For most of the day I never see the weather. I only feel the waves.'

We briefly got on to the subject of Nouméa, the capital of New

Caledonia, where we're bound for after Tahiti. Vitali said, 'Ah, very interesting place. You know, Nouméa is the transvestite capital of the world. When you try to walk out of the port into town, you cannot move for so many women-men!'

Vitali is young and, like his name, full of vitality. He can never sit still for long. He looked at his watch.

'I have to go,' he said, suddenly springing to his feet. 'See you later alli-gay-tor. In a while croc-o-dile.'

Vitali is always coming out with unexpected expressions.

At 15.25 hours we were 1307 miles, or about three or four days, away from the Sobrero Passage, which is our intended route through the islands of the Caribbean. More things were floating past. For about an hour we sailed through a spate of giant brain-like splats of elfin-green seaweed. Then, with mini binoculars pinned to face, I saw what looked like a dumping of porn mags drift by – the marine equivalent of cycling past a discarded cache of double-page spreads splayed in the bushes. Only on a ship you can't stop to have a look. Then I espied a crocodile. But there again it could have been a dead body. Or maybe even an interestingly shaped lump of wood.

An hour passed and then Ian moseyed on to the monkey deck still looking, in this uncomfortably sticky and sweaty weather, as if he was dressed for the office. I made much light of this and wondered what it would take for him to peel off into T-shirt and shorts. He said he was keeping his legs covered for the sake of humanity.

'I wouldn't want to inflict their ghostly white knobbliness on anyone, not even Llewellyn!' he said.

Though Ian's knees remained unseen, he did reveal the shocking fact that he has come away with an astounding twenty collar-and-cufflink shirts. Later on I noticed that he had changed out of his thick blue corduroys into a pair of lighter-weight trousers pressed to knife-edged crease perfection.

This evening the sign on the door to the officers' mess said: THE SHIP'S CLOCKS WILL BE RETARDED BY 1 HOUR TONIGHT.

In other words, we'll be three hours behind home. Things are moving on. And back.

Leapfrogging three hours ahead means that when it's ten in the morning, Gary will be eating a stack of doorstep sarnies on his half-hour dinner break. When it's 13.00 hours on board, he'll be stopping for his tea break. When it's four in the afternoon, he'll be at home, dunking more biscuits with his tea. When it's eight at night and I'm standing on deck in my shorts in the velvety air beneath a spangly sky of stars, Gary will be tucked up in bed. Not that he's on my mind or anything, of course. How could he possibly be when I've got a flotsam of crocodiles and corpses to watch being swallowed by the sizz of the waves?

### DAY 14

*The Atlantic, 12 November*

Sometimes I wish I was in a world that wasn't moving. The waves are still as big as buses and banging us around at fifty to the dozen. As a result the continuously uneven motion is surprisingly tiring. I'm amazed how anyone can do any work at all. I feel constantly exhausted. And all I'm doing is lolling around.

There again, everyone seems a bit listless. They're all a bit tetchy too. The weather doesn't help: there is a damp menstrual heaviness in the air, as if the clouds are retaining water.

I was in the middle of watching a sudden flurry of flying fish when Ian appeared. He was in a bit of a bad mood because the air-conditioning has gone on the blink. He's not too impressed with the services on this ship. He thinks Andrew Weir Shipping need to get their act together. After a few minutes of moaning, he switched subjects and started talking about Australia. He said that he preferred

Australia to New Zealand but he still thought both countries were very inward looking.

'And as for Western Australia,' he added, 'I have never been there, but I should like to see Perth, despite it being the arse-end to nowhere.'

This afternoon I was on the bridge with Mr Alex Sasha second officer Nepomnyashchikh. Sometimes, when I'm feeling in a not very sensible mood, I stand at the control panels and say, 'Excuse me, Mr Alex Sasha second officer Nepomnyashchikh, but what does this switch do?' And I make as if I'm about to flick on a switch. Mr Nepomnyashchikh always looks very worried, which makes me laugh. Of course I am far too well behaved to go around tinkering with unfamiliar knobs that have nothing to do with me. I also have the captain's words lodged in my head from when I first joined the ship: 'Please be careful where you place your hands on the bridge. Inadvertently touching the wrong button can cause a worldwide search and rescue operation to commence.'

While we are on the subject of search and rescue, I was rifling through a few of Mr Nepomnyashchikh's papers when I came across a copy of suggested things to hurl into the lifeboats should that heart-in-mouth moment come to abandon ship. Along with the obvious things like food, water, rubber ring and emergency swimming skills, I took special note of the 'ADDITIONAL ITEMS TO GO INTO SURVIVAL CRAFT':

MEDICAL
Along with First Aid Bags – all crew to bring sunglasses, body bags for hypothermia, pillows for injured.
NAVIGATION
Pencil, rubber, sextant, charts, Nories Table, Pilot Book.
MORALE
Playing cards, bible and prayer book, books, magazines, cigarettes, bottle of brandy and small measure.

Mags, fags, booze? Blimey. This survival lark is all beginning to sound like a hedonistic knees-up in Ibiza or Faliraki. I don't mind saying I'm even quite looking forward to it. But until that moment comes, I shall keep a step ahead by bundling up my morale and stowing it away for safe keeping in an emergency pack beneath my bunk.

As if all this wasn't enough for one day's excitement we passed over another submarine mountain today, this one like an inverted ice-cream cone of prodigious proportions. Then, to counteract this flamboyant absurdity of nature, the ice-cream cone fell away into a devilishly deep rift. At the moment the seabed is 2,500 metres below us, but when we chugged over the rift it was 7,000 metres below our very insignificant old hull. Put another way, the rift was almost 23,000 feet deep. That's a scarily deep five miles (give or take a furlong) – or an hour's laden cycle uphill. The thought of having such a bottomless abyss beneath us makes me feel quite giddy. I think I had better go and have a lie down to recover.

**DAY 15**

*The Atlantic, 13 November*

You might have noticed I've started to count the days. I think that's what you're supposed to do when you're incarcerated. It's only a matter of hours now before I start to carve tally marks with my penknife into the wall above my bunk. As if you haven't already guessed, I'm feeling a little stir crazy.

I got an email from Mum this morning. She says she's swept up a few deathwatch beetle carcases she's found on my bedroom floor. She also says the TV licensing people are threatening to take me to court because I haven't got a TV licence. The explanation is easy: I haven't got a TV licence because I haven't got a TV. Yet no matter how many times I write to tell the TV licensing people this, they don't believe me and dish out another red-letter court summons, kindly informing me I am risking prosecution and a fine of up to £1000. At first I wrote quite polite letters. But when they kept ignoring them and telling me they were going to send round a man to drag me away, I finally returned one of their red-letter letters across which I had satisfyingly shouted in a blue-in-the-face-scrawl: 'I'VE TOLD YOU I HAVEN'T GOT A TELEVISION! I LIKE RADIOS. AND BICYCLES. SO PLEASE GO AWAY!'

These days, it seems you're automatically deemed a criminal if you don't own a television. Well, I'm sticking to my guns, as well as my radios, and saying: UP YOUR BOTTOM BRACKETS THE LOT OF YOU!

There, I feel better now.

While we're on the subject of televisions, I haven't got round to turning my cabin one on yet. Not that there's any television to see, mind you, as the ocean wave provides zilch reception. It's just for watching videos. On the deck below there is a small dark windowless room containing a whole cupboard stacked with videos. Every now and then I walk in there to select a film for the night. And I walk out with a book. There's a cupboard loaded with books on the opposite wall from the videos. I like books. They're much easier to turn on.

Most of the crew are addicted to videos. Whenever I pad past their cabins in the evenings they've got some big detonating Hollywood blockbuster emanating at ear-shattering volume from the doorway of their curtain-pulled cabin – each one competing explosively with their neighbour's.

I was talking to third mate Young Alex this morning and he told me how his Spanish mother met his Cockney dad. It was when his dad was working as a chief engineer. One day his ship docked in Valencia and on his few hours of shore leave he wandered down to the beach, where he was much smitten by the looks of a Spanish girl. When he finally got back to England and had some time off, he jumped on a motorbike and rode back down to Valencia, where he hung around the same beach for a few days until he saw the same girl again. They then got married. But they are now divorced.

Up on the monkey deck this morning in my usual sea-staring trance, I started thinking about single-handed sailors. I found myself marvelling at their ability to sail across an ocean for so many weeks on so little sleep. Oceans may look big and spacious and empty, but you can't just flop out on your bunk and go to sleep for half a day like Ham Man. Things like ships, icebergs, whales, oil drums, logs as heavy as medieval battering rams and semi-submerged containers that have fallen off container ships like this one can appear out of nowhere all waiting to rip your hull in two. So you have to keep a watch out for what's around you (not that I imagine you can do much about whales, drums, containers or the like, because they tend to be upon you before you know it) and snatch sleep while you can in cat-napping bursts of maybe fifteen, twenty or, at a push, thirty minutes or more – depending on your limits of dare. When I stand up on the monkey deck, a hundred or so feet above the sea, the horizon seen from here on a clear day circles me at a distance of about ten miles. But from the deck of a small yacht, the distance would shrink to around three miles. The single-hander Peter Nichols explains in his book *Sea Change* that:

> Beyond three miles, a ship will be 'hull-down' below the horizon, only its superstructure visible. Eight miles away, the whole ship will be below the horizon. Conditions of haze, cloud, rain, fog, or a large swell on a sunny day can reduce this to yards. A ship moving at eighteen knots (the speed at which the average container vessel ship might travel – many travel faster), unseen when you come on deck and make your periodic scan of the sea around you and then go below again, can steam up over the horizon and run you down in twenty minutes or less.

Without doubt, it's up to the little yacht to keep well out of the way of the big ship. If you're alone on your small boat you first have to spot the ship, then you have to watch it like a hawk to work out its course, and then you have to be ready to spring into action to alter your course to avoid it. Peter Nichols says, 'If you don't have an engine,' (he didn't), 'you'd better hope the wind is blowing.'

I know the chance of us mowing down a small boat is about as unlikely as seeing Ian in shorts, but I still can't help feeling more than a little concerned for the welfare of the way-down-there wave-farer. In bygone times, ships would have a man posted on the bow or in the crow's nest peering out into the night or scanning the waves in the day. Nowadays, a few shipping lines might still have a watchkeeper on the bow in radio contact with the bridge, but this is a rarity. Crew cutbacks means that most big ships are, if not short-handed, then working with the bare essential of crew. These crews are more likely than not overworked and underslept. (I've read in the International Transport Workers' Federation *Seafarers' Bulletin* that in a major survey co-ordinated by the MMR Unit – not the Measles, Mumps and Rubella Unit, but the slightly more long-winded Maritime Medicine Research Unit of the University of Southern Denmark – looking into the health and working environment of nearly 7,000 seafarers, only one in ten worked for 60 hours or less a week. Six out of ten worked 70 hours or more a week, and three out of ten worked 80 hours or more, and all of them seven days a week.) Some crews, depending on their nationalities, are expected to stay at sea for upwards of eight months, or sometimes nearly a year. If you work that hard for that long in often pretty nasty conditions, you're not going to be exactly razor sharp for spotting things like a little boat bobbing about on the mass of lumpy sea. Big ships can be seen, but little sailing boats can go completely unnoticed.

Before I came on this trip, I had to go to my doctor to get a letter showing I had a clean bill of health. Although Dr Hallatt had been my doctor for years, I had never met her up until that moment because fortunately I hadn't been ill or injured enough to warrant a visit to the surgery. She asked me why I needed the letter so I told her I had to have it in order to join a Russian freighter that was to take me to New Zealand. This got her quite excited.

She asked me which way I was going, and I said through the Panama Canal, and then she said she'd been through the Panama when she sailed to Australia six years ago with her husband and eighteen-month-old baby during their round-the-world voyage on their fifty-five-foot yacht, *Ocean Dream*. This was riveting information and I spent the rest of my ten-minute consultation firing Dr Hallatt with questions. I never knew a visit to the doctor's could be so much fun. Of course there was far too much to talk about in the allotted ten minutes. I said that I could suddenly make myself very ill and come in to the surgery to see her every day for the next week. But that didn't seem quite right. So we stayed in touch.

The point of telling you all this is that on one occasion when I was talking to Dr Hallatt's husband, Paul, he told me that whenever they saw a big ship he would call it by VHF radio. For one thing it was nice to have a chat with someone different (crossing the Pacific they would only see another ship about once every ten days) and it was also useful to find out any news, or whether the freighter, or whatever ship it was, had seen anything unusual, or what the weather was like up ahead. More importantly he would ask the officer on watch if he could see them on the radar. And sometimes he couldn't. 'They often turn down the sensitivity of the radar,' Paul told me, 'so that the officer doesn't get woken up by every wave or large piece of rubbish drifting by.'

On these big ships, according to Peter Nichols, 'Lookout may be by radar alone, and if the radar doesn't pick you up, you're invisible. Yachts, particularly wooden yachts, do not make good radar pictures. They're small, their radar echoes may be lost in "sea clutter" – you may look like just another wave on the radar screen. And the radar, as I've often found when calling a ship by VHF radio to ask what sort of radar picture my boat made, may be turned off.'

At night on the *Speybank* there is always a Russian watchman positioned on the bridge along with the officer on duty. During the day there is just the officer who, along with trying to keep a lookout, often has his hands tied up doing a lot of other things as well: studying the chart, plotting a course, checking the weather fax, taking sea and air temperatures, making a coffee, having a smoke down the side wing. This is normal but I am worried there are whole swathes of ocean that are passing by unwatched.

There have been cases when a cargo ship has run down a small boat and not even known it, ploughing on at twenty-odd knots regardless. Paul Hallatt told me that, in the Red Sea, large ships don't pay any attention to the small stuff. Returning home that way, he was one day talking to the Port Authority in Yemen. The Port Authority man (let's just call him PAM) told Paul that he had been talking to a captain of a container ship about his having hit a yacht. The captain told PAM he had not hit a yacht. PAM insisted that he had. The captain insisted that he hadn't. So PAM led the captain up to his ship's starboard bow from where the ship's anchor always hung when not in use. Tangled up in the anchor were the remains of a mast and rigging of a yacht. Neither the captain nor any of his crew had realised they had run down a yacht. No trace of the yacht, or its crew, was ever found.

It's no big leap to imagine being on board a small yacht when you've just woken from a brief twenty-minute doze, climbed sleepily up the companionway into the cockpit, and looked up to suddenly see the towering bow of a megalithic ship carving its shadowy death path towards you. And it's this thought, along with the horrific image of being dragged down and then carved up by the screwy churn of the ship's monster propellers, that keeps me sweeping across the surface of the sea with my binoculars. I can't help feeling that on a boat, no matter what size, you can never have enough eyes looking out.

Just before midday I found another email from Mum. It said she's worked through my pile of post and found another letter from the TV licensing people. This one says that there's going to be a mob of TV bailiff-like types arriving unannounced on my doorstep to search my premises and remove any articles they find suspicious. (What, like a small stash of deathwatch beetles? Well, in that case, they are very welcome to them.) I wrote back to Mum to say she was not to worry about a thing and that I'd set Gary on to any undesirable types with a sledgehammer.

At lunch there was no sign of either Ham Man or the French-men. Ham Man, who had told me he was suffering from 'abject boredom', has taken to either getting triple-boosted doses of sleep or watching wall-to-wall videos throughout the day (he likes big noisy car-chasing bomb-blasting Hollywood blockbusters), while much of his nights are given over to radio hamming. The French-men, who rarely venture outside, likewise spend a lot of time sleeping or watching videos. They read quite a bit, too.

Conversation at lunch revolved around the demise of Concorde. At least it started off as a conversation, mainly between Llewellyn and Ian, but rapidly turned into a monologue from Llewellyn about what a disaster Concorde was and the huge amounts of money it lost. Ian confided in me that he thought Llewellyn was talking rubbish. Later, up on the bridge, Llewellyn told me that he thought Ian was like a coconut and that he's always throwing a ball at him to knock him down. I didn't quite know what he meant by this and I didn't ask because I didn't want to get involved.

Maybe everyone is so bristly because the weather is so hot and oppressive. The air feels angry, as if at any minute all hell is going to break loose in the form of a detonating storm. There's been no show of the sun today, just a weighty and grubby sky. The Atlantic is a mass of heaving greyness. The *Speybank* seems to be making heavy weather of this wide open ocean, wallowing with a ponder-ous rhythm as she heaves her bulk at thirteen painful, creaking knots through the long swells.

For some reason I keep finding myself staring at the lifeboats. The more I stare at them the more I wonder what will happen if we have to use them.

Up on the monkey deck in my usual lookout position looking for something unusual, I saw what I thought was a piece of aircraft wreckage sliding down the side of a sea-trough. It disappeared, then reappeared. Quickly I homed my binoculars in on it. It looked like a piece of torn wing off a small plane. But then I lost it again. And then I found it again. I was about to go rushing off to alert the captain when I thought, oh, it's a surfboard. Or maybe even an ironing board. Or maybe just a plain bit of board. It's a bit hard to tell when you're pitching about in the ocean going one way, and it's dipping about in the waves going the other, with a lot of slosh in between. It's also a bit hard to know when to act to inform the officer on watch that I've seen what I think I've seen when it's nothing of the sort. Not that I know that I know that it's nothing of the sort. In all this see-sawing sea I don't think anyone can be really sure they know what they are rescuing until they are up close or broadside. But, at least in my case, it's probably an idea to get a slightly firmer picture of just what it is exactly that I have espied floating astern or abeam or asunder. Otherwise, if I wasn't careful, I could attract a raft of embarrassing headlines: *PASSENGER CAUSES RUSSIAN FREIGHTER TO DIVERT COURSE MID-ATLANTIC TO RESCUE DROWNING IRONING BOARD.*

I also feel that in my novel position as a novice watchkeeper it is probably best not to alert the chief chaps to everything suspicious that I see or else we would be forever going round in circles and then we would run out of fuel and then we would have to take to those two interesting-looking lifeboats and then we would drift on this huge ocean for weeks with nothing to eat but our comrades, which means someone has to be killed, which means it would probably have to be me because, unlike me, all the *Speybank* crew have useful nautical skills while all the passengers have something they can offer of varying usefulness for survival. Ian would be good at telling us we were 180° off course; Ham Man could radio ham for help on his fishing rod by alerting an Aussie truck driver stonking along the Stuart Highway through the red-dusty Simpson Desert in his fifty-two-wheeled kangaroo-bashing road train to our plight (though the truckie would probably just crack open another XXXX and say, 'Good on yer, mate!' by way of response); Llewellyn and Eleanor could set up a makeshift air-traffic control centre and guide a search and rescue plane to our port door, or at the very least, inform us when any aircraft was about to crash into the sea (the floating wreckage could come in handy for a spot of craft-surviving DIY); the Frenchmen could doff their caps and don their army fatigues and shoot dead any pirates, whose meat and bone marrow we could then dine on with relish (seaweed relish, that is).

Yes, thinking about it now, it's a worrying realisation that all I'm any good at is cycling, which really isn't a proficiency that is in much demand when it comes to surviving in a lifeboat lost at sea. There again, if there was some way I could convert the lifeboat into a pedalo, thereby unleashing all my pent-up energy into propelling us over hill and wave, we'd be laughing all the way to the sandbank and home and dry by tea. So on this supposition, I think eating me would be a very bad idea indeed. Let's eat Llewellyn instead. It would be kinder on the ears.

At 16.00 we were 22° 26′ N, 55° 19′ W on a course of 242°, which meant we were about 500 miles east of the Sombrero Passage. We hit our highest speed of the voyage late afternoon: a dizzy-making 16.1 knots. I don't think this was due to any abrupt power surge from the engines, but more to do with a sudden storm that hurled itself at us, resulting in the ship being propelled in a catapulting fashion off the surfing crest of a prodigious hold-on-to-your-hats wave. If 16.1 knots sounds hair-raisingly fast, bear in mind that most container ships these days steam along at around 25 knots as a matter of course. Modern racing yachts, which tend to look more like hydrofoils than yachts, can hit thirty-or-more knots. Skimming that fast across the waves is said to feel like being on a tube train completely out of control. Thirty knots without an engine. We can scarcely go half as fast and we've got not just one engine, but two. I think I might have to go and have a word with second engineer Boris. I suspect he might be having problems with his perforated inlet manifold gasket.

Towards the end of the squally-skied day, Ham Man finally stirred from hibernation and crawled up to the top deck in an advanced state of comatose torpor. As it took a while for him to gain consciousness, we sat side by side on the bench saying very little. In one prolonged burst of silence we both became transfixed watching a small notch of wood blowing back and forth in an eddying wind across the deck in front of us. Then we both started laughing, marvelling at how we had been reduced to finding the observations of a mere speck of wood as the height of high sea excitement. When we'd finally exhausted this entertainment, Ham Man revealed he didn't like the Atlantic at all. Everyone had told him that after the Bay of Biscay it would get all blue and calm and doldrummy.

'But instead the weather has deteriorated and everything is always rattling and crashing and rolling around,' he lamented, scratching his beard in troubled thought.

I said that I was loving the Atlantic – that it was everything I had ever imagined it to be, with wild seas and skies and screeching winds and big churning waves piled high.

'But have ye no' noticed the noise in our cabins? Everything is constantly vibrating and humming and rumbling and buzzing. I just cannae sleep well with such a rrracket!'

Ham Man is right. There is a lot of noise in our cabins. But when I lie down to sleep I've managed to attune myself to blot it out, or at the very least, shove it right down the bottom of the food chain of all annoyances, because if you just lay there concentrating on it, it could drive you barmy. Ham Man, it seems, is going barmy.

'If you're having trouble sleeping,' I said, 'try watching the light cord.'

Ham Man gave me a sidelong look. So I explained.

On the flimsy plastic wall beside the head of our bunks is a mini striplight, switched on and off with the help of a little dangly cord. Attached to the end of this cord is a small plastic cylindrical noddle of a light-pull, which tends to act as a miniature pendulum as the ship rocks back and forth. You can gauge the roll of the ship by the distance the noddle sways across the wall (sometimes it travels alarmingly far). Watching it is very hypnotic. And if you've fallen into a hypnotic state, you are one step away from slumber.

Dinner talk tonight featured Papua New Guinea, which is one of the *Speybank*'s ports of call. I said that I had read quite a few books about the place and would love to go there. That prompted everyone to gang up on me by saying that I was very naïve and that if I ever went there it would be guaranteed I'd get raped or robbed or murdered or eaten alive.

'It's a very primitive place,' said Llewellyn, 'full of primitive people and dangerous tribes.'

He then launched into a long story about how in the Second World War the Americans arrived in Papua New Guinea and they went into the jungle to cut out an airstrip and build an air control tower to enable planes to land and disgorge food and goods and equipment. All this, said Llewellyn, was watched by Papua's 'primitive' people, who then went away to another part of the jungle to copy the white invaders by building their own airstrip and tower.

'They then sat back watching the sky to wait for the giant metal flying beasts to appear and land on their strips to discharge strange offerings to them,' said Llewellyn. 'But of course no planes ever arrived.'

This evening I walked into the bar to fill up my water bottle from the bar sink's tap and came across Ian and Purser David having a drink. I joined in conversation and after a while asked David how long he had been working as a purser. This set him off and he told us in quite some detail how he started off his career by going to catering college and then working as a waiter for years on P&O cruises before moving into the kitchens and then working on container ships. At one point he mentioned that he lived in Wiltshire with his eighty-two-year-old mother. Unfortunately this prompted Ian to say, 'You know why you can't get any fried potatoes in Wiltshire, don't you?' Pause for dramatic effect. 'Because they've got no Devizes for Chippenham!'

A little closer to home at the moment than Chippenham, we passed over the latitude of 23.5° N today, otherwise known as the Tropic of Cancer. That means we're now on a level with the middle of Taiwan as well as Aswan in Egypt and the Tuareg's Hoggar mountains in Algeria and Havana in Cuba and Cabo San Lucas in Mexico. At last I feel we're getting somewhere.

## DAY 16

*Somewhere just below the Tropic of Cancer, 14 November*

Suddenly we are on an emergency mission. At three o'clock last night Mr Alex Sasha second officer Nepomnyashchikh, who works the midnight to 4 a.m. Graveyard Watch, was contacted by the US Coastguard on Puerto Rico. A telex-style message rattled out of one of the many machines on the bridge, which Mr Alex Sasha second officer Nepomnyashchikh later gave me to stick into my diary. This is the gist of what it said:

UTC Time: 03-11-15 . . . SAR Safety Call to Area: 20 N 62 W 200 – PosOK

THE U.S. COASTGUARD IS ENGAGED IN A SEARCH AND RESCUE OPERATION WITH A 42 FT SAILING VESSEL NAMED 'ALWAYS SATURDAY' A 42 FT KETCH WITH 2 MASTS. A MEMBER ON BOARD IS SUFFERING FROM A HEART ATTACK. LAST KNOWN POSITION IS 20-25N 062-09W TAKEN AT 20:00Q 14TH NOV 03 HEADING AT COURSE OF 240 TRUE. THE U.S. COASTGUARD IS REQUESTING ANY VESSEL THAT MAY PROVIDE ANY ASSISTANCE TO SAILING VESSEL 'ALWAYS SATURDAY', TO DIVERT TO LAST KNOWN POSITION. 'ALWAYS SATURDAY' CAN BE REACHED ON VHF-CHANNEL . . . OR BY SAT PHONE AT . . . U.S. COASTGUARD SAN JUAN, PR CAN BE REACHED ON . . .

ANY VESSEL ABLE TO RESPOND IS REQUESTED TO CONTACT THE U.S. COASTGUARD AND PROVIDE AN ETA TO POSITION. THE U.S. COASTGUARD IS SCHEDULING TO BE SENDING A U.S. COASTGUARD CUTTER AND AIR-CRAFT TO ASSIST AT FIRST LIGHT OF THE 15TH NOV 03. ANY VESSEL ABLE TO RESPOND IS REQUESTED TO PROVIDE COMMUNICATIONS RELAY OR MEDICAL ASSISTANCE. SIGNED U.S. COASTGUARD SAN JUAN, PR.

The weather is diabolical today: the sky roiling in with biblical wrath, the sea swirling in a furious turbulence of high-waved confusion. Sometimes in the deep hollows between the waves, the collapsing spume gives way to strange whirlpool-like eddies before momentarily turning eerily smooth like oil.

The estimated time for arriving at the yacht is 16.00 this afternoon – fourteen hours after receiving the signal from the US coastguard to divert course. 'Captain' Ian says we are 350 nautical miles from Puerto Rico. I can't stop thinking how every hour must feel like a week to the heart-attack man. There's been quite a lot of contact between the *Speybank* and *Always Saturday* by VHF radio. There is a crew of three men on board, including the heart-attack man, and one woman – his wife. The condition of the heart-attack man, who is sixty-six and a paediatrician, seems to be deteriorating fast.

As the day progressed the weather worsened. The wind increased and the rain poured down like a waterfall. The visibility reduced by the minute. By late morning the latest plan of action was to pick up the heart-attack man in one of our lovely-looking lifeboats (oh no!), before transferring him back to the *Speybank*. We would then sail full steam ahead towards Puerto Rico until we were within flight range for a US Coastguard helicopter that could winch the man on board and whisk him to safety.

I couldn't concentrate on anything today. Being on a rescue mission was just too exciting. I sent an email to Gary telling him what was happening and he sent one back telling me to hang on tight. He also said that everywhere at home has gone on a high security alert fearing some sort of major terrorist attack to coincide with Bomber Bush's visit this week. I suddenly realised this was the first piece of news I had heard since leaving home. Having no newspaper or radio or television makes the whole world feel as if it has gone AWOL and slipped off the edge of the horizon. The thought of people shopping or farming or driving cars or going to school or bustling through the noise of a city or answering a string of querulous telephones seems like another planet away. Life on the

*Speybank* revolves around a world of sea and sky and three dozen people. It's all rather nice and all rather simple. If something happened back home now which needed me to be there, there is nothing I can do. I'm stranded in the middle of this vast primeval soup from which we all once crawled.

By four o'clock visibility was down to only a few hundred feet. The wind was howling, the seas thrashing and thundering. The windscreen wipers on the bridge were having trouble clearing the seething wash of rain that the wind was hurling against the glass. The captain was in an understandably edgy state. Nothing was showing up on the radar and yet, according to the distressed and raspy voice emanating out of the static of the VHF giving *Always Saturday*'s current position, we should have been practically on top of it. When the weather worsens, and the air thickens with blinding rain and spray, the imprisoning circle of the radar constricts. Out in these stormy conditions where the sea is indistinguishable from the sky, it was like David looking for a needle in the haystack of Goliath. The last thing the captain wanted to do was to run the yacht down. Binoculars were pinned to faces, scouring the fast-darkening greyness. When you're on board a 550-foot long behemoth, a hundred feet above the convulsively churning swell of the waves, it's very hard to visualise what a forty-two-foot ketch is going to look like down there.

The bridge was filled with a heightened air of anxiety. Apart from the rain drumming down on the wheelhouse roof, the whirring and static electrical buzzes of the equipment, the suddenly stern calling of orders from the captain to the helmsman and the occasional disembodied voice from the VHF, the only sound was silence – an all-pervasively agitated and jittery silence. I kept well out of the way in a corner, not daring to murmur a word. At least not until, scanning the almost impenetrable gloom with my keenly roving binoculars, I suddenly blurted out, 'There it is!' as I picked out a feeble light swaying from side to side on top of a murky mast.

Then it was all action. An engine was killed, another throttled right back to virtually nothing. The *Speybank* approached from windward, hoping to leave the yacht becalmed in a short chop to starboard. Even so, *Always Saturday* appeared to be reaping little relief from the fraction of protection we offered from wind and sea. Once the *Speybank* was in position, a small lifeboat team of Russian crewmen in hard hats and carrying a stretcher were summoned to their stations.

I couldn't believe how insignificant the yacht looked. When you see a forty-two-foot sailing boat tied up in a marina it looks big – like standing next to a whopping great two-trailer truck. But out here in the hugeness of the stormy ocean it looked like a toy – the sort of thing I used to shunt around in the bath with my squeezy duck that squirted jets of water out of its bottom. Even though the shambolic swell of the sea had lessened a touch, the ketch was still being maniacally tossed about by the jousting waves.

Now that all the attention was focused on the starboard side of the ship, a rush of people had washed up into the part of the bridge overlooking the lifeboat and flailing yacht. Ian, who liked to think he was in command of operations, stayed put on the bridge. As did Llewellyn and Eleanor and the Frenchmen. Neither Ham Man nor I liked the feeling of getting under the captain's feet so we took ourselves off to the wind-screeching rain-strafed monkey deck.

What happened next was not reassuring. The team of Russians who had been dispatched to lower the lifeboat were having trouble releasing the boat. They couldn't seem to unshackle it from the cables or budge it off its davits. Precious minutes passed and still the boat refused to move, appearing far too content to remain where it was, apparently welded to the hoisted launch pads of its mother ship. But Russians are not the types to give up without a fight. So, a lot of ripe Russian language, urgent semaphoring and dicey manoeuvres later, the recalcitrant lifeboat suddenly and unexpectedly dropped by several feet. It looked like it could have plunged right into the sea were it not still rooted to an unyielding cable.

Eventually the lifeboat was stabilised. A handful of men then dared to climb into and onto the craft (I hope they were being paid 50,000 extra dollars for this act of heroism) while those left stationed at the winches attempted to lower it again.

In an ideal world lifeboat lowerings run like a well-oiled machine. But sadly, I wasn't in an ideal world. I was in a much-battered-about ex-Russian navy icebreaker of advancing years. As a result the lifeboat, with the aid of what looked like the swinging thwacks of a sledgehammer applied in desperation to the heavy metal shackle anchored to the aft chain, lowered in jerky and jolty spasms. A few of the men had now wriggled down through one of the hatches and disappeared from view. Two other men were perched precariously on either end of the boat, gripping on for dear life to the lowering cables. I presumed their job, when and if the boat ever reached the water, was to release the cables swiftly, allowing the lifeboat to accelerate away quickly and safely before it was smashed against the hull of the *Speybank*.

All this time, the captain marched in and out of the bridge looking grim-faced, shouting orders into his radio.

By now Alexi, the chief officer, who was on board the lifeboat and in charge of the rescue operation, had appeared head and shoulders out of the hatch. Miraculously, and being the top man that he is, after what had evidently been more than a spot of bother, he had managed to get the engine of the lifeboat going, ready for its mercy dash mission away from the ship.

The really scary part was only just beginning. The lifeboat was dangling a fair way down the side of the hull when the effect of an almighty wave flung it out sideways before sending it back crashing into the hull. Somehow, the two men clinging to the chains on the outside of the boat managed to hang on without being catapulted into the sea. Ham Man and I stood in the pelting rain watching all this in a state of shocked disbelief. I felt almost certain I was about to see someone killed before my eyes. It's a strangely surreal feeling, like an out-of-body experience, to watch a drama unfold before your eyes. Even so, I wanted to shout down to the crew below to haul the lifeboat back up double-quick and then think of a new plan. But of course I couldn't, because the

captain was in command and what he said went. Anything else was
mutiny.

Meanwhile, *Always Saturday,* poised close by in a position to ease
collection of its seriously ill crewman, was having trouble trying to
keep steady in these horribly roiling seas. All of its sails were of
course down, so it had to keep motoring away before looping
round into position again, hoping that this time the lifeboat would
at last be safely released and steaming towards them. Ham Man disappeared down to the bridge for a moment before coming back
up to report that the yacht's skipper had been on the radio to say
he didn't know how long they could keep up circling round and
round, because their fuel levels were dangerously low.

From the monkey deck, and with the aid of my binoculars, I
could see three people on the yacht. They were all in life jackets
and getting completely thrashed by the wind and the rain. One
man held the helm while another crouched in the bows with a coil
of rope. The heart-attack man's wife held on tight in the cockpit.
Who knows what was going through their heads. In horrendous
conditions and with a dying man on board, they had travelled
through the night and most of the day to meet us and now, for one
long agonising minute after another, they had been watching a
hopeless attempt at lifeboat launching.

Half a lifetime later the lifeboat hit the water, albeit still hobbled
to its fetters. Yet the swell and swash of the sea was such that one
moment the boat was semi-submerged by water and the next, as
the *Speybank* rolled to port and the sea was sucked away, the boat
would be left hanging high and dry with the shrieking propeller
wailing like a banshee. Even if the chains could be released with
efficient speed, it looked virtually impossible to time the release so
that the lifeboat landed in the water without being pulverised by
the crushing hulk of the *Speybank* rolling back over to starboard. In
addition to this intractable nightmare, the lifeboat was still being
repeatedly smashed into the side of the hull.

In the unlikely event that the lifeboat ever got released, I couldn't
understand how it stood any hope of being retrieved and winched
back up, as both of the end hooks of the cables would have to be

engaged simultaneously with the couplings on the lifeboat or else the whole thing would up-end in a scene of unimaginable disaster. As far as I know, lifeboats are designed to be jettisoned from a sinking ship as fast as possible. The recapturing of a lifeboat by its original host is not quite so crucial. Obviously this boat-retrieving exercise is a lot easier to do in a lifeboat drill when the crew are practising in the sheltered waters of a millpond-still harbour. But out here in the banzai seas of the Atlantic, where the big and buckling waves are anything but obliging, lifeboat ensnaring is rather more complex.

As the lifeboat continued to be slung recklessly into the unyielding cliff face of the *Speybank*, it didn't look like the two crewmen on the cables could hold on for much longer. Word came from the bridge that as the lifeboat could neither be safely launched nor retrieved, the crew on deck were to haul it back up. So up it came in jerky fits and starts as the heaving team flung their crashing weight on the winches and chains.

At this stage I was hit by a fit of nervous laughter. Throughout most of this astonishing charade of events, Ham Man had been dropping a spiel of wholly inappropriate but highly entertaining doom-mongering remarks. There's nothing quite like being on an ageing tub in the middle of a storm in the middle of the ocean with a lifeboat that can't be launched. It's like watching your main chance of survival being washed clean down the drain. All we needed now was to be sucked into the Bermuda Triangle.

Just as we were wondering what would happen next, an arm of the rear crane swung out over the ocean pointing in a vague direction towards the oscillating yacht. This looked like the most desperate measure yet. A big fat hook the size of a butcher's block hung menacingly off the end. I could only imagine the planned objective was to hook the heart-attack man by his belt and then rein him in like one might a large fish. I'm not sure whether the health and safety authorities back home would approve of such measures. There again, it's probably a method not unknown to the National Health Service. If crane-hooking was the only rescue option available to the heart-attack man, surely it would be much kinder simply to hit him over the head with a hammer?

It seemed the crane method of attack was the bright idea of a break-away faction of Russians. As soon as the captain saw the swung-out arm of the crane he stormed out of the bridge into the pelting rain furiously waving his arms at the crane driver, signalling him to stop while yelling, 'LISTEN TO YOUR RADIO! LISTEN TO YOUR RADIO!' Then he stomped back inside, effing and blinding to himself as he went.

Quite what the yachting crew had made of this line of attack, I don't know, but it can't have fired them with much confidence. In fact, judging from what happened next, it seemed they had decided that being left to their own devices was immeasurably preferable to any rescue attempt by the wallowing *Speybank*. The skipper on *Always Saturday* got on the radio to say thanks, but no thanks, and that he was going to about turn and make a bee-line for Puerto Rico.

It was a terrible sight to see the forlorn-looking yacht turn around, its exhausted crew – their hopes shattered – raising the sails, before drifting away into the gathering night and strength-ening storm. My last memory of *Always Saturday* is watching it being bounced and tossed around like a toy by the wildly pitching waves before disappearing into an amorphous nothingness. I felt like crying.

A mini hurricane hit as darkness fell. And then the *Speybank*'s engine refused to restart. Luckily we had another engine lurking in the wings. And luckily it was still working, though it was any-body's guess how much longer it would continue to do so. With one engine down, it did rather beg the pertinent question that if one engine could so easily fail, could not the other just as easily follow suit? And then what? Put your life in the hands of the scary lifeboats? I think I'd rather swim. I said to Ham Man, 'I might just put my swimming costume and Speedo goggles on in preparation for an evacuation. I want to be suitably attired if we're called upon for a spot of fast crawl.'

And so the *Speybank* floundered onwards into the night at a disabling seven knots.

Dinner tonight was supposed to be a Welcome-to-the-Caribbean barbecue extravaganza for the whole crew on the monkey deck. Purser David, the grub organiser, wisely noted that it was not perhaps the most opportune time to conduct such a feast. Instead there was ravioli del Roma and banana split in the normal place. The only people on the top table were the captain, Purser David and Chief Phil. I detected the mood on this table was not good. No one said anything to anyone.

The trouble with the rain is that I have to shut my portholes. And the trouble with my portholes is that they leak. And the trouble with them leaking is that we might sink. And the trouble with us sinking is that we're up the creek without a paddle. But there again we have got a lifeboat that can't be launched, so it's not all doom and gloom. One should after all be grateful for small mercies even if they do involve an inevitable drowning in writhing seas.

By 20.00 hours, the weather had deteriorated into an electrical storm of ferocious proportions. I stood in the darkness of a corner of the darkened bridge holding tight on to the rail beneath the window. Shards of lightning cut the sky and lit up the sea like daylight. There was nothing so dainty as raindrops in this. As it strafed the decks it was just a cubic mass of falling water, pounding against the wheelhouse with a fearful din. Thunderous explosions cracked above our heads, some so shockingly loud they made you instinctively cower. The therdunk-therdunk of my heart beat harder and harder. The only other people on the bridge were the captain and third mate Young Alex and, over in the far corner, standing with his back to me, the dark form of the watchman who I think was Zhenya Sotnikov, but it was quite hard to tell as he stood as still as a corpse. And all the time the eerie whirring teeth-grinding sounds of the out-of-the-ark Russian auto-pilot giros filling the bridge with worry.

After a while the captain went down to his cabin. I couldn't stop thinking about what a nightmare it must be to be stuck out in all this on *Always Saturday*. And after what they had already been through too. I said to Young Alex, 'I hope they're all right.'

Young Alex said that he had managed to get hold of them a couple of times on the radio and they seemed to be doing okay. 'Though I don't think that heart-attack bloke is feeling too rosy.'

Lightning continued to shatter the sky, throwing the night into brilliant confusion. Rain fell in torrential waves. In those short periods when it would ease off a fraction, the lightning illuminated an eerily flattish sea. But in those moments when the full ferocity of the rain returned, the wind shot up to storm force, whipping up the waves into a spume-flying frenzy. It was at these times that the tearing wind slammed into the ship with a shrieking awfulness.

Around ten o'clock the rain moved up a gear, flinging itself at us with a new intensity. Before long the bridge began to leak. Water was dripping in fast through the roof and the windows. As I had my head-torch strapped around my skull (I liked to be prepared in case I was called upon for a spot of sinking-ship pot-holing) I was scrambled into action to fetch containers and buckets and to mop up the steadily growing lakes forming around electrical equipment with the torn-up remnants of the Russian crew's underpants. Fortunately there was no short supply of these. In one of the back storerooms I had found two big dustbin bags, bulging with worn-out pants.

I was mid-mop when all of a sudden an almighty detonating crack had us practically flinging ourselves to the floor, as in scenes of time-honoured Hollywood blockbusters. Lightning had hit but streaked straight down the sides. Luckily we were still floating because we are in a Faraday cage (or so I've been told – apparently it's something to do with fending off electrostatic nastiness). But less fortunately both GPS's had gone down and so Young Alex had to start navigating by the Robinson Crusoe method of dead-reckoning (a half-art, half-science method of navigation whereby a position is plotted based on speed and elapsed time, and a course

steered from a known position). This caused momentary conster-
nation as to what part of the world we might end up in next.

Of more immediate worry to me was the plight of *Always
Saturday*. I couldn't see how anyone on a yacht could survive out
there in conditions like this. Young Alex agreed.

'This is no bloody weather to be stuck in a small boat,' he said.

He tried raising the yacht on the VHF radio.

'*Always Saturday, Always Saturday, Always Saturday*. This is
*Speybank*, this is *Speybank*, this is *Speybank*. Do you read? Over.'

Apart from a terrible hissing, there was nothing.

At this point I had an idea to go in search of Captain Ian and
his GPS. I bumped into him on the stairs and he swiftly went back
to his cabin to fetch his hand-held equipment. When he returned
we forced our way out on to the side deck through the heavy wind-
hammered bridge-wing door and fought our way into the full fury
of the elements until we reached the railings. We worked as a team.
I directed the beam of my torch on to Ian's screen while he leant
out over the side, his mad-professor side-wings of hair flapping like
lunatics, to try to get a reading of satellite-bouncing data. Not that
we needed two people to do one job, mind, but in times of need
it's good to kill as many birds with as many stones.

We were both soaked in seconds but at least we hadn't sunk
yet or crashed into a country that wasn't supposed to be there.
Captain Ian, displaying signs of advanced smugness for at last being
able to play a crucial role in emergency procedures, eventually
registered some numbers on his upmarket toy. Jubilant, we both
dripped back to the bridge with the result. Ian conveyed his
bearings to Young Alex. Young Alex jotted them down and became
very pleased with himself. His dead-reckonings had been spot on.
So we weren't going to end up colliding into Greenland after all.
A bit disappointing really, as I've always fancied going there.

I told Ian that Alex hadn't been able to raise *Always Saturday*
on the radio. I turned my back for a moment to do a tad more
extreme pant-mopping and the next thing I knew Captain Ian,
apparently flushed with the success of his previous critical mission,
was on the radio himself, trying to summon life from the fatefully

bedevilled yacht. I couldn't believe my ears. I thought only a Captain Ian Cumming could be so unbelievably brazen. But it turned out he was much practised in this field (or at least he liked to think he was), having owned for many years his own yacht. As it was, Alex had unbeknown to me granted Ian free rein with the radio, seeing as he was rather tied up with tallying up his dead-reckonings with the configurations of the GPS.

'*Always Saturday, Always Saturday, Always Saturday,*' repeated Captain Cumming in his elevated tones. It would have all been very amusing had the situation at the other end not been so serious. 'This is *Speybank*, this is *Speybank*, this is *Speybank*. Do you receive? Over.'

*Sssssshhhhhhhssssssshhhhh* were the only ominous sounds of radio-wave static to greet us. I was hit by a sudden sinking feeling in the pit of my stomach. As if *Always Saturday* had been swept clean off the planet. Four people who could be dead who could have been with us.

But there was no time to dwell on such gloomy thoughts. All of a sudden an emergency red warning light started flashing in a loud and berserk blipping and blurping manner. It was just like the noise and flashings that you see in war films when a submarine has been hit by enemy torpedo. Any moment now I was expecting to hear the urgent shout of 'Go! Go! Go!' as fit lithe men in tight white vests somersaulted through the hatches from one end of the sub to the other. In our case, things weren't quite so fast moving. The Russian lookout man remained sitting motionless in a state of advanced rigor mortis. As for Captain Cumming, he moved an inch or two to smooth down his mad-professor wings that lived a life of their own. And as for me, I merely had a little nervous twiddle with the adjusting beam of my head-torch. It seemed like an apposite thing to do – twiddle and test, but only because I felt that at any moment I was going to be called upon to locate more than a mop of pants, more like a lifeboat. (Oh no!) The only person to rouse himself was our heroic Young Alex. He declared that the red flashing light indicated that the second (and last) engine had failed. Yikes! Does that mean we now have to start rowing or fashioning sails out of a few old sheets? But before I had a chance to set about this assignment, Young Alex declared the emergency over. It appeared the red flashing light was a false alarm. Just rain-water in the electrics, I believe.

# 5

# A Cut Above the Rest

## DAY 17

*Somewhere a bit off course but quite near the Caribbean,*
*15 November*

Dreamt about dead-reckonings and drownings last night. But apart from that, what little sleep I did manage to glean was surprisingly pleasant. This morning couldn't lie in starker contrast to when I went to bed; the sea is smooth and blue, the sky all loose and wispy. It's steamy hot too.

I spent the early morning getting very sweaty jumping up and down on the railings to unleash some excess energy. The seas are alive with flying fish. They're bouncing all over the place. I think flying fish are just frustrated birds that haven't yet come out of the closet.

Now that we are down to one engine, I'm certain we are going round in circles like a one-oar rowing boat because I'm sure I've seen that bit of sea before. But no matter how many bits of sea I've seen before, it has occurred to me in the calm of this morning what a fortunate thing it is that the *Speybank* had this other engine skulking down below. Means we can still notch up a knot or two without having to relocate to the lifeboats (ha!) or lassoing a line around the sturdy chassis of a conveniently passing turtle.

When I first signed up for this scintillating joyride on the *Speybank*, my two fat-tyred wheels were scheduled to be skimming across the clean green lands of New Zealand by the middle of November. By my estimations, that's where we are now – plonk in the middle of Thomas Hood's 'no shade, no shine, no butterflies, no bees, no fruits, no flowers, no leaves, no birds, November!' (The miserable sod – I think it's a very nice month myself – I mean look at it, the seas are all lovely and turquoise.) But now, thanks to all that French flour that took a lifetime to load, and abortive rescue attempts and engines conking out, the days are falling by the wayside. The latest ETA for New Zealand is the end of December. That will be two months at sea. I always wanted to go on a long boat journey, but not this long.

Talking of rescue attempts, word has it from Mr Alex Sasha second officer Nepomnyashchikh that the US Coastguard from Puerto Rico picked up the heart-attack man some time this morning, though whether he was still alive is a moot point. All Mr Alex Sasha second officer Nepomnyashchikh could tell me was, 'Maybe he dead. Maybe he not dead.' All I can say to that is: oh dear. Because there's quite a lot of difference between the two. As a result, I'm feeling very terrible. I hope he has survived.

Just before lunch we hit the Caribbean. The sky didn't look much like the glossy holiday brochures. It had transmuted into a dirty dishcloth, all overcast and dull, and the air felt warm and watery. As if another storm was astir up its sleeve.

And then, lo, land! The first earth and trees we had seen in a month of blue moons. These were islands. A small scattering of Virgins and over there St Croix and, somewhere way beyond that rocky outcrop, Puerto Rico with its hospital and heart-attack man. Some of the islands seemed to be sprouting carbuncles, which careful analysis through my binoculars told me were monstrous cruise ships – each one looking as incongruous as a fallen sky-scraper. There were lots of yachts too, flitting back and forth in what looked like a very pointless manner, as though him-on-the-helm was saying: *We'll go this way!* While her-with-the hair was bemoaning: *But I want to go that way!* Either that or they were lost. Ah yes, that must be it. I can see it now: the wives all have maps in their laps which they are trying to read upside down. We upset things further by carving a big barging trail through their paths.

The top-deck barbecue happened tonight. All afternoon the Russian crew moved half of the contents of the lower ship to the upper ship. Every time I went into my cabin I would see a table or bench or box of speakers or crate of beer or sack of firewood dangling on a rope outside my porthole like snaffled contraband. Every so often the booty would snag on a ledge or a railing or a jutting, which always evoked a rapid burst of enthusiastic shouting as the Russians hauling up the load and those attaching it half a mile of decks below bellowed to each other in a fusillade of incomprehensible Cyrillic vocabulary. Sometimes, just to complicate matters further, I would stick my arm out of my porthole and grab whatever was passing my way. It was always fun to hear the Russians shouting to each other.

It was a bit touch and go whether the weather would hold. A storm had been dickering with us all day, the clouds looking bruised and apprehensive. But in the event it held. In lots of heat and little clothes, the whole heap of crew and passengers (apart from Alexi, the chief officer, on watch) sat, stood, ate, drank or danced on the monkey deck. Unfortunately the muscling wind had swung round to the rear, which was good in that it pushed up our one-engine speed to a reckless 12 knots, but inconvenient in that it blew the putrid black fumes over our food and into our mouths.

It was good to meet those Russians whom I barely saw. The ones who tended to vanish into the labyrinthine decks of the lower ship. Though their English was more impressive and applicable for the current environment than my phrasebook Russian ('*Gdyeh bleezhighshahyah* **poch***tah?*' – Where's the nearest post office, please?) it still fell rather short of the mark so we resorted to that old onion, and most amusing (for them) standby, of me trying to pronounce and remember their names: Yuri Basalaev-the-Bosun (a bullet-headed and once professional violin teacher); Ivan Chirkov-the-Fitter; Dimitri Prokopev-the-Engineroom-Oiler; Leonid Pushkarev-the-Deck-Engineer; Yuri Vasyutich-another-Oiler; Nickolai Flimin-yet-another-Oiler; Ilya Kuzmin-the-OS (Ordinary Seaman – a junior seaman); Nikolai Schukin-the-other-OS; and the four ABs (Able Seamen): Zhenya Sotnikov, Leonid Lasko, Alexi Guriev and Alexander Fokin. Alexander Fokin, a thickset, good-natured giant of a man, is a keen cyclist so we did at least manage to exchange phrasebook-speak cul-de-sacs concerning the size of his down tube. Which as it happened was amazingly large. Quite an eye-opener, in fact.

At one point the captain took a seat alongside and told me that he had a son of eighteen and a daughter of sixteen and that he hadn't had Christmas at home for fourteen years. On the other side of the table, Chief Phil was telling jokes: 'What's the difference between a Kiwi and a pot of yoghurt? A pot of yoghurt's got more culture!' Ha, ha.

When chief officer Alexi appeared after finishing duty on the bridge, he told me that he had only been to England once and that what surprised him the most was what a white and fluffy state the sheep were in. He had been most amused to learn that they got sham-pooed and washed. 'In Russia, all our sheep look as dirty as pigs.'

Meanwhile Ham Man, who had at last woken up and was now

proceeding to get a little merry, told Purser David how unhappy he was with the ever-growing delays of this ship. Ham Man called the *Speybank* 'Fawlty Towers On Water'.

I said to Purser David, 'At this fine rate, do you think we will even reach New Zealand this year?'

Purser David, who was in an ill-advised Hawaiian print shirt, hunched up his shoulders and splayed out his arms in a beseeching manner and said what he always says whenever any of us ask whether the *Speybank* has the stamina to reach the Panama Canal, let alone the other side of the planet. '*Ensha'llah!* If God is willing!'

Not a comment to fire us with confidence.

**DAY 18**

*Somewhere in the middle of the Caribbean Sea with no land or ships in sight, 16 November*

It's 34 degrees today and at last the swimming pool has been filled, with a fat hosepipe sucking in a small amount of that appealing turquoise sea over which we are sailing. Only something weird happens to the turquoise the moment it enters the pool: it takes on the not-so-inviting hues of a bilgy sludge. All the other passengers say that nothing, not even large sums of money, would entice them to climb into this water, never mind the actual pool. Because, as we know, the pool is not so much a pool, but, as Ham Man says, a ballast tank with its top sawn off situated on top of the engine (the working one).

Feeling in need of a challenge, I immediately scampered up to my cabin, peeled off into my swimming costume, wrapped a towel around me and flip-flopped down the six flights of stairs, passing the odd raised-eyebrow Russian as I did so. By the time I'd made it

all the way back down below, stubbed my toe on the fifteen-inch
door sill (fitted on all doorways to help to prevent flood water from
flooding various compartments – though sills on the upper decks
are generally much lower), relocated my shoulder after dislocating
it for the fiftieth time while ram-opening the ten-ton submarine
hatch-door and picked a path through the cigarette butts, I discovered that the water level of the swimming pool had sunk by
several inches. Either a very fat man had belly-flopped into the
slosh of a puddle of the pool, sending a small tidal wave flooding
into the lower reaches of the ship, or the swimming pool had a
leak. As the ship didn't contain any very fat men, I deduced without too much active involvement of grey matter that the pool had
a leak. Thus, in order to get a swim, I had to act fast.

It was only when I had entered the water that I discovered the
tank was just long enough to perform either one stroke of breast
or half a stroke of crawl before I crashed into the other end and
it was time to turn around again. In the event, I decided I would
get far more exercise by simply treading water. But owing to the
steadily draining water, even this proved a race against time. Before
long, the water level had dropped by such an extent that in order
to avoid a painful scraping of flesh, I was forced to tread water with
my knees around my ears. It's a slightly unnerving feeling to be
bobbing about in a tank in an enclosed room beneath sea level
and watching the four small grimy blue-green walls around you
growing higher and higher and higher as you disappear lower and
lower. It was like reliving one of those nightmares I had as a child
when my bedroom walls started inching inwards, threatening to
crush me. So before I experienced the unpleasant sensation of my
legs being sucked down the plughole, I made a life-saving leap for
the rusty bottom rung of the short dangly ladder dangling high
above my head and heaved myself out.

Word had it today that, during the night of that abortive rescue,
fifteen inches of rain fell on us within two hours. That's more water
than can fill the swimming tank. The US Coastguard told Mr Alex
Sasha second officer Nepomnyashchikh that fifteen inches of rain
fell on Puerto Rico too. Well, if you've got to have fifteen inches of

water falling on you then it's just as well you're in an ark – even a leaking one.

At lunch, after the others had retreated to their quarters (Ham Man to sleep off hangover, the Frenchmen to fill up on videos, Ian to scratch brow in worriment while reassessing one-engine predicament) and before I had a chance to escape to my lookout nook on the monkey deck, Llewellyn nailed me to the table to give me another one of his air-traffic disaster stories. This one involved the mustard, the butter dish, the chilli sauce and the horseradish. Llewellyn, being the chilli sauce, overheard a conversation taking place between the mustard and the horseradish, respectively a controller and a cadet. They were both looking gravely at the butter dish (radar) and the cadet was saying he had lost contact with the Cessna though it was still showing up on the screen. Straight away Llewellyn saw the mistake the cadet had made and ordered him to tell the pilot of the Cessna to climb immediately, as the plane was in mountains. Moments later the Cessna disappeared off the butter dish screen. Llewellyn sent orders to send out a search and rescue team. Not long after, the wreckage of a Cessna was found. It had flown into the mountainside because of controller error. All four men on board were killed. Llewellyn put in a report about the incident but his supervisor tore it up and told Llewellyn not to mention the incident to anyone so as not to damage the air-traffic control reputation. Ten years later, Llewellyn witnessed four near-collisions within twenty-four hours. Llewellyn put in another report, and his supervisor told him to forget it, to go and have a drink, and then ripped up the report. So Llewellyn walked out.

The weather is all steamy and moody and up to no good. A series of surrounding squalls seems to be lording it over us. I'm glad this weather is all at sea with itself, because it's much more exciting than all that Caribbean balmy blue mollycoddling calm. I was up on the monkey deck this afternoon surveying the scene around me with my usual periscopic head working overtime and wondering what the weather was going to throw at us next, when spiralling down from a menacing black monster cloud I suddenly saw what my brain registered to be a tall white cliff. A moving one at that. But unless I was missing something I didn't think we were supposed to be on a land-ramming course for Dover. So I felt it must be more a mass of angrily luffing sail attached to an absurdly large schooner. Then, grabbing my binoculars for detailed analysis, I realised with a flutter of nervy excitement that it was the ghostly white tornado plume of a waterspout kicking up its tail.

I'm not quite sure why it took me so long to recognise that fearful shape of the funnel cloud. Several years ago when cycling across America I had found myself unintentionally riding through an area that is known in Kansas as 'Tornado Alley'. As a result the eerie colour and heart-stopping shape of a funnel cloud forming and falling to earth became an all too familiar sight. Like tornadoes except that they occur over water, waterspouts are whirling dervish columns of screwy cloud that work themselves up into a frenzy, creating a freestanding vortex of intensely low atmospheric pressure stretching down to the water and stirring up a terrific mess. They can measure from hundreds to just a few feet wide. As for their speed, some move as fast as 80 mph, others 2 mph, and the swirling wind within the spout can vary from 60 to 120 mph. Rather disappointingly, this one amounted to nothing more than lashing up a wall of white foam before deciding it had better things to be doing and collapsed in on itself.

Apart from my being nearly decapitated by a massive dragonfly that suddenly helicoptered past at a rate of knots (the first insect I'd seen since England), the only other moment of note was at dinner when Ian set about eating his cob of corn with a knife and fork, adopting a highly ineffective kernel-sawing method. I found this sight most amusing and said, mid-gnaw of my cob, 'Ian, why not just gnaw it?'

Gnawing at something was not part of Ian's dapperly cufflinked bearing. So he continued to wrestle with his cob with unsatisfactory results.

**DAY 19**

*Somewhere in the Caribbean between Nicaragua and Colombia,*
*17 November*

Another sky-shattering electrical storm hit the ship in the night. Thank heavens for Faraday cages, I say. Otherwise I might now be having an overly close encounter with the seabed of the Caribbean. Either that or the internal workings of a shark.

It was still raining cows and horses at 4.30 this morning as I battled on through my daily leg-humming bout of step-ups on the monkey deck railings. But I kept going, as it was warm rain charged with ions and felt electrifyingly exotic.

I went down to inspect the state of the swimming tank and was surprised to find some water in it, albeit only a large puddle. I climbed in and found it came to thigh level – not deep enough for swimming or treading water, but quite fun for running on the spot in. At least for the first five minutes, until a pointless tedium took hold. But I forced myself onwards for half an hour, hoping all the time that no Russians came in for a sauna. I would struggle for an explanation as to exactly what it was I was doing.

After breakfast Ian cornered me on the stairs about the Great Conspiracy. He is trying to garner support to form what sounds to me like a Boat Moaning Group. The idea is to rally together a mutinous faction – so far Ham Man and the two Frenchmen have signed up – and then, bearing arms (the ones attached to their shoulder joints), to march upon the cabin of Purser David demanding an explanation as to just what the bloody hell is going on with the cack-handed nature of our engines and itineraries.

'David is simply not doing his job of keeping us informed,' said a very disgruntled Ian to me as I stood trapped by his towering frame in the corner of the stairwell.

But I held my ground and declined his offer to form a rebellious uprising because, as I explained to him, broken engines and haywire schedules don't bother me in the slightest. Unlike all the other passengers with their meticulously planned agendas, I have no schedules other than just trying to get to New Zealand this side of 2010. And anyway, who wants things going to plan when they can go to pot? The unexpected is always far more exciting than a guaranteed certainty.

By mid-morning the rain had been usurped by a deep blue sky populated with a dense flotilla of clouds, all spinnakering west. A lusty breeze played havoc with the pages of my diary. Along with the temperature (it's 36 sweaty degrees today) the wildlife was hotting-up too. A few gull-sized noddies made an appearance, skimming across the sea with rushed and rapid wing beats, looking as if they were late for the train. Next on the scene was an august but rather pugnacious-looking peregrine falcon in yellow sunglasses that landed on a deck crane before boldly swooping on to a nearby railing, allowing me to take its portrait. Then a giant moth the size of a saucer landed on Llewellyn as he took a turn about the monkey deck in his dapper blue shorts, his reedy legs trailing out of them like a heron's.

It seems Ian's revolt has produced a frisson of a result. After lunch we were all summoned into the bar by Purser David, who told us that he was awaiting word from London (i.e. Andrew Weir Shipping HQ) re the conked-out engine.

'We're seeing if we can get a new engine part flown out to Panama,' he said. 'If that is possible, then we will have to spend three or four days in Panama for it to get fitted. We would then arrive in Tahiti on or around December 6th.'

Everyone, especially Ian, gave a moan and looked very grave. Ian questioned Purser David on what he thought the chances were of having this replacement engine part sent out to Panama.

All Purser David could do was throw up his arms and say, '*Ensha'llah!*'

I asked Purser David what was the bit of engine that we needed. But there was no willing God helping with this answer. He didn't know. He looked very uncomfortable throughout the whole little inquisition and, before we knew it, he had beaten a hasty retreat back to the safe haven of his quarters.

Ian said that at this laborious pace, he would miss his flight connection from New Zealand to Australia and hence miss spending Christmas with his daughter and grandchildren. He translated what little Purser David had said to the Frenchmen. They both looked very grim-faced because they had a flight booked back to France from New Caledonia on December 7th. Mickael stood throughout with his elbows cocked and his hands jammed angrily into his rear pockets.

Meanwhile Ham Man was feeling exasperated, because at this rate he wouldn't be in New Zealand in time to meet his fiancée flying in from South Africa, let alone all the hotel bookings, car bookings and inter-island ferry bookings that were going up the spout at considerable cost to him. Llewellyn said that he had so far lost over £2,000 in hotel bookings, which sounded like daylight robbery to me. For that excessively large sum he and Eleanor must have been planning on staying at the most exclusive top-notch hotels in New Zealand. I was glad I had a tent. It tends to make life a lot simpler.

\*

Back in position on the monkey deck, I was not so much on the lookout for noddies as for pirates. As I was passing through the bridge on my way up top, Mr Alex Sasha second officer Nepomnyashchikh had handed me a copy of a piracy report that had earlier been regurgitated by the telex machine. It said:

THIS BROADCAST WARNS SHIPS IN PASSAGE IN WEST AFRICA, SOUTH AMERICA, CENTRAL AMERICA AND THE CARIBBEAN WATERS REGARDING PIRACY AND ARMED ROBBERY.

But all the current excitement was taking place off West Africa. The dispatch reported three incidents that had occurred in the past few days. The first one happened at 1030 UTC during a river passage in Warri, Nigeria. Pirates in three boats armed with machine guns surrounded a refrigerated cargo ship and tried to block her passage. Two minutes later pirates fired two shots at the hull. The ship increased speed and took evasive manoeuvres and the pirates gave up the chase. The pilot aboard contacted the authorities but no local assistance was received.

The next occurrence took place about one-and-a-half miles from Dakar Pilot Station in Senegal. A bunch of pirates armed with knives boarded a refrigerated ship that was underway. The general alarm was raised and the crew mustered and chased the pirates. Dakar Port Control was informed and they sent a police boat to escort the vessel to berth.

The third case proved more fruitful for the pirates. At 2248 UTC in Lagos Roads, Nigeria, another gang of no-gooders boarded a chemical tanker from a speedboat at poop deck level and stole the ship's stores. Before anyone was hurt, the crew raised the alarm and the pirates escaped at 2300.

The words at the bottom of the report said:

SHIPS ARE ADVISED TO MAINTAIN ANTI-PIRACY WATCHES AND REPORT ALL PIRATICAL ATTACKS AND SUSPICIOUS MOVEMENTS OF CRAFT TO THE IMB

PIRACY   REPORTING   CENTRE,   KUALA   LUMPUR,
MALAYSIA.

As the officer on watch was tied up with his other duties, I felt I
could be playing a crucial role sitting on the monkey deck with a
swivelling head keeping a keen lookout for any suspicious behaviour
of approaching craft. And as I did so I thought what a fine word
'piratical' is. It's not a word that often enters my vocabulary, but in
future I shall endeavour to apply it to my conversation wherever
possible.

Then there's 'piracy'. Whenever I hear this word I can't help
conjuring up images of seventeenth-century buccaneers with skew-
whiff eye patches, hidden treasure, skull-and-crossbones and
belt-swaying cutlasses. But for seafarers the reality is a world away
from the mythology as the armed attacks on both themselves and
their ships are becoming increasingly more violent, ruthless and
catastrophic. In recent years there has been a scary profusion of
cases in which ships have sailed at full steam through busy shipping
lanes with no one at the controls because the crew have been tied
up or taken hostage and held at gunpoint by pirates. There has
been a rash of other incidents too, where the attackers have fired
M16s, rocket-propelled grenades or even shoulder-launched missiles at laden tankers and gas carriers. Usually, the main aim of
these ambitious and well organised gangs is to hijack entire ships:
they kill the crews or set them adrift in life rafts, sell the cargoes
and in the most elaborate schemes repaint and rename the
hijacked vessels while at sea to avoid detection, turning them into
'phantoms', which, posing as legitimate ships with the necessary
paperwork, pick up new cargoes and vanish. One of the most violent pirate attacks occurred at the end of the 'nineties when a bulk
carrier named the *Cheung Son*, loaded with steel-mill slag, was
hijacked on the South China Sea by pirates dressed in Chinese customs uniforms. The pirates lined up the twenty-three crewmen and
systematically clubbed them to death before attaching heavy
objects to their bodies and heaving them overboard.

The *Seafarers' Bulletin* reported that there have been more than

2,635 pirate attacks on ships in the past decade (1,228 of these occurred between 1998 and 2002). With the increasing numbers, the levels of violence are escalating too – there are more than 3,300 cases of crew members having been killed, injured, assaulted, taken hostage or threatened since 1993. According to research carried out in Japan, these figures are just the tip of the iceberg; barely one-third of attacks are reported.

The most likely place for the *Speybank* to be attacked is in the South China Sea – two-thirds of piratical activity is concentrated in this one region alone, which includes the waters of Indonesia and the Philippines. Purser David told me that when they sail through this region, in order to make any intending pirates aware that they are keeping a good watch out for anything unusual, they have the high-pressure hoses rigged, floodlights and watchkeepers doubled. They also have all accommodation doors locked. Seems things are going to get a bit more strict in the next year or so; to comply to the New International Regulations that are coming into place, the *Speybank* will have to have combination locks and padlocks on all outside doors as well as regular security drills. As the security situation stands at the moment, I feel slightly worried for the crew because, if the *Speybank* were to be hijacked in bad weather, the pirates couldn't even give the crew a sporting chance by setting them adrift in the lifeboats – not unless they maybe fired one of their shoulder-launched missiles into the cable shackles of the lifeboat cradles in order to release them without a massive amount of effort. Well, I suppose if it's to be any consolation, at least the dog-eared state of the ship should deter any would-be attackers from thinking there was anything about the vessel worth their while to purloin. There again, an undercover piratical re-painting could be just what the *Speybank* is waiting for. It doesn't look like anyone else is going to give it a fresh lick of paint in a hurry.

## DAY 20

*Still in the Caribbean but homing in on Panama with Colombia to the east and Costa Rica to the west, 18 November*

It's so hot today that even the shadows are suffocating. The wind has dropped away to nothing, turning the sea glassy and smooth. Hanging over the railings I can see quite a lot of rubbish drifting by – mostly polystyrene, plastic bottles and wood and something that looked like a dead flamingo with a laundry basket caught round its neck. But by the time I had scuttled round to the aft deck for further identification purposes, the flamingo-basket had been sucked into the screwy churn of the wake.

I thought that this part of the Caribbean would be crowded with ships (of both piratical and non-piratical varieties) all bearing down on the Panamanian shortcut sliced through the middle of the Americas. But apart from a couple of distant horizon-gliding hulks, we have the sea to ourselves. Where are they all? There are 43,000 monster merchant ships – container vessels, tankers, bulk carriers – that wander the world, plying the open freedom of the oceans among an indeterminate number of smaller coastal craft and carrying nearly all the raw materials and products of international trade on which our lives depend. I know the Atlantic is big (more than thirty-three million square miles – roughly the size of all the world's landmasses combined), but I am still surprised how few ships I have seen on it in the past two weeks – barely a handful. I always imagined that in the build-up to the Panama Canal, we would be sitting in a veritable bottleneck, fending and bumping off each other like fairground dodgems.

Just before lunch all passengers were called upon by Purser David to assemble in the bar. So in we all piled, only to be told that there were no spare parts available until we reached Tahiti. Thus, we would proceed limping onwards to Papeete (the capital and main port of French Polynesia) on one engine. That's a long way to travel at a hobble: 4497.4 nautical miles, according to Captain Cumming's calculations – or about six months of cycle touring, depending on the mountainous terrain encountered and the state of one's knees.

Ham Man was angry. So were the Frenchmen, who had travelled to Tahiti before on the French CMA CGM container line. They told us their ship had left on time, arrived on time, and shot along at 25 knots (the food was top gourmet fodder, too). This meant that by the time it's taken the *Speybank* to dilly-dally to just outside Panama, the CMA CGM ship would already be in Papeete.

Ian sat slumped, looking very depressed. Then he suddenly roused himself. 'This service is diabolical!' he declared. 'This is no way to run a business!' And with that he marched out of the room saying he was going to email his daughter in Australia to investigate flights out of Tahiti. He wanted to jump ship at the earliest opportunity.

Llewellyn was as morose as the rest of them. He told me he had powers to see into the future and that he had never been wrong. He claimed he had even correctly predicted the death of a man who had once approached him in a Manchester pub asking him what his future held. (How lovely!) He now said that our future on the *Speybank* looked very gloomy indeed.

'I think even I could have told you that,' I said to Llewellyn.

But Llewellyn was not amused. He said, 'I'm serious.'

'So what's going to happen to us?' I asked. 'Are we going to sink?'

'You don't want to know.'

'I do,' I replied. 'I'd like to be prepared.'

'One can never be prepared enough in life for anything,' he said in a sort of philosophically swings-and-roundabouts way, which didn't really make much sense to me because you'd think if one knows one is definitely going to sink, one could do something about brushing up on one's emergency swimming skills, or at the very least set about building a lifeboat that works. I was just thinking about what else I would do if I knew I was fast drifting towards a guaranteed sinking (email Mum, perhaps, and tell her, 'We're just about to sink. But don't worry. I'll be fine!' On second thoughts, maybe I should write something a little more doleful along the lines of the letter that Margaret Fuller – the first female American journalist, champion of women's rights and nurse – wrote to her mother in 1850 just before she boarded a big full-rigged ship in Italy bound for America: 'There seems somewhat more of danger on sea than on land . . . I hope we shall be able to pass some time together yet in this world; but if God decrees otherwise – here and hereafter, My dearest Mother'), when Llewellyn added that he was also able to see into the present, from afar.

'I do that every day,' I said. 'With the aid of binoculars.'

Oddly, this isn't quite what Llewellyn meant, and he told me so.

'Well, in that case,' I said, 'can you tell me what Gary is doing right now?'

'You don't want to know,' he said.

'Yes, I do,' I replied, feeling I had been here before.

'Being unfaithful,' he said before stomping off.

My only response to that is a recommendation that Llewellyn brush up on his far-reaching telescopic telepathic abilities. Checking the email machine, I found Gary had sent me a sixth-sense email a mere minute earlier, explaining how he had just got back from Selborne where he had been tenderly tending to Mrs Dolding's taper burn marks on her mantelpiece. There are those, I'm sure, who would read something differently into this. But I know better.

**DAY 21**

*At the mouth of the Panama Canal, 19 November*

We arrived here at 03.00. It was most exciting. Lots of noisy grinding and clanking of unravelling anchor chains and shouting of Russians as they moved unseen about the main deck far below. There were lots of flickering lights of nearby ships at anchor, too. As I stood alone in the dark on the monkey deck looking out over the illuminated shapes of these ships, I wondered how many of them might have fallen prey to any previous piratical actions.

Now that it is daylight, I can see we are surrounded by twenty-four gargantuan ships at anchor. The sea has a sullen, oily look to it. With the help of my binoculars, I can read the names of nine of the ships: *Wallenius Wilhelmsen*, registered in Tönsberg (a place in which I remember getting lost on my bike, just south of Oslo); *Yasaka Bay*, registered in Georgetown; *Pac Athena*, registered in Singapore; *New Explorer* and *UBC Salvador*, both registered in Limassol; and *Vega Pioneer* and *Bright Laker*, both registered just over there in Panama. Panama, incidentally, is the largest maritime nation on earth, followed by turbulent Liberia.

I used to think that the name of the homeport painted on a ship's stern was the port from which the ship had hailed. But these places of registry, generally known as 'flags of convenience', mean nothing of the sort. The ships don't even have to come from anywhere near these homeports. Nor does the country of registry have to have a coastline. There are ships that materialise out of La Paz, in landlocked Bolivia. There are ships that materialise out of the Mongolian Desert. I find it all very confusing. Does that mean that a Ship of the Desert is really a Camel of the Ocean?

What is certain is that these resulting arrangements, though deeply subversive, have placed the oceans increasingly beyond governmental control and given ship owners something that has grown into extensive freedom. A lot of the time, it works fine, but it also means that there is a worrying amount of registries of convenience out there with shoddy track records and reputations for allowing owners to operate their vessels nearly as they please. All of which suits potential pirates and terrorists very nicely indeed.

The other two ships anchored in our vicinity are *Bow Mariner* and *Spring Deli* but both are too distant for me to read where they've been registered. Probably somewhere like Alice Springs and Sutton Coldfield. Having time on my hands I have just conducted a small survey of the surrounding area, and I am pleased to announce that I am standing on the most visibly ramshackle ship of the lot. What a magnificent achievement.

*

Ian was uncharacteristically cheerful at breakfast.

'I'm feeling so much better,' he said, 'because I've now got a parachute.'

'A *parachute*?' I said. 'You don't need a parachute on a boat, Ian. You just need a lifeboat that works.'

But before I became baffled further, he explained, 'I've had an email from my darling daughter who has booked me on a flight out of Tahiti on the ninth of December. That's the sort of efficient service I expect from my children!'

Later Llewellyn said to me, 'The sooner he buggers off, the better!'

It was long gone noon when a refuelling vessel, its decks a tangle of pipes and hoses, drew up alongside to pump in 910 tonnes of bunker oil. At US$180 a tonne, that's nearly $164,000, or the equivalent of about 100,000 tip-top touring bikes. Seems like an awful lot of money to spend just to feed an engine when we're only travelling at sailing speed. I'm sure it would be a lot more cost effective to simply hang up a few old sheets or catering-size underpants and to blow very hard.

The next ship to draw alongside looked a lot more promising in my eyes, loaded as it was with crates of drinkable and edible provisions to replenish our dwindling food supplies. I was pleased to note several boxes of bananas disappearing through the hatch of the foodstore hold. For the past ten days we have been eating squashed black-skinned bananas. Or at least I have. No one else fancies them. Lucky thing this ship isn't superstitious; many sailors nurture nautical myths and beliefs, one worrying one being that if anybody should board a boat carrying a banana (or umbrella), woe betide that ship and its crew. There's a bottomless tank of other such maritime superstitions: black cats are considered lucky to have on board a ship, but rabbits are bad news: should a rabbit lollop across a sailor's path while he is on his way to his boat, he must immediately turn round and go home. Over the centuries it has been believed that for a vessel to survive a voyage it must never be boarded by a woman, a red-haired virgin, an ordained minister, a solitary bird, any land bird except a dove; and bizarrely, a citizen of Finland. Sailors shouldn't board a fishing vessel from the port side or whistle for wind unless they want to get in a fix. Nor should they have their hair cut at sea (except during crossing-the-equator ceremonies, when heads of novice sailors are shaved). To bring luck, a skipper ought to renew his crew every year. While at sea, it is considered bad luck to point a finger at another ship, which rather makes a mystery of how you are *supposed* to indicate a nearby vessel (a semi-pirouetting semaphoring ballerina-type outstretched leg, perhaps, before toppling overboard?). In one of those moments that one has from time to time when, raising your gaze skyward, you are greeted by a sight that you weren't altogether expecting to see, the crew must make haste to the halyards should a black bear be espied taking a turn on a yard aloft, for the animal's acrobatic antics presages a gale. But undoubtedly the most convincing superstition that has got to be nothing other than wholesomely credible is the one about a drifting coffin: if it's found to contain an open Bible, a wreck is nearby.

Along with the bananas, I also noticed a sizeable stash of cheap Panamanian bottled water being lowered by deck crane into the hatch. I made a mental note to buy some of that off Purser David, because all the ship's normal water supply comes through its onboard desalination system and tastes pretty horrible.

Another peregrine falcon (oh no, bad luck!) has joined the ship and it's currently engaged in massacring any lesser bird that is imprudent enough to land on a part of the ship for any more than half a second. Apart from that, this is the other wildlife so far spotted today: pelicans, egrets, boobies, herons, frigates, flamingos, spoonbills, black terns, laughing gulls, a possible osprey, dolphins, bat-sized butterflies and a massive multi-storeyed cricket that jettisoned out of yonder jungle and landed on me on the deck twitching its probing proboscis the size of barbecue skewers. (Just in case you think I've turned into a nautically twitching Bill Oddie, there's a bird book on board which I'm digesting fast by the minute. A lot of the Russian crew are also very on the button with their birds, so they are telling me what's what.)

Rumour has it that we shall go through the canal tomorrow

morning, though I'm not holding my breath because that's the fourth change of time in about as many hours. Anyway, an additional rumour emanating from the bridge has it that it's very unusual for the *Speybank* and other similar rusty tubs to travel through during daylight hours, because that's usually the time allotted for the dazzlingly white high-and-mighty cruise ships, which are given precedence so that their jewel-endowed passengers can see the sights. In the time we've been anchored here this morning I've seen two of these leviathans, the size, apparently, of ninety-eight football pitches, or maybe 600 double-decker buses. Or Wales. Whatever, they are all huge and rammed with rich punters lining the decks as they glide haughtily past the riff-raff that have been swinging at anchor for days.

Despite his parachute, Ian has gone all grumpy again. It's all this hanging around. It makes him irritated and crotchety. Delay equals supreme inefficiency in Ian's book. He likes things to run like clockwork and he likes things to be within his control. Anything else is anathema in his eyes. Beats me how he's survived this long without jumping overboard. But I'm glad he hasn't. Despite his occasional shortcomings and lofty puffiness and prejudices, he's not a bad onion, is Ian. He's the best of the bunch for conversation and I feel he's the most trustworthy. What's more, being the ship's jester, he's always unfailingly amusing to observe. In fact, unlike Llewellyn and co., I'm even a little upset he's found a parachute in the form of Tahiti. I'd really quite like to go the full hog with him to Auckland. How else will we cope without his elaborate course-plotting toys? Why, it was only the other day he informed the captain that, by taking the globe's magnetic variation into account, we could shave off precious time by maintaining a tighter course that kept a truer line to the curvature of the earth. There can't be many passengers who come out with such entertaining hogwash as that. Even if it is true.

Talking of Ian and his plottings, he's just told me that it's 2,458 nautical miles from Tahiti to Nouméa in New Caledonia. And from Nouméa it's another 985 miles to Auckland. Add that little lot to the sizeable heft of the Pacific, plus a few wrong turns here and there, and that's not much short of 10,000 miles yet to go. Or about a year's cycle touring with panniers loaded to the gunwales. Blimey, what a thought! I think I might start looking for a parachute.

At one point today a pointy-nosed pilot boat called *Pike* ('stupid boy!') drew up alongside and a couple of pilot men clambered up the rope ladder that had been hurled over the side of the *Speybank*. These were the first Panamanians I had seen up close and, what with their mafia shades and pistols in hip-holsters, they looked like gun-slinging cowboys. After they had done their business and sped away in *Pike*, word had it that we would definitely be travelling through the canal during the day due to the substantial amount of French ammo we've got on board. I think the authorities want to keep an eye on us to make sure we don't blow anything up. Like a lock gate or two.

I spent the rest of the day up on the monkey deck peering out at the distantly hazy terminal port of Colón and the jungle-clad mountains as well as at the constant comings and goings of the various exotic, and sometimes eccentric-looking, birds and ships that passed through the outer anchorage. One bird that flew by (I have no idea what it was) looked like a mixture between a seal and a flying hoover. Not even Mr Alex Sasha second officer Nepomnyash-chikh could put a name to this feathered conundrum.

The mast above the monkey deck is fluttering very festively at the moment because a string of pennants has been hoisted in preparation for our moving into the inner harbour. Among all the colourful signal code flags snapping in the hot humid wind there are also the house flag of Bank Line, the courtesy one of Panama (one red quarter, one blue quarter, and a red star and a blue star each on white) and a red flag with an arrow notch cut out of the end indicating that we have dangerous cargo on board.

Through my binoculars I've been following the passage of several ships constantly crawling inbound and outbound, all of them monster container vessels, freighters, tankers or bulk carriers. Around thirty to thirty-five ships make the nine-hour transit through the Panama each day (about 12,000 a year), including the odd liner and the occasional warship or yacht. Whatever the type of ships cutting their way through the mountainous isthmus that joins the North and South American continents, all of them are saving themselves 8,000 miles and three weeks of sailing round the perils of Cape Horn, the scorpion-tail tip of South America. (Before the canal was built, the usual way to travel by ship from New York to California would have been by 'rounding the Horn', a journey of a month and some 15,000 miles.) And because of this, all of them seem quite happy to hand over the thousands of dollars in canal tolls – the average vessel paying approximately $40,000 for the privilege of shaving off the better part of a month and some very hairy seas.

Talking of shaving, Valeri, the Vinnie Jones fourth engineer who drove across Russia in his Japanese truck, is tempting fate: he appeared at dinner tonight with no hair. When I last saw him (at lunch) he'd had quite a thicket. But now it's all gone, shaved off in a flash and thrown overboard with the booze bottles.

Which reminds me of a dream I had last night that for some reason featured Valeri. He was racing a tandem recumbent (one of those lie-down bikes) late at night through pitch-black muddy woods and then he stopped by to pick me up (he still had hair at this stage, so luck was still on our side) and I climbed on the back and we went racing off through the mud and we hit 80 mph and then I got a bit panicky thinking I should never have got on board because we're going to die and the next thing I knew I was on a hill on a sunny evening dying for a pee when what should I find before me but a brand new dazzling white toilet bowl (minus the seat and cistern) and I thought: well, how handy is that? Only trouble was the toilet overlooked a busy road and I kept getting more and more frustrated waiting for a break in the traffic so that I could proceed with the peeing process without being spotted but the cars kept on coming in one steady stream and I was desperately cross-ing my legs hopping up and down completely baffled by the amount of traffic when I suddenly remembered it was late-night shopping which explained all the busy comings and goings. And then I woke up and had a pee in my vacuum toilet, which was a much safer bet anyway.

No email from Gary today. I presume he must still be caught up in Mrs Dolding's taper burn marks. But I had one from my next-door neighbour Val. She's just got back from a Christmas fair in the village hall and when she was asked by various local folk what was I up to these days, she told them I was rowing single-handedly across the Pacific. And they believed her. Maybe that's the para-chute I'm looking for.

**DAY 22**

*Still at the mouth of the Panama, 20 November*

The weather has turned explosively stormy. Lightning lit up my cabin for most of the night and the thunder was so extreme I could feel it zinging through the ship, vibrating the walls and tingling my skin. And it's still storming this morning, the intensity of the rain marching across the sea in huge dark dolloping waves that blot out the land and the straggly gaggle of ships idling at anchor. With day disintegrated into night, all the ships' lights are blazing.

I've just had a bit of a revelation, thanks to spending rather a lot of time staring at the sinuous squiggle of Panama on various maps and charts. I always imagined that a ship transiting the canal from the Atlantic to the Pacific would be heading due west. But instead it travels southeast. Because of the country's snaking 'S' shape, the Atlantic lies to the west of the canal, the Pacific to the east. As if that doesn't sound silly enough, we're also going to be travelling slightly uphill; a quirk of the Coriolis effect means that the Pacific Ocean sits about nine inches higher than the Atlantic.

The latest news is as usual very unclear. It all boils down to the indisputable fact that we may or may not be off in the morning. With all this non-activity the other passengers seem to be turning increasingly angry and slowly insane. I must be very annoying for them because I feel completely fine. As the *Speybank* is for once relatively still, I've put our time at anchor to good use by mending bits of camping equipment that I meant to do before I left home but never had time, and sewing and adapting my custom-made attachments of webbing straps and various toggles and Velcro to assorted tent, clothing and panniers – a task that is impossible to tackle when the ship is continuously rolling from side to side. I've tinkered with my bike too, which is always good for the sealed bottom brackets of one's soul.

**DAY 23**

*The Panama Canal, 21 November*

Just when you least expect anything to happen, it happens, with a wild flurry of sudden activity. Around 3 a.m., at the clunking sound of the anchor being raised, I fell out of my bunk in a dreamy dead-headed state, foggy with sleep. No matter how tired you are, you can't miss a minute in this game or else you'll find a chunk of the

Panama Canal has passed you by. Once I'd got my shoes on and
senses together I was up on the monkey deck in a jiffy, draped in
binoculars and cameras. Not that there was much to see, mind,
apart from a lot of inky dark shimmering water and flickering
lights.

And then the engine was thrust into forward and we were under
way, slowly sliding into the beginning of the 51-mile transit of the
canal. The *Speybank* edged her way carefully past the widely scattered sluggish brood of ships dozing at anchor, the shy slapping of
the black slack sea smacking against the bow. We entered the channel from Limon Bay at the Cristóbal breakwater. With the powerful
aiding nudge of *Esperanza*, a tubby snub-nosed tug, we were soon
easing into the first of the canal's three sets of locks, each of which
has two lanes and massive steel gates seventy feet high. The crew at
this stage tended mostly to sit back and watch, as we now had our
Panamanian pilots on board (since 31 December 1999, Panama
has taken over full control of the canal from the Americans) plus
a shadowy mob of about twenty local deckhands in hard hats, all of
whom took over the highly specialised job of guiding us through
the lock chambers which fit a big ship like a glove, often with just
a couple of feet to spare on each side. The biggest of ships able to
fit through the canal are called Panamax size. Measuring 965 ft ×
39 ft, they are designed specifically for the canal. There are plenty
of vessels that can hold up to 300,000 tonnes of cargo, but the limit
for the Panama is 65,000 tonnes. The *Speybank*, being a mere 18,000
tonnes, feels pretty pocket-sized in comparison.

Although vessels use their own propulsion for the greater part
of transiting the canal, they are assisted when passing through the
locks by electrically powered locomotives called *burros* (mules)
which use fat cables to align and tow the ships. These mules are
fantastically strong silver-sided creatures adorned with jaunty traffic lights and Panamanian flags on their cabin-heads. What they
lack in hauling speed, they make up for in a constantly high-
spirited repertoire of clanging bells and chirpy whistles.

Up ahead in another chamber of the same lock sat the *Bow
Mariner* from Singapore, while sinking into the dark cavities on the

other side and travelling in the opposite direction were the *Cabo Virgenes*, flagged in Valparaiso, and the *Stolt Confidence*, with the words 'George Town' shabbily painted upon its stern. Treading water outside the lock with its tug, *Guia*, and its teetering heights of LINEA MEXICANA containers hovered the *Cielo Del Canada*, registered in Leer. Just a small handful of the ships, cargos and crews that travel through the Panama every year to and from every country on earth.

It took the *Speybank* around two-and-a-half hours to clear the triple locks at Gatun – locks that effectively act as water lifts, elevating us twenty-six metres above sea level to Gatun Lake. This lake, which acts as a water 'bridge' covering a third of the distance across the isthmus, supplies all the water and hydroelectric power required for the lockages – each lockage using approximately 200 million litres of fresh water (45 million gallons) that is ultimately flushed into the sea. Were the locks to use salt water it would have to be pumped all the way up from sea level, which, apart from being exorbitantly expensive to install and maintain, would corrode the lock mechanisms and destroy vegetation.

As the ship's clawed arms of rusty anchor sploshed into the khaki-green soup, the sun, a fat fireball of blood, began to crawl its way up into the early morning haze of humid sky. Surrounding this immense artificial lake, created by the damming of the Chagres River, are thickly knotted mangrove swamps and hills and mountains carpeted in dense tropical jungle and astonishingly noisy with baboons and thousands of insects and colourful birds. (On the map, Panama may look little more than an emaciated waistline – a skinny coil connecting the two overweight Americas – but there are almost as many bird species here as there are in the whole of North America and Europe combined.) A fretwork of islands – summits of drowned hills – scatter themselves over this lake, all of them topped in a canopy of jungle.

Through my binoculars I homed in on the outlandish sight of giant white and electric yellow flowers blooming as big as dinner plates on the rooftops of some of the weirdly primeval-looking trees. I wondered how long I might survive if I were to be plucked from the ship and dumped in this jungle. When Gatun was being flooded, an engineer, inspecting the lake by canoe as the water rose, noticed a semi-submerged tree covered with what appeared to be black leaves. He paddled up to the tree to investigate whereupon he got a terrible shock and abruptly skedaddled away as fast as he could paddle. What he had mistaken for foliage was in fact thousands of tarantulas, clinging to the branches to delay their inescapable drowning.

Never mind what spiders might be lurking close by, the waters of the canal are not ones you really fancy taking a dip in unless you want to come eye to evil eye with a crocodile. With all the surrounding land edged in swampland, these stealthy long-jawed predators are lurking all around, ready to chomp through half a torso in a trice. But at least one man refused to be deterred by what might be lying in wait to pull him under: in 1928, Richard Halliburton paid 36 cents in tolls to swim the length of the Panama. It took him ten days to complete the journey.

Not surprisingly, his was the cheapest toll ever paid for a passage through the canal. The most expensive is credited to the *Coral Princess*, a liner belonging to Princess Cruises, which forked out an astounding $141,344. I've just worked out that if the *Coral Princess* took the usual nine hours to slide through the canal, then it cost the cruise line nearly $16,000 an hour. That's a lot of bottom brackets to the pound.

Various ships were anchored nearby awaiting instructions to move further along the canal. One of the container vessels had 'P&O NEDLLOYD' painted in vast lettering down its hull and was loaded to the hilt with CMA CGM and CHINA SHIPPING containers. When the ship swung round I read the words 'AIGOA' and 'Monrovia' upon its stern. I was giving it the once over with my binoculars when I saw a crew member on the poop deck peering back at me through his binoculars. Still with binoculars pinned to faces, we both flipped up an arm and waved.

Occasionally, big bird-size butterflies flapped lazily out of the jungle, flopping for a moment on to the railings to recharge their batteries. It was when the Frenchmen were with me on the monkey deck together with Ham Man, and with Llewellyn and Eleanor in a corner, that a strange kind of bee, its body a whirlwind of swirling psychedelic yellows, greens, oranges and blues, plummeted in a demented 'ged-me-oudda-here' fashion down the front of my shirt, causing a rapid undressing down to my bra. Everyone found this most amusing, though I don't know why.

By 13.30 and in a sudden and tremendous tropical downpour (the area receives about ten feet of water per year – mostly in short, intense head-hurting bursts) we were off again to cut through the eight-mile-long chasm of the Gaillard or Culebra Cut (the authorities can't seem to make up their minds what to call it). This is where the Panama Canal carves its remarkable way through the 400-foot cliff faces of the Continental Divide. It is also where the labours and tribulations of all the thousands of men who struggled to build the Panama become dramatically evident. Ever since 1513, when the Spaniard Vasco Núñez de Balboa allegedly became the first European to see the world's greatest ocean, Panama has been a routeway from the Caribbean – and Atlantic – to the Pacific.

Small tribes once dotted the region, but it was the conquistadors who were the first to spot Panama's narrow isthmus as the world's greatest shortcut, and hammered out the *Camino Real* (King's Highway) to lug booty from Peru to Spain without having to go 'round the Horn'. In those days, the only available transport for the crossing was by mule train and Shanks's pony. By the time the mid nineteenth century rolled along, the Americans had completed the world's first transcontinental railway – a forty-mile-long extravaganza of track cutting through the jungle. Then came the canal. It was the French who embarked on building this grand waterway. They started the canal in 1879 but because of the apparent impossibility of the project, which was to be the largest civil engineering work the world had ever known and which involved the deaths of 22,000 men, they abandoned it after ten years, leaving behind a very deep ditch.

Panama had achieved freedom from Spain in 1821 but

remained part of Colombia until 1903, when an American-inspired revolution led to Panama's declaration of independence. A year later Panama signed a treaty with the United States giving America control of a ten-mile-wide 'Panama Canal Zone' for a down-payment of $10 million, plus $250,000 a year. In 1904 the Americans took over the building of the canal, pumping $350 million into the project, which took another ten years to complete. The labourers were mostly Americans, West Indians, Indians, Chinese, Spaniards and Greeks and they all disembarked at the quays along with tractors, cranes, steel, timber and every conceivable building implement. By the time the first ship transited the canal in 1914, the whole construction of the waterway had cost the lives of 26,000 men, including those killed during the initial building effort of the French.

It took the rest of the day to trundle through the incredible enormity of the canal. For years I had imagined the Panama to be a bit like a Dutch canal – dead straight and narrow with the odd duck and dyke on the side for good measure. Instead it was a spectacle of the most unexpected beauty, wide and winding among mountains and tall craggy cliffs and jungle. Strangely, if the world's weather continues to grow wild, extreme and unpredictable, in the next half a century the Panama Canal could be in competition with another 'Panama Canal' higher up the globe. As parts of the Arctic are now so warm (Inuit were amazed to find a wasp in the Canadian Arctic last summer – they had never seen one before and had to be warned not to handle it), ice is melting so fast that it has been predicted that within fifty years it may be possible for ships to sail across the north of Canada and Russia. As a result, it has been nicknamed the 'Panama Canal of the North'.

By the time the mules were hard at work hauling us through the Miraflores Locks, the last locks of the lot, darkness had fallen and the nearby jungle was coming alive with the noisy sawings and chisellings and high-pitched grinding sounds of the nocturnally busy insects and creatures hidden within.

We rumbled slowly onwards, slinking past the glitzy Miami-like skyline of Panama City, shimmering and alight in the near distance, before gliding beneath the towering and spot-lit meccano-like structure of the Bridge of the Americas. High above our heads dinky toy trucks and buses, festooned with fairy lights, were busy bustling back and forth along the bridge and that most fantastic of roads – the Pan-American Highway, which, save for the virtually impenetrable jungly swampland of the Darién Gap, stretches 16,000 miles all the way from Barrow in Alaska to the Argentinian port of Ushuaia in Tierra del Fuego. One day, I thought, I'm going to cycle across that bridge on my way from Anchorage to Patagonia and I'll look down and remember that hot and steamy Pacific-bound night, standing on the monkey deck, the bridge and the road and the canal shrinking into the darkness behind me, as the *Speybank* nudged her nose out into the night, and into the greatest ocean on earth.

# 6

# *The Pacific*

*Off the Panama Coast, 22 November*

If I thought the Atlantic Ocean was big, the Pacific is almost too big to comprehend. It has a rapacious appetite, its area swallowing a third of the entire earth's surface in one easy mouthful. That's double the size of the Atlantic. Just for the sake of superlative comparison, when you look at the Indian Ocean on a world map it is huge. In fact it is so huge that you can fit India twenty-eight times into the Indian Ocean. And India itself is no minor morsel; fourteen United Kingdoms fit inside a treat. I spent months cycling in India and nowhere near reached the bottom. Or the top. Or the sides. And I used to cycle quite far and fast in those springy-kneed days. Yet the Pacific is almost three times the size of the Indian Ocean, which, put another way, means it is as big as nearly ninety Indias. Or four hundred United Kingdoms. There, I think you get the picture. Blinking massive.

But wait. There's more. The Pacific is the world's deepest ocean, with an average depth of 13,780 feet (4,200 metres), which is half the height of Everest. Its deepest known part is 36,200 feet, almost seven miles – or a slow hour's cycle away. Makes you wonder what monstrous creatures dwell down there – hopefully not ones the size of double-decker buses (or Wales) with seven-mile-long sucker-bearing arms and a taste for container ships.

As if that isn't quite enough unrivalled superiority for one day, the waters of the Pacific make up half of the World Ocean. The Pacific also contains oceans of other seas, including the Bering Sea and the Sea of Okhotsk in the north, and the Sea of Japan and the China Sea in the west. Then there are the Philippine and Indonesian island groups which enclose the Banda, Celebes, Seram, Flores, Java and Molucca seas. Over in the southwest slop the Arafura Sea, the Coral Sea and the notoriously stormy Tasman Sea – the latter lying in the Roaring Forties between south-eastern Australia, Tasmania and New Zealand and which I hope to cross by ship to

Oz once I'm done in Kiwi land. About ten years from now, then, at this snail-in-labour pace.

The islands in the western Pacific are considered part of Asia. But the main volcanic and coral islands of Micronesia, Melanesia and Polynesia (which we're inching towards now – though we won't get there for another two or more weeks, or not at all if the other engine packs up) are included in those happy shimmering isles of Oceania.

But that's a long way off. All this morning we headed south into a smooth blue sea, with scarcely a williwaw of wind passing over the surface, at around ten knots while following the long jutting-out mountainously hazy coastline of Panama. Only then could we hang a right and nudge out west into the remote and monumental hugeness of the Pacific proper. The *Speybank* is currently under aerial attack from a bombardment of gannet-like boobies (blue-footed ones) all going great guns across the bow, while aquatic assault is underway from a flotilla of flying fish busily plinking into the water.

By early afternoon the sea had opened up to a wide expanse of ever-darkening blue. The heat was intense, the sky scattered with big dollops of cloud, some of which pelted us with heavy hot showers. The wind blew from behind, sweeping the black smoke that bellows out of the funnel into my cabin and over the monkey deck, making my head feel scuzzy from acrid fumes.

Llewellyn is turning progressively more curmudgeonly and loopy by the day. This morning he was in a terrible mood, huffing and puffing about how he has mistakenly deleted most of his digital pictures of the Panama Canal off his laptop. He's got the digitally minded Ian and Ham Man and Purser David and even the captain running to his aid. All conversation at breakfast and lunch revolved around nothing but emergency rescue procedures involving task bars, scroll bars, search companions, kilobytes, dialog boxes, inactive notification icons, floppies, hard drives, long drives ('Are we there yet?') and so on and so forth ad infinitum. For a non-computerised person such as myself, all this techie waffle went clean above my head so I took myself off and went for a swim in the Pacific instead.

The treading-water tank has at last been refilled (fortunately minus the man-eating sharks and other such sinister sea-patrolling creatures of the deep) but someone has tinkered with the plug so it now leaks a fraction slower than it did before. Means if I act fast after it's been topped up with the sea-hose, I only have to tuck my legs up over my shoulders instead of my ears in order to tread my daily waters.

Not that I like to be fussy, but another fault with this highly unrelaxing flotation tank is the noise. Talk about a bloody racket! Because the tank is situated on top of the cacophonous engine, it sounds as if I am partaking of my water sports above an army of bang-bashing ship-breakers and highway maintenance men digging up the road with bone-shaking JCB-mounted tarmac breakers, pile-drivers, Wacker plates and pneumatic drills. The constant juddering and reverberations of the tank walls are so skull-crunchingly intense I can feel the neurons in my brain being rearranged. If I manage to keep up this twice a day swim-sink routine I think I may have to steal a pair of ear-muffs off Chief Phil. Otherwise my eye sockets might rattle loose and drop with a flop to my ankles.

Traipsing puddles up the stairs on my return from my sea-dousing, I met Llewellyn.

'I have a very low opinion of your intelligence,' he told me.

'Why?' I said. 'Because I prefer treading water rather than getting involved in the inactive notification icons of your hard drive?'

He gave me one of his not-impressed, down-the-nose looks, as if I was nothing more than a drip in his way. Which I suppose I was, standing there in my sopping cozzie. Anyway, didn't stop me from wishing he would just bog off.

Later, up on the monkey deck, having a bit of a high-spirited anti-Llewellyn confab with Ham Man and Ian, I told them that so far Llewellyn had called me fat, stupid, naïve, unintelligent, under-aged, shoulder-hunched and doolally and said that I reminded him of his feisty daughter – another one of his offspring that he apparently is not too keen on. Ian and Ham Man laughed and commented that they were feeling a bit lacking in insults in comparison and tentatively awaited their adjectives of abuse. Ian said that so far Llewellyn had only called him 'a lonely man', whereas Ham Man had been called 'brave' for emigrating to New Zealand. 'Brave – for a man of your age,' is how Llewellyn had put it. Both Ian and Ham Man agreed they would try to gain a higher score on the Llewellyn Insult Stakes before the journey was out.

At dinner Llewellyn performed a spectacular change of subject mid-subject. Something he seems to be particularly adept at doing. Ian was telling a tale about how a group of immigrants had recently been found suffocated in one of the stacked-tight piled-high containers on board a freighter. While Ian was talking, Llewellyn kept trying to interrupt him, presumably because he wanted to add something regarding the story. When Ian finished talking, Llewellyn said, 'I'll tell you a sad story.'

We all listened, expecting another tragedy on a similar theme. Instead we got something wholly unrelated about how Llewellyn had once gone on a safari somewhere in Africa (it took about ten minutes for him to set the scene) and during this safari he had occasion to compose the 'most perfect picture' of an elephant across which arched 'the most perfect rainbow' stretching from one edge of his camera's viewfinder to the other. And then . . . (I could hardly contain my suspense – actually, I was more anxious to get going on the banana course) he pushed the shutter button and what should happen . . . ? Oh jeepers! The camera jammed!

A stunned silence prevailed across the table. And then I said, 'Oh, is that it? I'm still waiting for the bit about the containers.'

I got an email from Gary tonight. It started out on a promising footing, first referring to the MSc he's doing in timber frame conservation and repair, and then about how he had discovered a strain of *Donkioporia expansa* (which I could only imagine was a cheap imitation of Viagra that was flooding the markets) not far from Mrs Dolding's taper burn marks. (I later discovered it is known more commonly in the trade as *Phellinus cryptarum*, an oak rot fungus – how very disappointing.) With the nuts and bolts and undersquinted abutments out of the way, Gary then turned uncharacteristically soppy. Referring to a handful of my emails that seemed to have vanished into cyber space, he wrote, 'When your messages start getting lost, it loses this one precious connection I have with you.' Further down the page he said, 'I think my brain has accepted that I won't see you for a while. Doesn't stop the occasional staring into space though!'

Crikey! What's wrong with the fella? I'm only planning on being away for a year or two, for heaven's sake. Last time I looked he was a big burly builder with barely a sentimental word about his person.

Fortunately, though, by the penultimate paragraph, Gary had returned to more familiar ground explaining how he was just off to check up on the state of his *Quercus robur* (*pendunculata*) – which in any other language is simply an oak tree. Then, to finish off, and because I wasn't there to nag him to tend to his personal hygiene, he said, 'Seeing as I'm going out on the razzle later I spose I had best wash me pits and flip me pants inside out.'

Just as well I'm 10,000 miles away if that's how he's carrying on.

## DAY 25

*Not very far into the Pacific, 23 November*

News Flash! (Mk II). We are now six whole hours behind GMT. Just thought you'd like to know. Helps to put a scale on things.

There are a lot of noddies on the loose, too.

Apart from the days when the ship has been pitching and rolling about like a bucking bronco on amphetamines, I have managed to clamber out of my bunk at dawn every day since leaving Dunkirk to go striding and tripping about among the corroded leg-wrenching obstacles and pongy fumes of the monkey deck. Purely in the name of pointless exercise, you understand.

One of the best things about these early morning perambulations upon the inky green deck (which in places is so indented and gouged that large puddles of saltwater form only to evaporate in the sun to create mini Atacama deserts) is being alone. Unfortunately, since leaving Panama, Llewellyn and Eleanor have decided to try to get up early too in order to perform their carefully choreographed and precisely timed half-an-hour brisk stroll about the hazardous deck. The past two mornings I've had about five minutes of glorious peace before they come stamping up the steps, Llewellyn ready as ever to start laying in to me with criticism: 'You might as well not bother if you're walking that slow!' 'If you don't walk briskly and get your heartbeat up, you'll never lose weight!'

'Llewellyn,' I say. 'I've told you, I don't want to lose weight! And I don't want to walk fast! I just want to be able to think without you up my bum!'

Because it's impossible to walk at the same time as the perambulating twosome without causing a major pile-up, and because the more I look at Llewellyn the more ineffably irritating I find him, I just turn my back on both of them, cling to a corner railing and launch into a non-stop mad maelstrom of step-ups. I am so pent up at this stage that I almost feel like crying and I go completely berserk and pound myself for forty or more minutes until I'm completely exhausted and sweat is pouring down my face and my T-shirt is stuck to my back and bloody Llewellyn and Elliana have completed their perfectly synchronised marital stroll and descended to their quarters. Hallelujah! I'm on my own again.

It's at times like this that I don't half wish Gary was here. Having no one on board who's on my level of silliness is doing my head in and driving me slightly bonkers. I need a good cackle. More desperately I need a big hug. Not that a few Russians haven't tried to give me a big hug, mind you. Actually, they've tried to give me a bit more than a big hug. But I've held tight and haven't caved in, because for one thing I don't want any of them to lose their jobs and for another I've got Gary, somewhere over the horizon and diminishing in size by the day.

I had quite a turn this morning during my treading water ritual. There I was, cozzied up to the nines and flops flipped off, when, lowering myself into the slop, I noticed through the sloshing murk of the water a large and horrible wriggly thing writhing about on the bottom of the tank. I could only think that some deadly poisonous denizen of the deep had been sucked into the tank through the fat aperture of the sea-hose. If the ship would just stay still for a second, then I might have been able to identify what highly unpleasant creature was lying in wait to wrap itself around my windpipe. Unfortunately the sea was a lot rougher today, sloshing the tank water back and forth and blurring my vision of the *thing*.

I thought: 'Don't be silly. It's nothing. Get into the water. You'll be fine.' But every time I plunged half a leg into the tank I just as quickly yanked it back out. Big dilemma. I didn't feel brave enough to get into the water with whatever it was and yet I knew I had to because, no matter how murky the water or how venomous the beast, if I didn't have my twice daily slosh in the slop I would feel all fidgety and crotchety and ready to bite Llewellyn's head off even more than usual.

Finally, I flip-flopped out of the treading-water room, stubbing my toe on the high-rise door sill, and flipped up the stairs to my cabin where I grabbed my goggles, strapping them about my head for underwater exploration purposes.

Back down in the treading-water room I grasped an old frayed rope that dangled from the railing at the top of the tank and gingerly lowered myself head first over the edge, hoping my face wasn't about to be engulfed by some giant cephalopod sucker-bearing tentacle. Suddenly I slipped and the next thing I knew I was hanging upside down, still clinging to the rope, one foot gripping the rim of the tank, with my head under water. With my hindquarters in the air and another leg flailing wildly ('Please God,' I thought, 'don't let any Russians walk in on me now') I can't say this was the most dainty method of approach for entering a pool of water. It certainly wouldn't win me any prizes at the local swimming gala. But at least my head was under water, whether I liked it or not. This enabled me at last to identify what was squirming around on the floor of the tank. And quite shocking it was too. For it was none other than a severed arm. Or, at least, that's what it looked like, but only because my portside goggle started taking on water, resulting in a splonk of salty water in my left eye that made everything go lopsidedly blurred.

In the event, it was not so much a carelessly lost limb or even the torso-enwrapping sea creature of horror movie proportions I had imagined, but more an accumulation of gritty gunge and gunk that by slopping about on the bottom had formed a horrible and realistically writhing sea-snake of exceptional magnitude.

The Pacific isn't behaving particularly pacific-like at the moment. The crimped sea of this morning has turned into one of deep grooves, sending the ship into uncomfortable lurching motions. The heat is still debilitatingly humid and ferocious showers keep sweeping across the ship. I've counted more rainbows this morning than I have flying fish, and that's saying something as I've got flying fish coming out of my ears.

Because of the rain, I've upped sticks from my usual lookout slob-position on the monkey deck down to the bench on the covered and open-sided strip of deck outside the bridge wing door. The bench is wedged up against two hopelessly heavy doors upon which are plastered weather-worn stickers that warn:

CAUTION BATTERY DEPARTMENT. EXPLOSIVE GASES! NO SMOKING. EYE PROTECTION MUST BE WORN!

Oh well. Never mind. You can't really go anywhere on a ship like this that isn't a health and safety officer's worst nightmare. There's always somewhere or something that is surreptitiously crouched behind a corner just waiting to break your leg or explode in your face. At least no one has died yet, which is more than can be said of life on the old square-riggers. In *The Last of the Cape Horners*, Spencer Apollonio says that, on average, each ship killed one sailor a voyage. One of the ships was known as 'the floating coffin' as it tended to kill two or three men every trip it made. Betty Jacobsen writes that on one voyage alone the 'sailmaker died; another boy was killed in the rigging; a third was washed overboard; one of the officers went out of his mind; a cargo worker fell down the hold and was killed; and the captain slipped on the poop one night and broke his leg.'

It was in this outer bridge wing position, slumped against my pack containing binoculars, cameras, diary and books, that I was reading and writing and writing and reading and staring at the sea and seeing and staring. And thinking.

I was in an even more semi-prostrate position than normal, taking a break from Alexander McCall Smith's Botswanan-set *The No. 1 Ladies' Detective Agency* (starring the insuppressible Precious Ramotswe) by reading an old copy I'd picked up of the *Safety Digest – Lessons from Marine Accident Reports 1/2002* put out by the MAIB – Marine Accident Investigation Branch ('Case 6: Passenger Falls Down Open Hatch on Fast Ferry'; 'Case 7: Collision Between a Tank Barge and a Vessel Alongside'), when Llewellyn flounced out of the bridge door and said in testy tone, 'Do you *ever* read books?'

I'm not quite sure what he meant by this because he must have walked past me hundreds of times in the past three weeks when my head has been buried in a book. If I wasn't reading it, what on earth did he think I was doing – counting the spaces between the words?

'Er, yes, Llewellyn,' I said with remarkable restraint. 'I do read books.'

'Well, in that case,' he said, 'I wondered if you might like to read this.'

And he plonked a copy of *Time was Mine* by Derek Tangye on my chest before striding back to the bridge. As I slumped on the bench I flicked through the book. It seemed to be about Derek Tangye's account of his journey around the world as a young man in the 1930s. I found a bit about the South Pacific and read how in Suva: 'The heat was the kind that kept one's clothing perpetually clinging to one's body; and the natives were fuzzy-wuzzies with none of the attractiveness of the Polynesian.'

In Tahiti he was amused by the comments of a New Zealander he met there who told him: 'Raratonga is a damned sight better place than this hole. The natives are taught to respect a white man there – and they damn well get off the pavement when one comes along.'

I think they should have stuck to the pavement, myself. And shot the white man. Would have been a lot easier that way.

More excitement was had in the treading-water tank this afternoon. Because of a heavy swell, the *Speybank* was rolling quite heavily, causing the water in the tank to slop and tilt energetically from one side to the other. The angle of the list was acute enough that one moment one part of the tank would be as good as empty while the other was awash with a small tidal wave that slapped up over the rim flooding all the floors. Trying to tread water in this chaos of choppy slop was the most fantastic fun – like being tossed around in a completely idiotic wave machine.

Things became even more ridiculous when I was suddenly plunged into pitch darkness. A power cut had drowned out the lights of the whole lower deck. Only I didn't know that at the time – I thought perhaps we might be sinking. Unable to see a thing, it felt strangely unreal to feel your body being flopped back and forth in a stirred-up pit of agitated water. A bit worrying too. This was definitely turning into a flotation tank with a difference.

I waited a moment to see whether the lights would flick back on, but when they didn't I had to feel my way out of the tank and stagger my way in the lurching roll of the ship until I found the heavy submarine door that led through another high-stepped break-your-leg opening to a dark passage and the stairs.

Tonight I finally got round to watching my first video: *Das Boote.*

An incredible film all about the sinkings of German U-boats. They had a lot of power cuts, too. Come to think of it, maybe I should try and watch something a little more restful for the mind. Something potentially less sinkable. Like *Bambi.*

There again, maybe not.

**DAY 26**

*The Pacific, 24 November, 3° 38.5' N, 90° 11' W*

. . . At least, that's where we were at 16.00 when we were travelling at 10.9 knots. But we've probably gone backwards by now. If you look carefully, you might see the Isle of Wight drifting past through a portside porthole. Ah, there they are now – the Needles.

I think the boundless blank and monumental hugeness of the Pacific is getting to me.

It was the Portuguese navigator Ferdinand Magellan who gave the Pacific its name, because of his calm voyage that was blessed by fine weather and gentle breezes from the tip of South America to the Philippines in 1520–1521. But the Pacific is by no means always peaceful, particularly not to the west of the International Date Line and north of the 40th parallel, where it can be as awful and inscrutable and as ruthlessly lethal as any sea known. The highest wave in an open sea, measuring an estimated 34 metres (112 feet – that's over a third of the way up Big Ben) from trough to crest, was recorded in the Pacific during a hurricane in 1933. Still, the Pacific is for the most part well behaved. The volume and might of the Ocean may be almost unimaginably huge, but it is this enormous expanse of emptiness and unbroken smoothness of the sea containing no nuisance obstacles like vast islands or snowfields or sand deserts or rain forests or mischievous mountain chains to disrupt or deflect the wind, or raise or lower temperatures, that determines the general placidity of the Pacific weather system. The even-tempered steadiness of the breezes means that nowhere else on earth is the weather so dependably stable or less likely to get itself into a savagely destructive twist.

Ferdinand Magellan – or to give him his proper Portuguese name, Fernão de Magalhães – was an iron-willed admiral and remarkable navigator. He set off on 20 September 1519 with a royal mandate (in the name of Spain – he had washed his hands of his Portuguese citizenship, following a bit of a squabble) to search for a passage through to the *Mar del Sur*, the 'Sea of the South', in order to make sure that the Spice Islands (the Indonesian archipelago south of the Philippines now known as the Moluccas) lay within the Spanish empire.

Sailing around the world is not an easy pursuit at the best of times. Even with the most up-to-date charts and high-fangled equipment things can go very wrong, in much the same way as they can go wrong with Russian '*folklorique*' instruments (as I had already discovered). But in Ferdinand's day, it was even more of a challenge, not helped by the fact that Schoener's globe of the world as then known showed Japan a stone's throw off Mexico. (*Ahh so, desu ka?*) It was also thought that the Moluccas were to be found merely a short hop away from Panama.

With this view in mind, Ferdinand set sail across the Atlantic with a fleet of five vessels. These were ships that, until Ferdinand had improved them, had been hopelessly unseaworthy. The Portuguese consul in Seville made no attempt to conceal his glee that he was not part of the 277-strong crew. 'I would not care to sail to the Canaries in such crates,' he wrote. 'Their ribs are soft as butter.'

Once repaired and bodged back together, the Armada sailed across the Atlantic. It was a voyage not without incident, involving among other things a stream of woeful tales of sodomy and mutiny and yardarm punishment. Working their way down the unknown and unmapped coasts of South America, the sailors passed through untouched and unsullied territory sighting such oddities as penguins, or 'ducks without wings' as they called them, and 'sea-wolves', or seals. The seas became more terrifying by the day as the temperatures continued to plummet.

Nearing the barren bottom of South America, and after the wrecking of one of the fleet during a reconnaissance mission of the coast, Ferdinand and his crew encountered giant men whom they called *patagones* – 'big feet'. The land on which these big feet lived has been known ever since as Patagonia.

By this stage another serious mutiny had broken out, led by Spanish captains against their Portuguese commander. But Ferdinand was not a man to give in easily to animosity and ill-behaviour and with characteristic doggedness, ruthlessness and resourcefulness he quelled the revolt by executing one man and marooning another two, leaving them to their fate ashore. As the remaining four ships sailed off towards the open sea, all that stuck in the memory of the sailors on board were the pitiful screams and howls of the two men echoing out over the still waters of the inlet.

More trials and tribulations followed, but finally, after months of searching for a passage through to the *Mar del Sur*, the Armada rounded the Cape of the Virgins and entered the strait that Ferdinand Magellan had been determined for so long to hunt down and which later would bear his name. But passing through the passage was no plain sailing. Two ships were almost swept to their fates on to rocks when they got caught up in savage winds and mountainous surf and deathly skulking currents. Then a huge storm broke that seemed never to end. Men were washed overboard, one ship was dismasted and another narrowly missed being capsized several times. Just when it looked like the whole expedition was turning into a fatal shambles, the ocean they'd been looking for was sighted and the unshakable Ferdinand broke down and cried with joy. Others weren't so happy and felt it only prudent to turn back and head eastwards for the Spiceries. But Ferdinand dug his heels in. 'Though we have nothing to eat but the leather wrapping from our masts,' he announced, 'we shall go on!'

In the event only three ships made it through to the Sea of the

South, one vessel having deserted. On the way, Ferdinand named the archipelago dangling off the tip of South America and separated from the rest of the continent by the strait: Tierra de los Fuegos, the Land of Fire. He was inspired to call it this because of the striking sight at night of hundreds of blazing campfires lit by the local Indians. Today Tierra del Fuego, as it's now known, burns more with the huge spurting flames of offshore oilrigs than the lowly flicker of the fireside camp.

Bobbing about in the placid waters of the greatest ocean on earth, I thought about Ferdinand and his men as they sailed this way nearly 500 years ago. What really got me thinking about their voyage was a small tour of the steely kitchens and massive walk-in refrigerated ship's stores that Purser David gave me at my request. Though the *Speybank*'s food might not be up to gourmet Ian's high standards, it's still very tasty (Purser David told me he based most of the menus on Mrs Beeton's cookbooks) and would have been more than the emaciated and scurvy-ridden men of Ferdinand's punitive mission could ever have wished for. Andrew Weir Shipping allows a generous-sounding £4.70 per head per day. So far the *Speybank*'s food costs since leaving Le Havre have amounted to £11,500, and we're still weeks away from New Zealand.

While we have menus revolving around chicken chasseur, creamed rice Hawaiian, lamb chops in reforme sauce, casseroled liver, braised ox-tail jardinière with macedoine of vegetables and Garfield potatoes, pear belle Hélène, black mamba jelly, sponge pudding and custard, neapolitan sundae, cheeseburger toasted bap, turkey cazullah, Hot Dog in a Bun, trout Cleopatra, pork pie salad with diced swedes, Canadienne tartare (which turned out to be mince and potato pie) and Manchester tart ('Do I know her?' enquired Ian when he was offered a slice), the sailors sea-locked on board the ships *Trinidad*, *Concepción* and *Victoria* had no such fare. Six weeks out of the Straits men began to die. They became tortured by thirst and stricken by scurvy – their gums turned spongy and bled, causing teeth to fall out; they had sallow complexions and sunken eyes; their breath smelt horribly rank; huge boils erupted from skeletal frames; and haemorrhages, often massive, penetrated muscles and other tissues. Not surprisingly, they fell into a hollow and hopeless depression. All that these men needed to spare them from a hideous death was a little boost of vitamin C. And yet the regulated administration of lemon juice, at least in the British Navy, didn't begin for another 250 years. Even Nelson contracted scurvy. Incidentally, British sailors became widely nicknamed limeys when, in 1865, lime juice was substituted for lemon juice.

With neither lemons nor limes, the constant misery of the Magellan voyage grew more and more terrible. Men were dying like flies. The water supplies turned scummy and rank. The only food left on board – rat-fouled biscuits – ran out completely and the men were indeed reduced to eating the leather off the yardarms. Somehow, despite such privations, Ferdinand and his surviving crew eventually made it across the Pacific. The journey that he had thought would take three days had lasted three and a half months.

## DAY 27

*The Pacific, 25 November*

The temperature has dropped to 29°C today. Feels decidedly chilly. Might have to put my gloves on. Meanwhile the Pacific is just that – ironing board flat.

My favourite place on the whole of the *Speybank* is right up on the prow of the bow. Here I can stick my head through one of the gaping mooring holes in the side of the gunwales. By lying flat and holding on tight, it's possible to look straight down to the ship's big rust-rounded bulb plunging up and down through the dazzling sea. This is the only place on the *Speybank* that you don't hear any noise or smell any fumes. I feel very happy here, stretched out like a ship's figurehead with just the sound of the wind and the waves. It's very hypnotic, too, staring at the bulbous bulb sluicing through the swish of water, watching the jut of the bow slicing the sea in two.

Taking a break from his Zero Lima One Charlie Tango, Ham Man joined me to take the opportunity of this pancake sea to prowl around the whole of the main deck and up to the bow. We spent most of the time photographing each other while straddling over or hanging from or tripping over the multifarious obstacles like foot plates and deck ridges and hatch covers and knife-sharp flaps. There are lots of grimy bilious yellow ladders, too, all leading down into unappetising black holes deep below deck that stink of chemicals and fumy gases and reverberate with head-clanging noise. I feel for the Russians who have to work down there.

I recently read in the *Seafarers' Bulletin* that researchers looking into accidents and injuries on ships have found that seafarers have a one-in-eleven chance of being injured on their tour of duty – a much greater rate than for other occupations. Out of a survey of 550 seafarers, a third had fractured or sprained limbs, usually by falling, slipping or tripping, while death rates as a result of fatal injury were much higher on board ship than on shore. This doesn't seem very fair, because the sea is a treacherous enough place without adding to the hazard. Fishing and seafaring are by a long chalk the most dangerous occupations, which is why mariners once had to be press-ganged rather than volunteering their service. Only the brave, the foolhardy or the desperate would have contemplated a career aboard ship.

On our investigations of the ship Ham Man and I kept coming across the odd crewman busily on his way to do something busy but we were never quite sure what. I tried to extract some information as to his line of work from deck engineer Leonid

Pushkarev who, by wearing a pair of sinister shades and a white bandanna wrapped around his head, looked like a cross between a pirate and a mafia hit-man. But as his English is as good as zilch, and as my Russian extends only as far as asking for the nearest underground station, we didn't quite hit it off on the comprehension front. Still, we had a laugh and a photo and draped each other's arms over each other's shoulders.

Walking back down the narrow fore-aft side deck, overshadowed by the ominously creaking and groaning cliffs of containers like monstrous shoeboxes stacked tightly and high, we came upon the two cheery Irish cadets, David and Steven, and the rather dishy ship's fitter, Nikolai Schukin. He and the cadets were kneeling on the deck making a blinking awful racket grinding away at the rutted deck with grinding machines, presumably to make it less rusty and rutted. They had their work cut out for them in an ever on-going Firth of Forth bridge-painting sort of way.

All of this reminded me of the bit that I recently read in *The Last of the Cape Horners*, where the square-rigger apprentice Betty Jacobsen says that after cleaning out the pigsty and the water closets, and fetching the ship's cook his coal and water for the day, 'the real work begins – chipping the darned rust. There is always rust in a sailing-ship; in fact, some of them, I gather, are nothing but one big piece of rust held together by a little paint.'

In 1933, when my mother was a year old, Richard Sheridan, the eighteen-year-old nephew of Winston Churchill who shipped on the four-masted *Lawhill* from London to Australia, wrote that 'rust accumulates in such thickness that if it were not removed, the ship's life would not be more than a quarter of the number of years that some of these sailing ships attain'. He then goes on to say how 'one is puzzled after seeing the accumulation of rust from hours' chipping that there is anything left of the ship'. Sheridan hated the job:

When I was alone I used to go off my head at times. I would listen to the noise of one solitary hammer re-echoing the length of her huge hold, chip-chip-chip, in the darkness, 60 times a minute, 3,600 times an hour, 18,000 times a watch. My brain used to work with the hammer in a monotone keeping time, thinking the same thing over and over again. To-morrow-you-will-chip-next-week-you-will-chip-next-month-you-will-chip-chip-chip-until-you-go-mad-stark-staring-mad . . .

He describes the job as being a 'wretched enough existence, the cold, the lack of sleep, the misery, depression, loneliness of it all'. The third mate of the *Lawhill* was a Finn and Sheridan remembers how, near the beginning of the voyage, the Finn came up to him when he was trying to do his best at chipping and ordered him to 'Cheep faster . . .'

'Can't, sir.'
'Moost, moost!'
'Yessir.'
'Sheridan, do you ever vash?'
'Vash?'
'Yas, vash.'
'Do you mean wash, sir?'
'Yas.'
'Every evening, sir.'
'No – not.'
'I'm not a liar, sir.'
'Donkeyman say you never vash.'
'Donkeyman's a bastard, sir.'
'You vash tomorrow, or we take you forward and scrub you with deck broom.' (Howls of delight from the rest of the watch.)
'Yessir.'
'Horry up, cheep faster.'
'Chip faster, sir.'

\*

On the return leg from our explorations Ham Man and I stumbled upon a dead rat. It was about the size of an average cat, yet we felt sufficiently moved to give it an official burial at sea. Without argument I allowed Ham Man to hurl it over the side as far as he could while I gave it a double-crossed blessing of good riddance. Should the topic of the rat crop up in dinnertime conversation we decided that, to spare sending Eleanor into a state of advanced paralysis, it was best to refer to it under the euphemistic moniker of Romeo Alpha Tango.

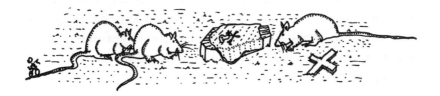

Climbing back up the inner staircase of the superstructure Ham Man and I suddenly decided to have a spontaneous hug, not because I fancy him or anything, but because . . . well, sometimes, especially after weeks at sea, you just need to have a hug no matter whom it is you're hugging. Actually, it does matter whom you're hugging, because I couldn't hug Ian as it would be like hugging a long stiff plank (he's a bit upright, is Ian). And I couldn't hug Llewellyn because I'd rather smack him in the chops. And I couldn't hug French army man Mickael Sailly because I'd rather do something to him far more interesting. And I couldn't go round hugging the Russian crew (more than I do already) because I'd be given yardarm and plank-walking justice. And so Ham Man had to do. One can't be picky marooned in the middle of the Pacific on a ship like this, you know. You grab what you can when you can.

As it turned out, Ham Man was quite good for hugging, but only because he's not very tall and I slot in under his arms a treat. So there I was, rammed in the corner of the staircase practically smothered by Ham Man, when who should suddenly step on to the scene but Llewellyn. Llewellyn stopped stock-still and looked shocked. As Ham Man had his back to Llewellyn he didn't notice him. But unbeknown to Llewellyn I was fully aware of the situation by secretly monitoring the current state of affairs through a chink of light beneath Ham Man's armpit. Because I wasn't feeling in a very sensible mood, I pretended I didn't know Llewellyn was there and started groping Ham Man's bum making it look as if we were having some serious schmoozing. Then for my next pretence act, I suddenly pushed Ham Man off while trying to look all hot and flustered and very embarrassed and said, 'Ooh, hello Llewellyn. I didn't know you were there!'

'Ah, I see,' said Llewellyn. 'So that's what's going on between you two, is it?' And with that he backed off out through the door with a look of disgust. It was all most amusing.

For the rest of the day I sat plonked on the monkey deck reading and writing and staring and thinking about how all this reading and writing and staring and inactivity can make your mind feel as if it's dissolving in on itself. I've never been one to look inside my head because I think that's a bit of an inward-looking self-analysing danger zone and that time can be better spent going on a brisk fifty-mile bike ride or tending to the finer lubrications of one's bottom bracket. But seeing as those two latter pursuits could not be accomplished with anything like ease on board a boat in the middle of the Pacific, I instead pondered in a cogitating fashion how the world has never felt so big or the horizons so unreachable.

Later on Ham Man joined me. Sweeping his arm from horizon to horizon in a grandiose manner he said, 'Look! Miles and miles of nothingness!'

Shading my eyes from the sun with a horizontal ledge of fingertip touching hands, I scanned the empty broad belly of the ocean and horizons as wide as the world.

'I can't see any nothingness,' I said. 'All I can see is somethingness.' Because whatever way you define nothingness, nothing is always something.

After Ham Man had retreated to his quarters to catch up on some easily earned sleep, I remained on the monkey deck staring at the sea for hours. During this time I had two thoughts. Actually I'm pleased to say I had a few more than two thoughts (the expansiveness of my thought process hasn't completely gone to pot yet – though it's a close run thing), but these are the two I'm going to give you. The first is a very deep and complex thought (so brace yourself for impact) and concerns Llewellyn and Eleanor. And the thought was this: what a lot of L's and E's they have in their combined names. I mean, Llewellyn has got four L's all to himself, for heaven's sake. How greedy is that? Also, when you say Llewellyn and Eleanor out loud, it's a very tricky combination of names to say at normal talking speed without tripping over your tongue. I'll just pause here a moment to give you a chance to have a go . . . There, see what I mean? A real stumbling block. And said fast, don't you find Eleanor comes out as enema? Or is it just me? So all things considered, I've been thinking it would be much easier simply to kill two boobies with one stone by combining their names when talking about them in combination and call them Lewellynor. It's kinder on the adenoids and has the added benefit of bearing a boating air about it: 'Quick! We're about to gybe! Grab the halyard and lower the lewellynor!'

Now, quite what my second thought was I've completely forgotten.

One of the strange things about this watery journey is that I have never slept so well for so long as I have on board this creaking vessel. Sometimes I go to bed at eight-thirty feeling utterly exhausted (from doing nothing) and fall into a comatose sleep as a warm balmy tropical wind (or a suffocatingly hot or stormy wet one) blows in through both portholes strapped back with bike bungees to prevent banging. (Can't have an annoying knocking and banging disturbing one's slumbers, you know.) I then wake up about five-ish. That's not far off ten hours' kip. Quite shocking! Must be something to do with the druggy ozone and the lullability of the constant rocking motion. I've also never had such busy dreams. Last night I dreamt Mum gave birth to a baby for me (I believe Gary played a part in there somewhere, involving something complicated to do with seed transfer) and then I found myself flying a Messerschmidt light German aircraft while simultaneously trying to breastfeed the baby (Mum was looking confused while holding on tight in the passenger seat). Then I said, with a degree of urgency, 'We've got to find a Tesco's!' This was because I needed to land in the car park to fill up with fuel and then I found one and Gary was there semaphoring me in to land but he was a little flummoxed because he thought I was supposed to be arriving in a 55-ton all-terrain six-wheeler, half-rigged, swinging cab crane with a 35-metre stick and a 25-metre luffing jib, and then I taxied over a whole lot of 4×4s (pleasingly crushing most of them in the process) on my way to the petrol station.

The calm of this morning seems to have been washed down the plughole. From afternoon onwards the sea has turned all agitated and edgy, as if it is up to some good-for-nothing tricks. How very un-Pacific of it.

## DAY 28

*The Pacific, 26 November*

Was up at 4.30 this morning in time to see an ashen pink sunrise defining the sea from the sky. Felt very happy with no one to be seen – just the big grumbling boat and a boundless expanse of sea and sky and the gentle gliding curvature of the earth. I managed to do all my madcap spiel of step-ups and slaloming speed-walk about the stumbling obstacles of the monkey deck before the annoyances of Lewellynor appeared on the scene. So that made me even happier. Then at 6 a.m. I spotted a distant container ship slipping over the horizon. First sighting of a ship in what feels like years.

The sea has now turned as flat as a tray. No whitecaps or big dents in it like yesterday afternoon. It's cloudy though, and only a chilly 25°C. I've detected goosebumps on my forearms jostling for position among a small forest of hairs standing to attention. What a fascinating discovery – especially when you haven't got anything else better to do. And 25°C isn't even cold. At least not by our northern climes. Isn't acclimatisation a strange thing? If I had gone from cold to hot I would now be boiling. But I've gone from hot to very warm and I'm now freezing. How silly is that?

The boobies are back in force. This momentarily strikes me as very odd. Where the devil have they come from? If you've got a minute, come over here, but mind your step and your head on the large radiation-emitting satellite pod, and follow the wide sweep of my arms and what do you see? Nothing but sea. I mean, we're in the middle of nowhere, for Pete's sake, even though nowhere is of course somewhere. But that aside, if you're a booby you don't just fly around in the middle of the Pacific for the fun of it, do you? After all, there is the serious lack of fuelling stations to consider. Yes, yes, I know boobies can fish, but surely they've got to have a little sit down and a rest every now and then, much like Mum does when she goes shopping. Ah, that is what I was forgetting. There is of course a very good service station not very far away in the shape of the equator-sitting Galápagos Islands – the location of Darwin's inspiration for *The Origin of Species*. GPS-clutching Ian tells me the Galápagos are about an hour or two's flight away for a booby. So that's a relief.

Ian seems to live among his abbreviations. He's got his PC, his PDA and his GPS among a whole host of other digitally abbreviated toys. I was flopped on the monkey deck, Russian phrasebook propped open idly on chest (**Dyehvooshkah nahs pryehrvahlee** – 'Operator, I've been cut off!') watching Ian leaning over the railings taking the latest reading with his handheld global positioning system when I suddenly blurted out, 'I.A.N. It's just as well you know the ABC of your GPS to give us an ETA in NZ, especially now we're in PDT, as it saves having to SOS PDQ anyone who might be in reach of our TEU-carrying tub.'

Ian looked at me as if I was minus an IQ or two. So I went back to my Russian *yah khahtyehl bi ahsortyee* ('I'd like some assorted appetizers').

It's late afternoon and the sky is full of fluffy cauliflower-topped but scrubby level-bottomed clouds skirted by dark curtains of distant squalls of meteorological liveliness. These clouds seem impossibly heavy, crushing the ocean flatter still. The threat of turbulence looks as if it is exciting the boobies more than ever. Their frisky antics are highly entertaining to watch as they sweep on a bow breeze with aerobatic ease. When one booby breaks away from the wind-surfing pack to divebomb like a refined military aircraft for its fish dinner, the rest of them follow in a sudden and noisy and elbowing squabble. And when they squabble they sound strangely like ducks.

All this staring at the sky has reminded me that I haven't seen a plane or vapour trail since leaving France several lifetimes ago. At home the skies seem to be a constantly droning and thrumming hubbub of the comings and goings of fat engine-thrusting jets and private choppers, their rotors pulsing a drumbeat. Lower down the aeronautical chain there are occasional gliders, flying strimmers (aka microlights) and small acrobatic two-seater planes doing loop-the-loops and heart-stopping engine-stalls all mixing among the treetop-skimming rooftop-strafing army Chinooks and balloon-gliding champagne-supping revellers. Out here in the bountiful and bright expanse of an all but infinite ocean there is nothing but an untrammelled sky. There must be planes crossing it somewhere, because planes from everywhere are crossing it from here and there all of the time. Wherever they are, they will all be far removed from the flimsy craft that first flew across the Pacific in 1928 when Charles Edward Kingsford-Smith, or Smithy as he was known, an Aussie aviator whose skill and derring-do had already notched up an impressive gauntlet in the pioneer age of aviation and long-distance flight (the previous year he had flown around the Australian continent in ten days flat), flew from Oakland, California, to Brisbane by way of Hawaii and Fiji, with a co-pilot, navigator and radioman. All this in the days before any accurate navigation systems existed. Apart from the phenomenal distance (7,200 miles), what's so astonishing about this courageous and skilful feat is that they flew in a decidedly makeshift and insubstantial wood-framed, cloth-covered 1920s tri-motor Fokker, which held about as much strength as a boy's Airfix model. Six hundred miles out from Honolulu things went a bit fokked when they slammed straight into a violent and hugely stormy weather system with bashing winds and boiling clouds of unknown ferocity. None of the men knew what to expect as no one had ever flown into such savagely frenzied weather before. For hours Smithy struggled to control the plane and keep it from breaking up as he and his crew were bounced about like polystyrene in high seas. Their rocky ride was made all the more uncomfortably perilous as the Fokker, so basic and primitive in design, didn't even have seats that were bolted down.

You wonder how Smithy managed to keep it together because, very inconveniently for a pilot, he was prone to incapacitating panic attacks when airborne. Following a childhood near-drowning experience he also had a morbid fear of the sea, which he called aquaphobia. And here he was flying across the biggest wettest puddle in the world in not much more than a winged matchbox. He was, though, about as equally addicted to terror as he was obsessed with fame. With the first trans-Pacific flight between America and Australia under his belt, he flew on and on, landing records all over the world like the first non-stop flight across Australia; the first flight across the Tasman Sea from Australia to New Zealand (he then flew back again); the first solo flight from England to Australia; the first westbound flight across the Atlantic (into the jet stream) from Ireland to Canada. Then in November 1935, he took off from Kent to attempt to break the 71-hour

England to Melbourne record and was lost somewhere off Singapore.

## DAY 29

*The Pacific, 27 November*

Here's a thought: I haven't walked on land for three weeks, three days.

And here's a fact: we crossed the equator at two o'clock this morning. Fortunately there were no fancy ceremonial dunkings or rituals involving being trussed up in King Neptune garb. But in honour of the Coriolis effect, I've conducted an experiment in the inner confines of my vacuum toilet area to see if the water goes out of the plug backwards. Unfortunately it seems to drain out in one sudden slurp – neither backwards nor forwards. I think I'll ask for my money back.

There are some things in life that you need to get to the bottom of, and one of these is my boobies. For days I've been wondering why boobies are called boobies. No one on board can seem to help me out here. I know why noddies are called noddies (in their displays of courtship, both males and females do a lot of nodding to show off their pale foreheads), but not boobies, boobies. So I sent my distant mother on an investigative mission to riffle through my bird books at home for an explanation. And this is what she came up with: boobies were named boobies because they are a bit thick and trusting at times, making it so easy for sailors to catch and kill. So there you have it. I can now concentrate on other pressing matters.

Every night at dinner Eleanor has worn a different outfit, mostly of a fancy frock nature. I said to Eleanor last night, 'Eleanor, have you got a bottomless suitcase?'

But as usual Llewellyn, acting like Eleanor's ventriloquist, answered. 'What you've seen is nothing,' he said. 'There's a whole untouched suitcase yet of cruise wear for the journey home on the *Aurora.*'

'Well, in that case,' I said, 'I think you ought to turf the whole lot overboard. That way we might pick up a spot of speed!'

They both looked at me as if I had just jumped on the table and dropped my shorts. Which I sometimes feel like doing.

This morning I was up at dawn. And what a spot of bad luck, because so was Lewellynor. I had about two minutes of peace walking around the monkey deck before Llewellyn clattered up the steps. I gritted my teeth and somehow managed to bid him a chirpy good morning. But no good mornings issued from Llewellyn.

'I've told you before,' he said, sounding a bit too much like a scolding teacher, 'if you don't walk at a fast pace you might as well not be walking at all as it's not doing you any good. It certainly won't get rid of any fat!'

I ignored him and, turning my back, leapt on to the railings muttering a fusillade of unsavoury thoughts to myself as I launched into a rant of step-ups. I could feel Llewellyn's eyes boring into my back. He was aggravating me beyond belief. I could feel my cross-hairs hatching. I was hot and sweaty and I felt like either throttling him or unleashing my tongue big time. But because I was stuck in a small space in the middle of a big ocean with nowhere else to go (a quick fifty-mile cycle and I would have felt fine), and because I didn't want to rock the boat as it could make the following weeks unbearable, all I said was, 'And don't look at my fat bits!' In no uncertain terms.

'I can't unless you turn round,' he said shouting into the wind, 'as they're all around the front!'

More treading water followed, and then by breakfast I was in a good mood again. But only because Ian came out with the word 'dastardly!' Which amused me greatly.

Here's a demonstration of how, when you're closely confined for weeks on a ship with people with whom you'd rather not be

confined, things can turn pretty petty. When anyone helps themselves to a drink in the bar, the drinker marks his drink against the
appropriate drink which is about to be drunk, with a tally mark.
Every now and then, the tallies are added up and the drinker then
pays Purser David the necessary sum in either dollars or euros or
pounds. Well, Ian didn't realise that the fifth stroke of a tally mark
amounted to five, so he had been overpaying. When Purser David
discovered Ian's mistake he said scoffingly to him, 'I thought every
child learnt how to tally in primary school!'

Ian, being a shiny gold cufflink shirt sort with a predilection for
the word 'dastardly', didn't take kindly to this comment. In fact he
got in quite a tizz about it and complained to me up on the
monkey deck how he thought Purser David had been incredibly
rude to him. I told him not to worry about it and that what he
lacked in tally marks he made up for in GPS positionings. But Ian,
who liked to hold himself in high regard, had been affronted and
he didn't like it. So after the insult had gnawed away at him all day,
he finally went to David and demanded an apology. Purser David
gave him one but I suspect not willingly. The atmosphere between
the two of them was all very frosty for a while, until Ian finally
relented and bought David a drink to make up. But this making up
is only a show, because Ian later said to me that he doesn't like
David at all. I think the feeling is probably mutual. 'Don't worry
Ian,' I said, giving him a little calming pat. 'Just count yourself
lucky you don't have to put up with David for as long as I have to
put up with Llewellyn!'

The height of excitement this afternoon occurred during my
afternoon session of treading water. For the first time in my career
as a treader-of-water, someone else appeared. It was the young
Boris Johnson look-alike, Vitali Agudalin, Second Engineer in
Waiting. He stripped down to his boxers and then brazenly, at least
for entering a sugarcube-sized tank containing a mere dribbly
sludge of water, belly-flopped on top of it – and me. Of course I
made no pretence that I didn't notice that the force of his flop had
washed his boxers down to his knees.

*

Outside the crew's mess.
*From left to right:* me, Zhenya Sotnikov
(Able Seaman), Yuri Basalaev (bosun),
David White (Irish cadet),
Dimitri Prokopev (engineroom oiler),
Steven Molloy (Irish cadet)

Grabbing a hold in the chartroom
with Mr Alex Sasha second officer
Nepomnyashchikh

Bridging a gap with
chief officer Alexi Khil

Welcome to the bunk of my boudoir

Ham Man in his cabin live on air

Purser David (nice socks!).
Mouth of the Panama Cana

Leonid Pushkarev
says if I want to
jump ship, leap
this way. Crossing
the Pacific

Ian
(*aka* Captain Cumming)

Natasha Kochmar
(*on left*) and
Elena Golubtsova
in full barbecuing
flow on the
monkey deck

I wonder what
happens if I pull this
and push that...
On board the *Speybank*

At work in the calm of the Pacific. Steven Molloy the Irish cadet *(on left)* with Nikolai Schukin (fitter/extra fitter)

Yuri Basalaev (bosun)

Passing through the Panama Canal

Refuelling tanker pulling up alongside.
Mouth of the Panama Canal

Peregrine falcon taking a break.
Caribbean Sea

Yuri-the-bosun out on a limb cable-greasing.
Mouth of the Panama Canal

Bike rearing to go.
Middle of the Pacific Ocean

Bike in transit to *terra firma*.
Nouméa, New Caledonia

At peace with panniers.
Moorea, Tahiti, French Polynesia

A local putting up his feet in front of the *Speybank* and the French CMA CGM ship.
Papeete, Tahiti

Christmas Eve in the ship's bar
*Front row from left to right:* Grigori Akulov (third engineer), Benji Evgrafov
(electrical officer), me, Valeri Ananin (fourth engineer), Ham Man
*Middle row from left to right:* Chris Baines (captain), Vitali Agudalin (the belly-flopping
second engineer – with a Pringle in his eye), Steven Molloy (Irish cadet)
*Back row:* Chief Engineer Phil, David White (Irish cadet)

Welcome to New Zealand at the height of midsummer. A torrentially raining
Christmas Eve, Auckland harbour

Today we've had some new boobies on the block. The blue-footed and red-footed ones seem to have been replaced by masked ones. These are big buggers with a wingspan up to five-and-a-half feet. That's bigger than me, for cripes sake! They seem to have an insatiable appetite for flying fish, which they catch either by snapping in mid-flight or by diving under water in hot pursuit. Some of their dives are most impressive, and certainly put the belly-flopping antics of Boris to shame. They soar into the sky, circling round and round. When they've got a good-size fish in their sights, they fold back their wings and plummet from heights of 60 to 100 feet into the sea with an impressive splash. Crashing into the sea from such height would give any other bird, if not concussion, then a stinking awful headache. But boobies, like gannets, wear the equivalent of in-built cycling helmets in the form of specially strengthened skulls that help to cushion the impact of their high-speed dives into water. The momentum must carry them quite a long way under because it's several long seconds until they reappear again. Sometimes, when they don't appear for more time than I think is natural, I find I'm on the point of kicking off my shoes and diving in after them on a spontaneous life-saving mercy dash. That's how involved I've got with their magnificent diving procedures. Other times on their way down from a dive they somehow manage to catch flying fish just as the fish re-enter the water. I feel like applauding.

I can't believe all the others would rather stare at their computer screens than watch boobies. These birds' antics have me completely transfixed. And to think I was almost not going to bring a pair of binoculars with me on this voyage because of weighty pannier concerns. They've been virtually pinned to my eyes ever since we left.

But boobies aren't the only entertainment on the cards as there's also been a smattering of petrels and frigates. There I was worrying over a booby's ability to be so far from land without a proper square meal inside of it, when all along it probably just gets refuelled with a splash of petrel. Actually, the boobies seem to go nowhere near the petrels' stations. They've got to watch it because they can have a frigate on their back if they're not careful. These frigates are quite something. Apart from their monumental wingspan (up to seven feet) and the fact that they have been known to have flown at a height of 4,000 feet – almost qualifying for the mile-high club – they have a very piratical streak in them. A flying booby that has just swallowed a fish is no match for these swift noisy marauders. The frigate bird (being the Mafioso of seabirds) attacks the booby, pummelling and jostling its victim until it either drops or disgorges its catch. Then the frigate grabs the fishy morsel before it disappears into the ocean. At first I couldn't work out why they didn't simply go fishing themselves rather than attack others. It would be a lot easier than all that piratical savagery and would conserve energy, too – so much fighting and squabbling must be very draining on one's precious reserves. It would also help the nerves and go some way towards keeping an even keel on oceanic oscine relations. (Even if they are non-aubergines, I mean, non-passerines.) But then I noticed frigates do go fishing. They skim along just above the waves, wetting no more than their bills, to snap up fish, and apparently they also adopt this method for catching jellyfish, squids, young sea turtles and scraps of carrion. Further observations have told me that they are definite skimmers, not swimmers. Like cats, they are best advised to keep out of water. This is because if a frigate is forced to settle on the ocean's surface, it is unlikely to rise again; it has no oil-producing glands to water-proof its yards of plumage. Unless a forceful gust of wind quickly lifts it aloft, the bird will probably drown. In this way I suppose frigates are quite like Smithy in his Fokker: constantly flying and dicing with death close above the sea, but utterly useless if they misjudge their moves and drop into it.

The frigates I've spotted round here appear to be particularly fond of flying fish, often catching them in mid-flight. They are fantastic. It's like watching a circus act. I'm on the edge of my seat wondering what surprises they're going to throw at me next.

I got an email from Mum this evening. She told me how she and Dad had stopped on their way to Devon for morning coffee down at some caff and caused a stir when Dad was loading up the tray with coffee and cakes by his suddenly dropping the lot on the floor. Heads turned to stare. Broken crockery everywhere. The woman behind the counter said it wasn't Dad's fault, that the sliding shelf was much too narrow for the tray. Aren't some people nice? If my experience of Dad and morning coffee is anything to go by, I'd have said he was piling on board a cake too many.

I also had an email from next-door neighbourly Val. She told me how someone in a fat four-wheel-drive had crashed on Milland Hill causing local traffic chaos. Then not much more than a day later a 4×4 was discovered upside-down in Durrants Pond at midnight. What a very unsensible place to park. Nobody was in it when found (how disappointing) but it was leaking engine oil and had most likely given the village ducks a run for their money. The trouble with this 4×4 fad is that the owners don't seem to realise that driving around on their roofs is not a good idea. My solution – hang, draw and yardarm the lot of them. Either that or incarcerate them on the *Speybank* with no one else but Llewellyn.

Val also said she had been down the road to visit a couple in the next-door village – Vi, 96, and Ted, 91 with two fingers missing off his left hand because he shot them off by mistake, otherwise fit as a fiddle, used to cut chestnut just over the way in Wick Wood. He told Val he went to Woolbeding school (just over the hill) age three and had his first caning age four for answering back sadistic flagellating woman teacher. Maybe we should set the likes of her loose on 4×4 owners who can't keep upright.

**DAY 30**

*The Pacific, 28 November*

It's taken me a day to realise this but since crossing the equator yesterday everything looks much the same in the southern hemisphere as it does in the northern hemisphere – lots of sea and lots of sky and nowhere else to go. The temperature has shot through the roof again, though. And the boobies have gone. Obviously they had better things to be doing. Unlike me.

We are now about as far away from anywhere as we are ever going to be. Five hundred thousand miles in every direction from any terra firma. At least that's what it feels like. Ian says we are now halfway between Panama and Tahiti, which means we're 2,500 miles from anywhere of any size. A distance that feels all the greater when you're travelling at the speed of a pedaloing worm. Or even a pedalling worm.

It's hardly surprising that the Pacific, which seems to like to hog all the biggest, deepest, wettest superlatives in the book, is also the place that contains the spot on the world's surface that is most distant from land. Where the lengthy longitude 118° 30′ W intersects latitude 47° 30′ S is an equal 1,560 miles from the nearest coasts of Chile, Antarctica's Peter Island and a tiny little uninhabited pinprick called Ducie Island – an island that the colonising British like to think is theirs after fishing it out of distant waters a very long time ago. Heaven only knows why the British couldn't just be content with nabbing islands closer to home like, say, the Isle of Wight. It's splat bang on their doorstep and, unlike distant Ducie, convenient to reach on Southwest trains. But unlike the Isle of Wight and its hankie-on-head holidaying hordes, Ducie does possess a slightly more exotic edge. It is a part of the Pitcairn group of volcanic islands that are renowned for their association with Fletcher Christian and eight other mutineers from HMS *Bounty*, who settled there with a group of Tahitian women in 1790, and whose descendants still live there.

Now that we really are in the middle of nowhere, even if nowhere is anywhere but somewhere, we are supposed to be hitting a blank spot of a black hole where no emailing satellites can reach us. At least that's what Purser David has told us. Well, blank spots or not, Gary still seems to be getting through. Maybe he's got a special tool bar that no one else has. His latest epistle (may contain nuts) is in answer to my previous cry for help re recipes for static exercises for mid-Pacific. Gary's got a set of weights at home with which he likes to wreak havoc on his muscles ('bicep now up to 16 inches, Jose!' he tells me) and he's never short of telling me about a new exercise or two. So in today's email he suggests I perform one called the plank. 'Lie face down supporting yourself on forearms and tips of toes,' he says. 'Seems to do nothing for a while then it really starts to hurt!' Well, thanks! 'Works your stomach muscles which shouldn't be necessary if you miss breakfast.' But I'm not missing breakfast. Eating is one of the major excitements of the day, especially when you haven't got any boobies left to watch.

I was busy plank-performing this morning up on the monkey deck when Mr Alex Sasha second officer Nepomnyashchikh stumbled upon me. Literally. He asked me what I was doing. I said I was in the middle of a plank. He looked blank. So I grappled him to the deck to try his hand at a plank. So there we were, me and the unpronounceable second officer, in the middle of the Pacific plonked out like planks. Only Mr Alex Sasha second officer Nepomnyashchikh's stomach, being of a rotund nature, kept him propped up instead of his elbows. Which I said was cheating. He said it was sensible and saved a lot of sweat. It was while we were having a good plank together that I rather hoped nobody else appeared. It's one thing to be caught canoodling Ham Man, but to be discovered planking the second officer is quite another ball game.

## DAY 31

*The Pacific, 29 November*

Weather update: Sizzling sun. Smooth blue seas. Precious little wind. Extra sweaty step-ups. Llewellyn calm to stormy and full of hot air. As usual.

Early this morning I spotted a schooner of tuna commuting to work across the prow with gay abandon. Three jumped in unison in line, looking like the arched back of the Loch Ness monster. At first I thought they were playful porpoises, which triggered off a memory of that ancient sailor's ditty of a weather rhyme that goes:

> When the sea-hog jumps,
> Look out for your pumps.

I think this is supposed to mean that when porpoises are spotted leaping close to the shore it's a warning to batten down the hatches and prepare your bilges (not gym shoes) for action, as stormy weather is on the cards. Not that it's a particularly applicable ditty here, mind you, because as far as I know we are about as far from land as we can be, and if by any chance we're not where we're meant to be, then hold on tight to your lewellynors because we're about to go aground. Added to the inapplicability of it all, chief officer Alexi told me they were tuna.

A bit later I was dusting myself off with arms all a-tremble following a session of the plank when Llewellyn and Eleanor appeared up on the monkey deck. I told them I had seen some porpoises which were in fact tuna.

Llewellyn said, 'Very common.'

I said, 'Well, they can't be that common. I've been scanning the seas for thirty-one days and they're the first batch I've seen.'

Then Llewellyn told Eleanor to go away as he wanted to tell me something. Eleanor looked hurt. I said, 'Can't you tell me with Eleanor here?'

Llewellyn said, 'No.'

So Eleanor went.

Then Llewellyn put his face very close to mine and in a soft tone of voice I had never heard before recited a poem full of philosophical questions, which included him saying something like: Which direction am I going and is there anything I must do? What is the price of this life I am journeying through? The poem rambled on for a good few lines. There was some concern about whether God was benevolent to man as part of this minute earth plan. There was also something about wraith and faith and what the wicked must pay and whether there was no one out there to help along the uncharted course of Llewellyn's wearisome way.

When I'd had quite enough, I moved my face back a peg or two and said, 'That's a lot of questions, Llewellyn. And I only told you I'd seen some tuna.'

Llewellyn said, 'Wait, there's more,' and asked me within his poetic refrain whether destiny might be waiting o'er some distant hill and would happiness end if he lacked the will?

I said, 'Probably not.'

Llewellyn said, ' I wrote that.'

I said, 'I think I'll go and have breakfast now.'

At breakfast I told Ian I had seen some tuna. Ian said, 'There was never a finer tuna than was played on a fiddle.'

'Ian,' I said. 'Don't you now start! I've already had it up to here with Llewellyn, and it's not even eight o'clock yet!'

I spent all morning as usual planted on the monkey deck, staring at the sea. At approximately 11.00 hours, I spotted what looked like an enemy attack of torpedoes rushing through the water towards the starboard bow. Yikes! I thought. That's where all the containers of French ammo are stored! I was just on the point of bracing myself for impact and taking evasive emergency action (by sticking my fingers in my ears) when I realised they were dolphins. There again, they could have been tuna. But I'm pretty sure they were dolphins. Tuna, as I had established earlier this morning, prefer to travel in a convoy of humps like the Loch Ness Monster. And as I've had more practice with up-close encounters with dolphins, like at Windsor Safari Park (though I can't say I saw any of these ones leaping through loops), I'd like to think I was able to distinguish my tunas from my dolphins. Supermarkets make this easy: one is supposed to be tinned, the other is supposed to be friendly. Also, these glinting torpedoes didn't seem to possess any spiky fin things like tuna, so I'm going to bet my bottom bracket they were dolphins.

At lunchtime Ham Man told us he'd had an email from Pippa (his fiancée) describing herself having a bath. Llewellyn's ears pricked up and he became very attentive. As for Eleanor, she simply listened to all this sitting as still and as unflinching as a heron watching water.

Later this afternoon Ian came and sat next to me on the monkey deck bench. He took a while to arrange himself, crossing his long furlong of neatly creased-trousered legs before sweeping his palms across his above-ear wildly sticking-out tufts of white hair. I think he was trying to tame them. In that case, he had a battle on his hands.

'I just want to let you know there's a deeper meaning to my comments,' he said, completely out of the blue.

'I'm sure there is, Ian,' I said. 'But I'd rather not go there if you don't mind!'

As he stood up to go back down to his cabin and his charts and his elaborate plottings, he said, 'I don't think the captain much likes me. He thinks I'm a snob. Which of course I am!'

Left alone on the monkey deck I stared at the sea and pondered on the very real possibility that we're all going slightly potty drifting about here in the enormity of the Pacific. Maybe the palpable sense of remoteness is exerting a strange hold on us. Scanning the horizon for so many hours, for so many days, has certainly made me feel transfixed by the emptiness. An emptiness that sends me in equal measure into elevated contentment as it does into whiffle-headed musings.

And so life drifts by as the sea slops on and we limp ever onwards.

### DAY 32

*The Pacific, 30 November, 4° 03' S, 111° 55.5' W*

Ian has just reported his latest GPS readings to me. We are now a mere 2,356 nautical miles from Tahiti and a slightly less mere 4,455 nautical miles from Auckland. Nearly there, then. What's that, Ian? Ah, I see. The 4,455 miles to Auckland doesn't include the wild goose chase diversion to the French ammo dump spot of Nouméa. Ian is not so interested in readings to Nouméa any more because he's jumping ship for his Tahitian parachute in about ten days' time. So I've been to see Mr Alex Sasha second officer Nepomnyashchikh, who says it's about another 9,500 miles to New Zealand. *Nine-and-a-half thousand miles!* Good grief! That's still nearly half a world away. I think I'll have to go and have a lie down after hearing that. Either that or go and have a plank.

Since leaving Panama, the engineering boys have been trying to mend the kaput engine, but so far without success. I suspect they might be having trouble with their rattly tappets. There again, it might be just down to a slightly knocking big-end-when-cold problem. Oh well, at least the wind has puffed up a bit. We hit 12 heady knots today. Even the Loch Ness tuna were travelling faster.

I've been thinking about sinking again, not because I harbour a particular penchant for doom-mongery, but because I've reached that bit in Peter Nichols' *Sea Change* where things turn from very bad to off-the-scale awful. Although in this case, in an awful sort of way, the awful is really very funny. Peter is now way out in the middle of the Atlantic and *Toad*'s leak has got worse and worse. In fact it is so serious that he has been on the VHF trying to call up ships to alert them to his severely leaking plight and that he may have to abandon ship. He manages to get hold of a near-passing Dutch ship and asks the officer on watch to radio (on their short-wave transmitter) the US Coastguard letting them know of his position and situation. He is totally unprepared for the Dutch ship's response: 'You need to get off now?' He is so unprepared for this question that he is silent.

'*Jacht*, you want to abandon ship now?'

'No, thanks. I'm hoping to make it to Bermuda. But my boat is leaking, and I may have to abandon ship later.'

'*Ja*, okay.'

And then the ship disappears and he's filled with regret:

Immediately, I start thinking I should have said, 'Yes, I'm sinking. I have to get off now. Please save me.'

What constitutes sinking? I wonder. Is *Toad* sinking? Even now, this is almost a new concept. It has a leak, but is it *sinking*? How bad is it? How accustomed to it have I become?

What if I don't see another ship?

When do I let go?

Peter works his pump for a long time but the floor of *Toad* is still covered in water. Suddenly a cheery voice appears on the radio, which he's left on.

'Hello, *Toad*! Little boat *Toad*!' An Indian accent. 'Hello! Hello! Hello!'

I pick up the mike. 'Yes, hello. This is *Toad*.'

'*Toad*, yes! Good morning! How are you?'

How am I? 'I am leaking, thank you. How are you?'

'Oh, yes, you are leaking!' A definite chuckle. 'That is what we are hearing! But we are fine, thank you! Very good, very good!'

The Indian accent, beloved of comics and mimics in England, is thick, and irrepressibly cheerful. It sounds like Peter Sellers, escaped from *The Party* and running amok on the high sea. If I were anywhere else – hearing this on the phone, say – I would know it was a joke.

And even here I say, 'Who is this?'

'We are the ship *Laxmi*. We are calling to see if you need help. How are you, really?'

'Where are you?'

'We are here!'

*We are here* is not a position a professional seaman would be likely to give. The sense of joke compounds, turns surreal.

'I mean what is your position, please?'

'But we are right here, *Toad*! Look! Look out the door, please!'

Still holding the mike, I step up on the galley counter and look out— A ship is *right* behind us, on top of us. I could whack a badminton birdie onto its deck. Big, black, rusty, a cargo ship of some sort. *Laxmi* written on its bow. The bridge towers overhead, and eight or ten grinning Indians are crowding the rail above my head, waving as if I were Prince Charles. I can hear them shouting: 'Hello *Toad*!' I wave back.

'You see!' says the laughing voice on the radio, 'We are here!'

'Yes, I see,' I answer back into the mike.

We all wave for a while.

'Well, do you want to come with us?'

'Where are you going?' I ask.

'We are going to Burma!'

'Burma?'

'Yes, Burma! You know, next door to India!'

\*

On my treading-water session today, second engineer Vitali belly-flopped on top of me again. He entered the tank looking very sweaty and flushed of face. He exited the tank looking much the same, because he only stays in long enough to belly-flop on top of me. He comes into the gunk tank purely to wash off the sweat. And he's producing rivers of sweat at the moment, as the temperature in the engine room is an asphyxiating 56–60° C. 'It's so hot,' he told me, rubbing a towel through his blond flop of locks, 'that we have to keep the tools in buckets of iced water or else they are too hot to touch.'

I hate to think what effect these astonishing temperatures are having on the engineers' sperm counts. Not that I want to have anything to do with their sperm counts, I hasten to add. I'm just concerned for their fertilising prospects. There's always something in newspapers or magazines these days harking on about how heat exposure is a particular hazard for male fertility. I recently read how men whose occupation involves working as either a welder, baker, firefigher, industrial laundryman or ship engineer are at particular risk. I wanted to ask Vitali if he wore loose breathable underwear and took long cool showers, but I thought if I wasn't careful things might get a bit out of hand. And that would never do.

Llewellyn collared me again the moment I was done with treading water. He presented me with a handwritten copy of the poem he had serenaded me with yesterday morning, apologising that he couldn't remember it exactly line for line. What's got into the man? Equatorial heat and endless miles of booby-less nothingness? Whatever the reason, he then told me, apropos of nothing, that in August 1979 he underwent major surgery at Manchester Royal Infirmary, during which he experienced the process of dying. He had written an account of this near-death experience and just so happened to have a copy of it about his person as he spoke, which he handed to me and suggested I read. There were reams of the stuff. Did he really expect me to wade through all this when I had more pressing matters on my plate like worrying over Vitali's perspiring sperm count?

But I did read it because I find people's NDEs (as Llewellyn refers to his near death's-door experiences) quite interesting. Maud Bridger had an NDE. Maud was a lovely old woman who used to live with Syd at the top of our lane in a small stone cottage that always smelt of roses and baking scones. Maud used to take me into the hills of fields behind our cottages to pick mushrooms when I was six. She lived just down the road from a smattering of other lovely locals who used to live at the top of our lane when I was small. People with names like Esme Strachey, Tilly Rook, Frank Holland, Edie and Daisy Boxall and Kate Pursley (a mad witch-like old woman with tangles of long wild hair who attacked people with sticks and axes and who lived in an overgrown hovel of a cottage with lots of cats and cardboard boxes until her home burnt down around her while she sat in a rocking chair in front of the fire). No one old lives at the top of our lane any more. They're all young and rich with big flashy cars and small shiny children, and planning permission.

Anyway, Maud once told me that when she was in hospital having an operation she died. Her heart stopped and the doctors thought they had lost her and she went into big colourful tunnels with lots of flowers and was enjoying herself immensely but then realised she had left some knitting unfinished on her chair so came back to finish it off. She stayed alive for years after that, knitting right up to the end when she died aged 94.

Llewellyn wasn't so keen on his dying experience. For at least ten years after the event he couldn't bear to describe what happened to him, not even to Eleanor, without breaking down in great distress. He says much of what happened to him will always remain indescribable and so bizarre that there were times when he feared for his sanity.

The boobies might have gone from the bow but we now have a swooping troop of two white-tailed tropicbirds in their place. These are beautifully peculiar birds with heavy eye make-up and bills like daggers. Even more strikingly, they look as if they have large pointy screwdrivers poking out of their bottoms. Maybe they have been sent by flying pigeon to provide the tools we need to mend the engine.

The flying fish are flying far. I don't know why they even bother swimming, as they seem to be able to shoot through the air, skimming above the water, at up to a hundred metres at a time. If I were a flying fish I'd stick to flying. The views are better and you don't get so easily eaten by screwdriven birds with spiky rears.

At lunch today Llewellyn said, 'I think I'm depressed. I can't get my computer to do what I want it to do.' So nothing new there, then.

Later, he asked me on the quiet, 'Have you read my piece yet? There's enough in there to keep you going for the rest of your life. You've got a lot to learn. You're still absorbing – but you'll know what you've been looking for when you find it.'

'Thank you, Llewellyn,' I said. 'But I know what I'm looking for. New Zealand.'

The Chiquita bananas that came on board at Panama are now completely black and squishy. But I still eat them because they are the only bananas we've got. Just thought you'd like to know that.

I swear it's getting hotter by the second. Everything is a shimmering and a soldering-iron silver-burning blue. It makes my eyes hurt and my head throb. It's too hot to be outside for long this afternoon as the air is melting my lungs. But then it's not much better in my cabin, as I stubbornly refuse to turn the air-conditioning on. At least it's darker shade. So I flop on my bunk with no clothes on reading *Enduring Love* by Ian McEwan and wonder what it must feel like to fall to the ground from a balloon (it's a riveting beginning). As well as reading I find myself staring endlessly at my map of New Zealand. I also stare at my bike strapped impotently to the chair and the table. I need to get cycling. And when I do I'm not going to stop. At least, not until my legs run out.

In the evening, when all the others were in the bar getting their free Sunday night drinks, I watched the sun plop over the edge of the world, melting a strip of sky molten red above the horizon. I do this every night, sun-plop watching. It's very hypnotic and gives my insides a rosy glow that all is well with the world. Even if it isn't. When darkness comes and if there's a moon abeam, I watch the oblique angles of moon-shining silver wakes of phosphorus marking the track of the gently undulating waves.

But on this night, and before the moon had risen, I went to talk to chief officer Alexi on duty on the bridge. It was the first time I had seen Alexi without trousers on. In their place was a pair of snazzy white shorts with a tidy razor-sharp crease.

'Nice legs,' I said.

But Alexi looked displeased. 'No,' he said. 'They are like sheep.'

'What, British sheep or Russian sheep?'

'British sheep. They are too soft and white.'

So I gave his thigh a little feel, and said, 'You're right. They are.'

Somehow we moved from sheep-like legs to piracy. Alexi told me that the pirates in the South China Sea know the exact cargo of every passing ship. I said in that case they had better keep me on board as a piratical deterrent, because I couldn't see too many pirates willing to risk their lives if they knew the *Speybank* was carrying a small shipment of cycling shorts with reinforced bottoms.

Alexi showed me a report from the International Transport Workers' Federation (ITF) which stated that twenty seafarers had been killed in the first nine months of that year, compared with ten in the whole of 2002. He also showed me a report from the International Maritime Bureau, which monitors attacks through its reporting centre in Singapore, warning of a major environmental disaster. Just a few days ago over in the Straits of Malacca two vessels were left sailing with no one on the bridge on the same night. The tanker *Jag Pranam* was left unmanned for an hour when pirates took the navigating officer below, while the 38,000 gross tonnage bulk carrier *Arabella* was without a bridge officer for twenty minutes while raiders collected valuables on board.

*

At dinner everyone was amazed how I could appear drunk on water and corn on the cobs. I told them, 'I'm not drunk, I just need to get cycling.' (I admit I'm behaving a bit oddly, but only because I'm feeling exceedingly fidgety.) It was obviously a 'get-at-me' night because then they all said how direct I am with my questions. Ham Man said he thought the English were always supposed to be reserved. I said, 'Ah, but I have got a mix of Scottish, French, Dutch and Mid-west prairie town blood in me.' Llewellyn said, 'I would far rather people were direct and honest. How many people say what they think you would like to hear, rather than what they really think?' If that's a compliment, it's the first one he's ever given me.

Llewellyn later cornered me beside the email machine to tell me that he had first met Eleanor when she was seventeen and he was thirty-one and married with four young children. He then got a bit carried away by giving me a lot of intimate details about his family.

'Llewellyn,' I said, 'why are you telling me all this?'

Before he could answer, Young Alex entered the bar to help himself to a beer and Llewellyn performed one of his amazing changes of subject by telling me how he was known in Shetland as the Dry-Stone Wall Man. Apparently he has brought back the art of dry-stone walling to the Shetlands. At that point Eleanor poked her head around the side of the door and said in an agitated tone, 'Ah, there you are!' And they both returned to their cabin.

**DAY 33**

*The Pacific, 1 December*

Same ocean, new month. Feels like something's happening even if it isn't.

Last night I started watching the Shackleton video, so I'm picking up some useful survival techniques just in case we find ourselves drifting on to an Antarctic polar face by mistake.

After that, I had a busy dream. I was watering plants round at Mum and Dad's when some sort of brick construction that Dad had built, on which to sit a plant pot, collapsed on top of me. Mum shouted out of the window, 'Look out, Jose! Behind you!' And I turned to see a massive wall of wave bearing down on me so I dived into the bottom of it and came out fine and the water crashed into the side of the house and round the back washing away the dustbins and then Mum appeared and I said, 'Lucky thing I had my swimming goggles on!' (I had put them on to water the plants.) Then I noticed the wave had caused a big crack in the side of the house so I started to plug it up with plastic bags and said that it'll be all right when Gary gets here with his mastic nozzle gun because he can fill it in with his Painter's Mate waterproofing potion. And when he did appear he mended it without a hitch. So that was a relief.

We have now resurfaced from the dead zone of the ocean where no satellites can reach us nor email machines work. Mum's written to say it's been too wet at home all week to cycle, so she's been washing the kitchen floor instead. What, all week? That's a lot of kitchen floor washing.

A sizeable epistle from Gary has spilled out of the computer, too. Says he's had a busy day building a square planned ogee profiled cupola roof with a semi-circular internal roof profile embellished with the correct dihedral diminished backing angles obtained via a plotted hip cross-section. There was also quite a lot about tea huts, as he keeps trying to dry out in the tea hut at work. For days the weather's been wet and howling, making all windows rattle and roads awash in mud and small branches. Gary says he was in the tea hut dunking biscuits into his steaming mug when he suddenly had the strong desire to clear off and spend the rest of his days wandering around the world with me. What, leave his super-tooled workshop and planted lead roll dihedral angles, not to mention Mrs Dolding's taper burn marks, for *me*? How rash.

\*

For the first time Ian is suddenly all cock-a-hoop. Bit cocksure, too. But that's because he's getting off in a week. He's booked into some swanky beachside hotel in Tahiti and says he's looking forward to good service and some decent food and wine at last. Says he'll cry if he's offered another Manchester tart before then. Funny that, because most men would give their back teeth for such a proposition.

Talking of interesting-sounding tarts, I've been reading about some of the sailors' own concoctions they used to make on board their square-riggers. One such delicacy was known on the four-masted *Ross-shire* as dandyfunk. Among the utensils required for the making of such a gourmet dish were a needle and palm (a hard shield worn on the hand by sailmakers to protect the palm) and a belaying pin. The needle and palm were used to make a canvas bag, into which was placed a heap of old biscuits. The belaying pin was used to pound the bag, smashing the biscuits to fine dust. The dust was tipped out on to a plate and water was added until the mixture formed a thick paste. After the addition of some molasses and jam, followed by a bout of vigorous mixing, the compound was carted off to the ship's cook, who put it in the oven. Basil Lubbock, the famous sailing-ship historian who joined the *Ross-shire* in San Francisco after several fruitless months of seeking gold in the Klondike at the end of the nineteenth century (much as my great grandfather, Hiram Myers, did), experienced the delights of dandyfunk at first hand. 'I thought it extremely good, and it had another excellent quality, it was exceedingly stodgy, and filled up the chinks nicely.'

Climbing up on to the monkey deck early this morning, I was pleased to see we still have our screwdriven tropicbirds in attendance. Reading about these birds last night, I was a bit disappointed to discover that it isn't actually a long-handled screwdriver they've got rammed up their bottoms but lengthy white tail-streamers measuring up to 40 cm. Crikey, that's 10 cm longer than my 30 cm school ruler. Well, whatever the length, they still look like screwdrivers to me from this distance. Either that or size twelve knitting needles.

It seems that these birds come with either yellow bills (like the ones we've got) or red bills. As with frigates and petrels, tropicbirds can roam across enormous distances searching for fish. But the odd thing about tropicbirds is that although they can fly, swim and dive a treat, they cannot stand or walk. So to move about on land the birds set their legs far back on their bodies. They then rest on their bellies and push and drag themselves along with their feet a bit like a broken wheelbarrow, which doesn't sound like a very dignified mode of transport for such a comely bird.

At lunch Ian and Ham Man had a right old rant together. They were very unhappy about the working, or more like non-working, of the ship. After finding that the air-conditioning had broken down again, Ian said, 'I'm fed up. It's just unacceptable. This whole voyage is a joke. If I wasn't getting off in Tahiti I would jump overboard.'

I just ate my Russian soup and let it all fly above my head. When there was a momentary pause in griping conversation, I said, 'Well, I'm enjoying myself! I'm treating the whole thing as an endurance test.'

They suddenly turned and looked at me as if I was skimming the fat off my Russian soup and pouring it into Ian's wine glass. Which is just what I was doing. Actually I wasn't. But I felt like doing it. Russian soup is very fatty.

'I think I might be a bit sorry when I finally get off this ship,' I said, to a scene of eyebrows in winged flight, 'as there's also something rather nice and secure about bobbing about on an ocean for weeks. There's no news or telephones or rush or pressure to do anything by any certain time and I don't have to worry about where I'm going to find food or where I'm going to camp and whether I will be alive by the morning. Apart from the fact that we could sink or blow up, I feel very safe.'

And I do. Unlike real life, there are no cars to mow me down on my bike and no road ragers to rage at me, and no men to attack me and saw my head off with a butcher's knife. Apart from all the men on board, that is. But they all seem like a nice bunch. With possibly one exception.

Sometimes I wonder if leaving this ship will feel a bit like leaving prison. Having to be integrated and rehabilitated back into society again and remembering how to do normal things like using money and finding your way in the hustle and bustle and fighting for space on the roads with the angry traffic and making conversation with someone other than the person you've seen every day for the past umpteen weeks that doesn't revolve around broken engines and infinite horizons and birds with screwdrivers up their bottoms.

I've been thinking about big waves today. Not just big waves but the giant freaks of 100 feet or more high (the equivalent of seven double-decker buses piled on top of each other) that can suddenly appear at sea with the potential to snap ships in two. And I've been thinking that I hope I don't meet any. For two thousand years sailors have reported such roguish waves but many scientists found the stories far-fetched and implausible. Recently there's been a lot of research involving Synthetic Aperture Radar (SAR) satellite surveys of the sea surface to study these monsters and they have been found to be more widespread than ever realised. Giant waves are caused by wind, weather and currents, distinguishing them from tsunamis (which originate with geological upheavals such as earthquakes), and can occur either alone or in groups. They can arise without warning, sometimes even in calm seas, and while some last several minutes, others can vanish after only a few seconds. Scientists have found that waves may combine into near-vertical walls of water, and the troughs they form can be as deep again as the height of the wave, creating a 'hole' in the water – a deadly combination of extremes that can sink ships so fast that there is no time to send distress calls.

Worldwide, two large ships sink every week on average and some of these calamities might be due to rogue waves. The causes have never been studied in the same detail as air crashes and the incidents are simply put down to storms and 'bad weather'. More than 200 vessels disappeared last year, twenty-four of them being big ships more than 100 metres long, and some believe that many of the sinkings were by rogue waves.

Among the most notorious losses was that of the British bulk carrier, MV *Derbyshire*, which disappeared off Japan in 1980, drowning forty-four crew. In February 1995 the passenger liner *Queen Elizabeth 2* encountered a wall of water 95 feet high in the North Atlantic. And within days of each other in 2001 the cruise ships *Bremen* and *Caledonian Star* in the South Atlantic met rogue waves nearly 100 feet high that smashed their bridge windows to smithereens, almost sinking the *Bremen*.

At dinner, Llewellyn was back on form. 'You don't listen and you don't learn!' he said to me like a very annoying headmaster.

Eleanor did one of those very rare things and opened her mouth. 'Yes she does!' she said standing up for me.

'Thank you, Eleanor,' I said, just as Llewellyn was telling her to shut up. 'I only don't listen to you, Llewellyn, when I think you've rambled on for too long. It makes my head go numb!'

At that point, Natasha, the sultry stewardess, came and gave me the rest of the bunch of the blackened bananas because no one else wanted them. She told me I could take them to my cabin. Llewellyn, as usual, made eyes at her. He then looked at my pile of bananas and said to me, 'And what are you planning to do with *those*, may I ask?'

'Eat them of course, Llewellyn. Why, what else did you have in mind?'

But Llewellyn didn't reply. He just rose from the table, pulled a face, and gave me a dirty old man sort of wink.

Bloody perv. Anyway, they're too soft for that.

**DAY 34**

*The Pacific, 2 December*

We are now eight hours behind home. And have been for a few days. I just forgot to tell you. Sorry.

P.S. I trod water four times in the gunk tank today. Apart from that it was too hot to do anything so energetic as think.

P.P.S. I keep catching myself bursting out with demented laughter for no apparent reason. People look at me sideways and then edge away. Maybe I'm going mad.

P.P.P.S. Everywhere: dark blue sea. Bleached blue sky.

P.P.P.P.S. Engine still broken.

P.P.P.P.P.S. Land not ahoy.

**DAY 35**

*The Pacific, 3 December*

We had news today. Not of engines or ETAs to Auckland, but of cannibals. One of Llewellyn's sons emailed him the headlines off the BBC website. There was something about Tony Blair trying to quell a tuition fees revolt as students prepared to lobby Parliament. But far more eye-catching was the bit about a German cannibal. Seems he has been accused of killing and partly eating another man who allegedly volunteered for his fate. I thought that's the sort of thing you're supposed to do if you're a shipwreck victim. Not a landlubber. But only once the stocks of turtles and fish eyes have run out.

Sometimes I find myself imagining that I've fallen overboard and am in the water watching the *Speybank* sailing away from me. Then, out of the corner of my eye, I catch sight of a shark's dorsal fin cleaving the surface on a determined course towards me. Out of all the thoughts I've had so far at sea, this is by far the most unpleasant. So I'm going to try and not think about it any more.

Although I've been on this ship now for a time-consuming thirty-five days, I still can't quite get over the vast expanse of ocean I can see from the monkey deck on a clear day. There's not a lot out there apart from water, waves and sky, but I can't stop staring at this all-encircling seascape because it's just so huge. I wouldn't have made a very good seaman in the days of the full-riggers, because after clambering up the miles of giddying rigging to shuffle aloft along the high-rise yardarm of the upper t'gallant, or even the sky-scraping fore royal, to bundle up the sail, I would probably have been more intent on admiring the view than watching my footing.

On his first trip aloft on the four-masted *Moshulu* in 1936 outward bound towards Australia, and clinging on over 150 feet above the deck, Alex Hurst was overcome with

> ... drinking in a scene the magnitude of which holds an enchantment beyond the comprehension of anybody who has not seen it for himself, for the tracery of the rigging below seems to culminate in some minute deck with which one feels no connection at all as if it were another world; the sunlit sails belly forth right beneath on all sides, and all around as far as the eye can see is the great curve of the sea's rim. The acreage encompassed from the truck [a round block of wood at the highest point of a mast] of such a tall ship is enormous, and on this morning, when the horizon was fifteen miles away, I could survey with the utmost clarity over 550 square miles of sea, with all the Baltic shipping dotted over it.

Sorry, sorry. I know I said I was going to try not to think about falling overboard any more, but I can't help it. I suppose it's just a natural reaction from splonking along in all this very drowny water. This time I'm blaming Frank Tatchell for having a bad influence on my thoughts. He was an English clergyman, the vicar of Midhurst, Sussex, in the 1920s. In his book *The Happy Traveller: A Book for Poor Men* (he was plainly something of an absentee vicar), I've just read his advice on how to avoid a watery grave:

> Should you have the bad luck, when at sea, to fall overboard, get your boots off and turn the coat pockets inside out; but do not take off your clothes, because they keep you warm. Make no attempt to swim anywhere, but just keep yourself afloat until you are picked up. If there are sharks about, keep splashing about.

To my mind, all that thrashing around in the water is a sure-fire way of getting the sharks to tear your head off and eat you up good and proper. They like a good broiling rumpus, do sharks. Frank, however, is a fountain of knowledge and goes on to provide all sorts of informative instruction such as what to do with cold feet ('Kneel on a chair or tree trunk for a few minutes . . .'); seasickness ('Try stopping both ears tightly with cotton wool.'); constipation ('Sip hot water before meals. Sea water is better still, if you can drink it without being sick.'); avoidance of colds ('Wash your nostrils with your fingers when they are soapy.'). I can find no mention in his book as to what to do with a drowned man (I need to know should I find one on my travels). This is where Charles Darwin's cousin, Sir Francis Galton, is of service. In his indispensable book *Art of Travel* he advises that:

> A half-drowned man must be put to bed in dry, heated clothes, hot stones, &c., placed against his feet, and his head must be raised moderately . . . All rough treatment is not only ridiculous but full of harm, such as the fashion – which still exists in some places – of hanging up the body by the feet, that the swallowed water may drain out of the mouth.

Another very splendid peregrine falcon dropped out of the blue today and landed on the arm of the aft crane. Who knows where this one came from (apart from the sky)? Then it swooped across to perch on the railings of the monkey deck. It watched me with a ratchet neck and eagle eyes. I watched it with a swivelly neck and human eyes.

Then I took its picture with my big-lens Canon AE1. Falcon-like birds always look like gangsters: mean and cross. Though I'm sure they have their lighter moments. Hopefully it will take out a few of our free-range Romeo Alpha Tangoes that are ratting around to no good on the lower decks.

Later on I saw two petrels fluttering along with erratic wing beats close to the water. I've now learnt that these are Wilson's storm petrels, though I haven't yet learnt who Wilson is. Maybe he's a tennis racket man with a fetish for birds. At six-and-a-half inches long, Wilson's storm petrels clock in as the world's smallest seabirds, which is good to know, as I like my superlatives. Even more pleasingly, petrels are small relatives of albatrosses. And albatrosses, as in those rather wonderful wandering ones, with a wingspan of almost twelve feet, are the largest of all flying seabirds, capable of flying 300 miles a day in search of food. But just because petrels are small relatives of albatrosses doesn't mean to say that petrels don't come big. A giant petrel, for instance, is larger than a light-mantled sooty albatross. And a light-mantled sooty albatross is larger than a lightly sooty mantelpiece. And a lightly sooty mantelpiece is smaller than a small horse and bigger than a badger. So there you have it, that's how big petrels can be. Come to think of it, maybe it's just easier to say that a big petrel is three feet long.

Ian appeared on the monkey deck for one brief moment this afternoon. He sat down on the bench beside me, and I stood up. Not because I didn't want to sit next to him: I just fancied taking his photograph. Unusually for Ian, he was no longer sporting his cufflinks as he had changed out of the customary office shirt into a short-sleeved nautically flavoured blue one. I felt that such a momentous occasion required documenting on film. And that's not all that was a step outside the ordinary – on his head he wore a baseball cap. I was in the process of reading his cap's caption (Hamilton Island – Australia) when I suddenly saw a shark's fin appear out of the top of his head like a devil's horn reincarnated. For a moment it looked a bit like he was wearing one of those joke caps you see some fat geezer wearing on holiday as he waddles along the seafront. The ones that look as if you've got an axe wedged in your head. I ran to the railings and hung over the edge. Ian, unaware of the dramatic events unravelling above his noddle, thought I was about to be seasick.

'I think I've just seen a shark,' I said. 'Either that or there's a man out there swimming underwater with an upturned flipper.'

I scoured the sea searching for Jaws with first my naked eye and then a dressed binocular.

'There it is!' I said, pointing to a point way off the port stern.

Ian looked, but couldn't see anything. By now it was difficult to tell quite what it was, but there was definitely something out there. Something big. With teeth. And probably a swimmer's severed leg in its gullet.

All this alarming activity proved too much for Ian and he soon retreated back to the safety of his plotted course and awaited parachute.

Meanwhile, I continued in the advanced pursuit of sea-staring. And it was while I was staring at the sea that I pondered upon my chances of survival should I fall overboard. They didn't look good. At least, not with shark-hats out there *that* big. So I decided to up my stakes and cogitate on my chances of survival should I fall overboard and land, very conveniently, in a life-raft. This looked more promising. Instead of minutes or hours, I could perhaps last days, if not weeks. As long as it rained and I didn't meet any rogue waves the size of a cliff face. I know from my cycling research (in case I took the wrong turning off . . . say, the B4096 to Lickey End and ended up lost in the Gobi desert) a human being can survive for forty to sixty days with water and no food, but for only a week without water. So every now and then I would need a nice fat rain cloud to empty its contents into my onboard receptacles that just so handily happened to fall overboard with me.

When I was about ten, I went through a stage of reading books about stories of survival, many of them several times over. One of these books was *117 Days Adrift* by Maurice and Maralyn Bailey, a couple from the Midlands who sold up everything they owned to build a boat. In June 1972 they set sail for New Zealand. Nine months later, after sailing across the Atlantic and passing through the Panama Canal, their yacht sank after colliding with a sperm whale some 250 miles from the Galápagos Islands. For nearly four months Maurice and Maralyn drifted in a rubber raft about 1,500 miles further out into the middle of the Pacific. If they had to spend a third of a year bobbing about in a life-raft at the mercy of the winds and currents, it was perhaps fortunate that they did so across a part of the Pacific known as the tropical convergence, where an upwelling current produces frequent rain and an astonishing variety of marine life. Although they were desperately short of water for the first couple of scorching hot weeks (surviving on a daily ration of one pint each) and had no conventional equipment for catching fish, Maralyn, having more of the practical Heath Robinson about her than Maurice, made fish hooks out of the first-aid kit's safety pins. She threaded a thin cord through the pin's spring hoop. The remaining meat of a turtle that she and Maurice had caught by hand provided the fish bait. Safety-pin fishing proved very successful. They caught hundreds of fish this way, trigger fish forming the bulk of their diet. Nothing went to waste, including the eyeballs (which they gouged out of the fish's head and sucked like Smarties for their thirst-satisfying liquid).

One of the amazing things about the Baileys' survival is that, despite living on a diet composed almost entirely of protein – fish, turtles (mostly green ones, but occasionally Ridley and loggerheads) and occasional boobies and small sharks (caught by hand!) – they showed few signs of scurvy when finally rescued after three-and-a-half months adrift by a Korean tuna-fishing boat. Captain John Duncan Walters, the surgeon from the Royal Navy of the Institute of Naval Medicine who studied their case, said this was because the relatively small amount of vitamin C in fish is concentrated mainly in the eyes, brain and pancreas, all of which the Baileys consumed with relish.

Captain Walters made another interesting observation. 'Energy requirements,' he said, 'vary widely according to circumstances as well as between individuals but, taking the adult population as a whole, the average male requires more energy input and has smaller reserves in the form of fat than the female. It follows, therefore, that the female of the species should fare better in the face of starvation and this would appear to be true since Maralyn was in much better physical condition at the end of the voyage than was Maurice.'

So in that case, if I was lucky with my rain clouds and safety pins, and could force myself to eat the eyes and brains of fish, I stood a good chance of survival.

More petrel sightings. For such a small bird, these Wilson's petrels travel ridiculously huge distances, commuting as much as 20,000 miles a year between both hemispheres in order to enjoy the most congenial seasons to their liking. I've noticed our petrels seem to have a problem with the hydraulics of their undercarriage – they fly along close to the surface of the sea with their legs dangling down instead of neatly tucked away like most birds. The best thing about them is the method they adopt for fishing on calm days: they stretch out their wings and hoppity-skip along the water in a pattering fashion on their gangly webbed feet, giving the impression that they are running across the waves. It's like a scene from the bible. St Peter would be impressed. Maybe they're Born Again birds. But amusing as it is to watch, it does seem to be quite an effective technique as they are constantly snapping up fish and snatching at other edible snippets from the sea.

## DAY 36

*The Pacific, 4 December*

Oh dear. There seems to be hormonal activity in play today. Am feeling sensitive to the nerve. A feeling not helped by Llewellyn. He came storming into the email room early this morning, the minute I had just begun an email to Gary, and glared at me. I felt an edgy little poke of irritation. But I kept it in check and said, 'Morning Llewellyn!'

He said (crossly), 'How long are you going to be?'

I said, 'I've just sat down.'

He said (very crossly), 'WILL YOU ANSWER MY QUESTION!'

I said, with hackles well risen, 'I am *bloody* answering your question!'

He gave me a brain-stabbing stare before saying a very school-teacher-like, 'WHAT did you say?'

I said in a very school pupil-like leave-out-the-essential-word, 'I said I am answering your question.'

'WHAT DID YOU SAY?'

'I said I am *bloody* answering your question!'

'That's what I thought you said. You've got a complex young lady!' And with that he went out and slammed the door.

I said chickpeas in Welsh. Chickpeas in Welsh is *ffa cyw*. Pronounced as you'd imagine.

And then my eyes pricked and I went all watery eyed. But then I thought: I've got better things to be doing than wasting a sob on bloody Llewellyn. Like treading water in the gunk tank. Which is just what I went to do. Big angry treading waters too, during which I let off a lot of Welsh chickpeas. Not that you could hear, because the one working engine is making such a flipping head-jangling racket. And then second engineer Vitali belly-flopped on top of me again. So I felt a bit better after that.

For the rest of the morning and at lunch Llewellyn played bolshie schoolboy and ignored me completely. Which suited me fine. He was still playing bolshie schoolboy this afternoon. Which was still suiting me fine. Though I thought it pretty stupid.

But then maybe it wasn't suiting me fine. At one point I walked into the lounge bit of the bar, where Ian and Ham Man were sitting having their usual moan together about the state and lateness of the ship. I'm usually quite conversational and silly with them but this time I wasn't. In fact I was so angry with Llewellyn that I could hardly talk. I just sat morosely looking at my feet, muttering the odd reply to their questions. I didn't want to be there at all, I had only come in to fill up my water bottle, and was a bit dismayed to find Ian and Ham Man lounging in the squashy upholstered seats when I had been sure they would be in their cabins – Ian directing navigational operations from the bridge of his bunk, Ham Man hamming it up on his Zero Lima One Charlie Tango ham radio.

I tried to scurry out, because I wanted to be alone, but they wouldn't let me. They had never seen me like this before and wondered what had happened. They were even quite concerned, which was rather touching. I said that it was nothing, and that I was fine, which is my usual response when I've slumped into a momentary pit of hormonal depression. But then they said, 'Is it Llewellyn?' And I said yes. And they asked what had he done. And so I told them in that sort of quivery voice that doesn't quite know whether it wants to laugh or cry. So I did both. Simultaneously. I said it was such a silly little thing which I had probably built out of all proportion. They said that it wasn't silly at all and that Llewellyn was a bastard and that they couldn't believe how much he got at me and wondered how I could have stayed conversational with him all these weeks and simply laughed off all his bullying asides.

Ian and Ham Man both dislike Llewellyn. Only about a week had gone by of the trip when Ham Man revealed to me that he thought Llewellyn was a 'fucking tosser!' He started racing down to every meal trying to bolt down his food in the first five minutes before Llewellyn arrived. Then he would leg it. But on those occasions that their eating overlapped, Ham Man more often than not would sit scoffing his grub without saying anything. 'Because, Jose,' he explained to me, 'Llewellyn is such an outrageously arrogant and irritating bore that I have to bite my tongue or else I know I could lose my cool and just shout at him to eff off!'

Ian has similar feelings towards Llewellyn. He thinks he's nothing more than a blustering and pompously conceited Welsh windbag. But being a well-bred and polite Charterhouse-schooled Englishman (even though he insists he's a Scot – 'My father was a full-blown Scot and I lived most of my working life in Scotland!' – an assertion that gives endless amusement to Ham Man), he sits and dines and drinks with Llewellyn with huge and admirable reserves of stoical tolerance. None of which means that he doesn't feel like marching round now to Llewellyn's cabin with Ham Man to biff the living daylights out of him.

They then got me a bit worried by declaring they were going to go to see the captain to explain to him what had happened and that he should go and have a stern word with Llewellyn to put him in his place. I said don't even think about doing that, explaining that I didn't want to start involving the captain in the trifling trivia of passenger domestics when he's got more pressing things on his mind like broken engines and hugely shambolic schedules to explain and rectify. I then surprised Ian and Ham Man by saying that, exasperating as I found Llewellyn, I also quite liked him. Which I do. In a funny sort of way I find him and all his long-windedly tall stories quite entertaining – stories that Ian and Ham Man both brush aside as whiffling baloney. Despite being so hugely aggravating, I'm sure Llewellyn means well. There just seems to be this thing going on between the oldest (him) and the youngest (me). He thinks that he knows all, while I think he thinks I think I know all, which I know I don't but he still thinks that I do.

\*

The trouble was, Ian and Ham Man did go to the captain. They wanted to see Llewellyn get his comeuppance. So there I was in my cabin, freshly returned from a dunking in the gunk tank, standing in an uncompromising position in the middle of the floor peeling out of my cozzie, when the captain knocked and entered (no one locks their doors – in fact most doors are mostly open most of the time during the day, with sometimes just a drawn door-curtain to contain a little privacy). The captain quickly averted his eyes from revealable bits blowing in the wind as I fumbled and desperately yanked at sodden straps while simultaneously having a rush of blood to the head. Then he said would I come to his quarters when I've got a minute. I thought, oh dear, now it's doubly more embarrassing. But once showered and dressed, off I dutifully slopped, cringing at the prospect, feeling as if I was being summoned to the headmaster's study.

As it happens, the captain's office was just like a headmaster's study – apart from the fact that it was gently rolling from side to side (yes, yes, I know headmaster's studies can still roll from side to side but that's only when you've imbibed in a little illegal naughtiness behind the bike shed) and that when you looked out of the window you didn't see a swag of guffawing pushing and shoving pupils kicking each other in the shins, but a large heap of creaking containers surrounded by miles and miles of help-get-me-out-of-here-I'm-going-slowly-CRAAAAY-ZEEEEEE Pacific.

The captain is a good solid salt-of-the-sea sort despite his bearing a slightly scary countenance. (I could imagine him getting very angry. Indeed I had seen him very angry during the can't-lower-the-lifeboats non-rescue fiasco.) He sat at his big burly desk and I sat on the opposite side feeling far from burly but surprisingly quite at home and we had a nice little preamble about his hometown of Preston and I mentioned how I had been cycling up that way recently through Lancashire's lovely wild empty moorland past such memorably named places as the Trough of Bowland and Swine Crag and Sniddle Holes and Shooting Box. And the captain's unshakably stern face cracked into a grin and I thought, oh good, I might have him on my side. But then I think I might have had him on my side before, as being caught at half-mast in one's treading-water costume can work wonders in some departments.

We then got down to the business of Llewellyn. Bloody Llewellyn, we said, bloody pain in the arse. Actually we didn't, though we said something similar, only the captain was a little more diplomatic. He gave a little laugh and said yes, he knew how Llewellyn could go on and on and how last time, when he was with Llewellyn on the *Speybank*'s round-the-world trip, Llewellyn had fallen out with most of the other passengers (about ten in all) and that in the officers' mess these fallen-out passengers had to move off Llewellyn's table as the atmosphere was so icy. And I said, 'I know. Llewellyn told me about that on the first day. I suppose I should have smelt a rat from the start and steered clear.'

The captain then went on to say something else quite diplomatic about how that was the trouble with life at sea on a ship like this – you're stuck for months with several dozen people in a cramped space with nowhere else to go if things come to blows. You can't just slam the door and walk out on the job and get in your car and drive home. You have to work and live and eat three meals a day with the crew so you have to get on with them as best you can. (I had noticed that when the captain is sitting at dinner with only Purser David and Chief Phil on either side, there is either complete silence or the conversation is usually exclusively about the ship, because after many months together the ship provides all that is left to be said.) The captain also said that Ian and Ham Man had come to him to report Llewellyn. And I said oh, and apologised for involving him in something that I didn't want him to get involved in when he had far more important things on his plate. He smiled and waved off the apology and told me not to worry about it and that he had to do things like this all the time. Which I thought was even more diplomatic of him. Surely there can't be even more problematical people in this world than Llewellyn and me? The captain then said he'd had a word with Llewellyn. I gulped and thought, oh dear, what a mess. Now Llewellyn's probably going to try and drown me in the gunk tank.

For the rest of the day Llewellyn insisted on point-blank ignoring me.

Early this evening, I was up on the monkey deck with Ian and Ham Man when I saw what looked like a body float past. We all ran to the back and I peered through my binoculars and said, 'It looks like Llewellyn!'

Ian said, 'That's a relief!'

We all found this hugely amusing. Which probably means it's high time to leave this ship. Llewellyn, as it happened, was a drowned piece of driftwood. What a shame.

## DAY 37

*The Pacific, 5 December*

Llewellyn is now talking to me again but only because, wrapped in a towel on my way down to the gunk tank, on the spur of the moment I walked into his cabin and said, 'Llewellyn?'

Llewellyn said nothing. He was sitting at his computer. But he did turn to look at me. Eleanor, who appeared to have swallowed an ironing board, was sitting unnaturally upright on the couch reading a book. She said nothing too, but her eyes watched my every move. They both looked a little bemused.

'I've just come to tell you, Llewellyn,' I said, 'that you're a bloody annoying cantankerous old bastard but as far as cantankerous old bastards go, you're quite a nice one. At least, you have your moments.'

I then pivoted at the door and walked out before, on second thoughts, walking back in. I flip-flopped over to Llewellyn and gave him a hug, trying hard to keep my towel from popping off.

And then I went to tread water.

## DAY 38

*The Pacific, 6 December*

I've been thinking (always a dangerous sign) that maybe men and women are destined always to make a small world in the midst of a big one. When I'm camping far from home in the middle of a strange land in the middle of mountains or a prairie or a desert or a dark and dripping wood, I make a little nest around me, whether it's in a tent or a bivvy bag. A homely nest made from all the essential clobber I cart around in my panniers day after day, mile after mile. And all these familiar things and routine habits I have are comforting and reassuring, even though I know I could hardly be more vulnerable if I tried. If a tornado or a hurricane or a madman with a psychopathic killing streak knocked at my flimsy nylon door, I'm only too aware there is very little I could do to prevent a nasty outcome. And the viciousness of the weather and other people (mostly lone men) sits like a constant threat on the hairs at the back of my neck. So I build a little familiar world in the middle of an uncertain one because it makes me feel better.

And here we are, on this insignificant lump of rusty metal making a small world in the enormousness of a very watery one. Life on board feels like living in a mixture between an office, a hostel, a sitcom, a restaurant, a factory, a soap opera and a football terrace all rolled into one. We all go about our daily routines and eat and read and sleep and work (just for the record, I work very hard at doing nothing – exhausting it is, too) and chat and drink and argue and laugh and video-watch and email and wash our socks. Just like on land. And yet we're not on land! How silly is that?

Instead we're bobbing about on the most ancient place on earth – a malicious primal force that plays havoc with human lives. The sea has remained unchanged, in every respect, for 3,500 million years. This swell of ocean, slapping against the hull a myriad long-dripping rust stains below my porthole, as well as all the other oceans of sea, slopped on to the scene in the depths of Precambrian time – the earliest of all aeons. That's old. Even older than my mother.

And here's a thought: there are just as many drops in the sea now as there were then. Well, almost. You can't say that about land. The sea eats land. Just the other day another slice of Yorkshire was consumed by the sea. All the time, all over the world, chunks of land are falling into the sea. Men might spend millions trying to reclaim land so that they can, metaphorically and biblically speaking, stand on water, but their money would be better spent providing another type of water – clean water – to the thousands who die every day without it. The sea, so uncertain and unique, always wins in the end.

Our little world is floating upon a sea which is like all seas the world over. It can turn on its charms and appear majestic and captivating and comely and serene and seductive and toe-dippingly gorgeous, but it takes just one simple mood swing to turn it into a lonely or dangerous or sinister or murderous monster full of vengefulness and rapacity. The sea is like a dominatrix, it holds a fatal attraction. Whatever its shifts and moods, whether it's feeling blue or bottled-up green, or has come over all commuter grey, or cloaked in hooded and cadaverous black, it is always powerful. In terms of an unremitting exertion of force, the sea is probably the most actively powerful earth-borne entity known. It is not user-friendly. It throws passions and rages. It is cruel. It deserves nothing but respect.

All seas and oceans are great, in the true sense of the word. Not, 'I had a great time last night' or 'I know this man called Llewellyn who is a great big pain in the . . .' But just simply, great. So great in fact that seventy-one per cent of the earth's surface is sea. It all but smothers the world, filling the hidden valleys and troughs and rifts and shiveringly deep dark dents pitted into the earth's crust. It tries to steal its way up freshwater rivers and creeks or is found lurking in lakes and swamps like stealthy and evil-eyed alligators, turning the water brackish and useless for thirst-wracked creatures. Stretching across the face of the planet it assembles into one colossal and complex but always interconnected body of water. It may be brimming with sodium chloride and other massive quantities of dissolved salts rendering it undrinkable for most living things, but in its own oxymoronic way, it kills us if we drink it, yet without it we would die. This sea, this wholly huge and whopping slopping sea that I see from the soaring heights of the monkey deck spreading itself in a tremendous 360° swoop over the distant curvaceous edges of the world, is king of all volumes, chief of all elements, both focal and vital to the existence of all life..

# 7

# *Land*

*Tahiti, 7 December, 17° 40′ S, 149° 22′ W, 10 hours behind home*

It's probably just as well we reached Tahiti when we did, otherwise who knows what state of advanced pottiness we could all be in. It's a tried and tested fact that proximity and prolonged exposure to the sea can render people a little dotty and unthinking. At one point in his long-winded trek across the Pacific in search of the Spice Islands, Ferdinand Magellan threw a fit of rage and flung his charts overboard. 'With the pardon of the cartographers, the Moluccas are not to be found in their appointed place!' he is said to have cried.

There must be something about the remorseless movement of the sea and its inhuman vastness that can make people turn slightly poggle-headed, if not a little cruel. These traits are not necessarily reserved for those all at sea, but can just as easily afflict people who live beside it morning, noon and night. Look at 'wreckers', the name given to those who earned – and can still earn – their living by scavenging from sunken vessels and who, particularly in the days of eighteenth-century piracy and nineteenth-century profiteering, were known to lure the ships of unsuspecting sailors on to local rocks by putting out false lights, imitating the sound of foghorns and even constructing crude 'stage sets' of harbours and cottages. Robert Louis Stevenson wrote a book of family memoirs in which he retailed a story concerning a ship about to founder in huge seas off an island hamlet in the north of Scotland. When the captain sent out a signal of distress, the villagers came rushing out of their houses, not to offer assistance, but to stand with folded arms and watch in silence the destruction of the ship and the drowning of the passengers and crew. Only then did they take to their boats to claim the cargo as their own.

Maybe it's all that howling wind and thrashing waves that can take a toll on people's sanity. Take composers and poets and writers and artists, many of whom live beside the sea. They may produce prodigious works of inspired brilliance, but have you noticed how many of them display an alarming tendency to go slightly off their rockers? And more to the point, have you ever heard any who talk much sense? Which is perhaps why they can be so likeable. Once, when I was cycling around the Hawaiian island of Kauai, I arrived hot and panting at the top of a steep hill only to be greeted by the sight of a man sitting at an easel, painting a most becoming scene of the sweeping coastline and distant crumpled cliffs. On his head he wore a brown paper bag, a pair of headphones and a snorkelling mask, minus the snorkel. I looked at him and he looked at me – through his underwater swimming mask. We conducted a perfectly normal conversation, me telling him I had found myself cycling around Hawaii more or less by accident, him telling me he was originally from Los Angles but had lived by the sea on Kauai for years. Then I asked him why he was wearing a snorkelling mask while sitting fully clothed painting a picture on top of a hill. He said that whenever he painted the sea he always wore his mask because it gave him more of a feel for what he was painting. 'Like a kind of sixth sense, I guess,' he said. I nodded knowingly while thinking: what a nutter! But he was all the better for being one.

\*

Over the past few days we have sailed past a handful of far-scattered desert islands floating on the horizon like shimmering mirages for Martini ads. Today we finally got to land on one. Tahiti may be more commercial pap than desert island, but at least it is land.

This much-awaited land was a bit hard to find at first. When I climbed up to the monkey deck at dawn this morning, I discovered that the burning blue of the past few thousands of miles had been replaced by a dish-rag sky which grew progressively more dirty the closer we slid towards Tahiti. The oppressive weight of these low scowling skies was of the sort that threatened rain in volume at any moment. How very unexotically welcoming of it.

By about nine o'clock, a dark brooding form was just visible squatting on the horizon beneath a mass of bad-tempered storm clouds. All morning, in between fierce bursts of torrential downpours, we inched towards this blackish bulk, which steadily grew in all dimensions until it no longer fitted into the tunnel of my binoculars. Instead I had to piecemeal it in magnified sections. Pale specks and smudges turned into houses clinging like limpets to the precipitous jungle-clad mountainsides. Ships and small boats ghosted out of the haze and became solid. Planes dropped out of the filthy sky to crash into the side of Papeete, the main port and capital of French Polynesia.

By 14.00 we had docked at Motu Uta, the small wellington boot-shaped bridge-connected island that sits in the port of Papeete. The Tahitian stevedores, some of them as magnificently round and fleshy as sumo wrestlers, wore winning grins and jazzy yellow uniforms. They appeared impressively efficient despite the overwhelming heat of the place, jumping on to fork-lifts and buzzing around like bees as the cranes swung into cargo-grabbing action. All of us passengers were itching to get off but we weren't allowed to do so until the customs men had checked that we were who we were. So while we waited to get our identities identified, I hung upside-down at the waist over the railings on the monkey deck double-checking I was who I am because sometimes, especially after so many weeks at sea, who you think you are is not what you actually see. And this time was no exception. Instead of finding myself in what I thought was me, I found Ham Man, albeit in inverted form through my legs. But that's only because he had come up to the monkey deck to see what was going on. Or more to the point, what was coming off. Containers. That's what. Loads and loads of containers to be exchanged for even more loads of containers, which were all piled brutishly high on the dockside awaiting their transit aboard the high seas and long trains and tall trucks of this world.

A small faction of the French army pulled up alongside the ship. It seemed they were after our ammo. For the first time in weeks, Mickael and Xavier stirred into life, looking uncharacteristically animated for a change. They were granted permission to leave the ship. As they trotted down the gangplank to meet their khaki-clad comrades, Ham Man and I tried to put them off their mission by shouting down. 'Xavier! Mickael! *Bonjour les Messieurs-dames! Attention la grande bang!*' A comment that I don't find remotely funny now though we did at the time, including even Xavier and Mickael, which is perhaps another fine example of how too much bobbing about in boats can play havoc with the mind.

A small white battered van drew up and out spilled a few Tahitian stevedore shift workers. They all looked skywards where Ham Man and I were standing on top of the *Speybank*. They smiled and waved, and so we smiled and waved back. Then a woman climbed out holding a small bare-bottomed baby in her arms. The woman was immense, with an abundance of cascading flesh that rippled beneath her flimsy dress. When she jiggled her baby up and down to make him laugh, her breasts were entities unto themselves. And when she walked back and forth alongside the van, her supremely generous thighs looked as if they were in charge of the entire operation of her body. She too peered up towards us and I quickly dropped my peeping-tom binoculars. She waved and I waved. And I called, 'Halloooo!' And she called, 'Alloorr!' And then she picked up her little boy's hand and waggled it too in a wave.

The next vehicle to grind to a halt beside the gangway contained two German engineers. One was built like a Panzer tank, the other a weasel. They both looked jet-lagged, surly and fifty-ish. They had been emergency air-freighted out to Tahiti at the urgent request of Andrew Weir Shipping to mend the *Speybank*'s wonked engine. The two men were escorting several weighty crates and trunks of what Ham Man and I presumed (and prayed) were spare engine parts and specialised tools. Either that or they travelled around with luggage containing sensationally heavy underpants requiring carefully crated supervision and industrial lifting devices. Unfortunately, there was no sign of any brand new easy-to-release-in-all-weather lifeboats. I was a bit disappointed as that would have been a very reassuring sight indeed to see turning up next on the dockside. Instead what we saw were two sauerkraut Germans lugubriously hauling themselves up the steps of the gangway while the Russians winched their crates of important equipment up high on to the ship by the aft deck crane, nearly losing the whole shebang into the water when an ill-fitted fixing rope slipped sideways mid-winch.

By 15.00 we were at last free to step from ship to land. Llewellyn and Eleanor were whisked away by chauffeur-driven car – friends of theirs. Ian and Ham Man teamed up together to traipse the three kilometres into town. Their first port of call was to be Europcar, as they fancied hiring a motor to drive around the island. Ham Man was desperate to get behind the wheel again. 'I miss driving more than anything,' he'd told me as my face turned blank and incomprehensible. As for me, I shouldered my bike down the slippery and quivery gangway and landed at last on a world that wasn't moving – never mind that the bodily one felt fit to capsize. 'Quick! Find me some land legs,' I thought. But the moment I flipped my feet off the ground and on to my pedals, the strange swaying sensation stopped. So maybe the balancing action of cycling is the perfect antidote to wobbly sea-leg syndrome.

To the cries and jestings and light-hearted abuse from a trouble-making gaggle of the Russian crew (notably Mr Alex Sasha second officer Nepomnyashchikh – I'll give him a good planking later) who were supposed to be supervising the unloading of the cargo instead of hanging over the ship's railing watching me mount up, I sped off on my wheels.

It wasn't an easy ride. First I had to play Russian roulette by suicidally weaving around the forklifts and straddle-carriers that were tearing up and down the waterfront with big cyclist-crushing containers dangling from their arms. Then I had to slalom round the barriers of Port Control (the Port Control sentry-box man looking more than a little puzzled as I did so) before fending off two vicious mud-coloured dogs that came rushing at me from a heap of rubbish they had been sniffing and clawing through. Once over the busy truck-laden bridge (quick aerial view of French naval ships, schooners, fishing vessels, small freighters and murky litter-swashing water) that straddles the Chenal de Taunoa, I was out of the port proper and into the snarled-up traffic of the town. I had about three hours of daylight left and, leaning into a roundabout shadowed with dented signposts, about ten seconds to make a plan of action.

The plan wasn't difficult to make. Tahiti is a big round mountainous lump of an island (Tahiti Nui) attached by an isthmus at Taravao to a smaller offshoot of an afterthought (Tahiti Iti), making it altogether look rather like a turtle swimming with head outstretched. Tahiti Nui is crowned by two ancient volcanic cones, the highest, Mount Orehena, peaking at 7,352 feet, and is covered in a dense thicket of tropically tangled vegetation and deeply dissected by valleys. The island has only one road that gets anywhere in a roundabout way. It starts in Papeete and ends in Papeete. If I follow this road northeast out towards Pointe Vénus, it's called an imaginative Route 1. If I follow it southwest out past the airport it's called a mouthful. Or, to give it its more official title, RD0-RT5. Somewhere out near Punaauia (a vowel-filled meal in itself) RD0-RT5 decides it's had enough of its double-barrelled haughtiness and takes itself down a peg or two to a more worker-friendly Route 2. Altogether this one island-encircling road of multiple R's, D's, T's, 0's, 1's and 2's and 5's is about 120 km long.

Eighty miles in three hours on two unconditioned cycling legs seemed like a lot to ask of a body that for the past six weeks had felt more at home slumped on a deck or throwing wobblies at Llewellyn. But what sort of excuse is that? So, as I've always been attracted towards the more masochistic side of exercise (my motto: what's the point in cycling round a mountain when you can kill yourself riding over it?), I gripped my bars and hit the road and pedalled like a person deprived of their pedals for far too long by . . . well, cycling round the mountain instead of over it. My excuse? A mental aberration of uncharacteristic sanity. My salt-addled brain had asked me where was the sense in cycling up and over a mountainous volcano when there was no up-and-over road? To which my sea-sozzled mind said, 'Search me!'

So round the mountain I went. The rain fell, the puddles splashed, the tyres swished, the dogs chased, the cars crashed, the girls waved and the boys called, '*Je t'aime!*' So did the men. Most of these men seemed to be lying semi-prostrate in the back of passing pick-ups. And most appeared to be drunk. As did the drivers. They swooshed past my elbow, swerving all over the shop. A man who looked like the King of Tonga had a squinched red flower lolling above his ear. He was shirtless and sprawled in the tray of a pick-up with another king-sized man. As they chugged past in a thick cloud of black fumes, Mr Tonga drunkenly slurred the ubiquitous words of love and tossed me his flower. But it fell short and landed in a slop of dirty puddle.

Fierce rays of sun shot down obliquely in between torrential bursts of rain – rain that did little to dispel the sweltering tropical heat. Sweat stung my eyes and poured down my back. My panting gulps of breath were nearly suffocated by the air itself. Coral reef-fringed Tahiti was the original South Seas paradise, yet I saw nothing of paradise on this ride. The traffic was mad and chaotic. The roads were fume-filled and booby-trapped with enormous potholes and straggling road-construction. Streams and small riverbeds dribbled with drab-looking water but were mostly choked with the miasma of stinking rubbish. Black volcanic beaches, ranked with bonce-conking coconut palms, swirled with litter, precariously pock-marked with glass. Roadside shops and houses appeared run-down and shanty. Everywhere, corrugated iron, a lot of it topping angular cliffs of cinder blocks. Other corrugated dwellings lay neck-deep in vegetation. As for the dogs, they were either trying to tear off a fangled mouthful of my fast-spinning shin or lying sprawled and decomposing in gutters.

But no matter how far from paradise this part of Tahiti may have fallen, it felt head-poppingly good to be cycling again, to be free from the constraints of the ship, to see faces and colours so exotic and extreme from the past few weeks. I rode on and on, just revelling in the sense of self-propulsion, the whirring of wheels, the hammering heart and the throb of muscles in shock. From the saddle I saw gutted cars and glimpsed snippets of life: men drinking, men smoking, boys fishing, boys surfing, boys sitting in beach-perched 4×4s with their explosive boom-box music threatening to blow out the sides. I saw women chasing after girls, girls chasing after chickens, chickens chasing after air. And not every dog was out to rip off a chunk of my leg. One was more interested in a cat, but unlike my panicky pedal-blurring defence mechanisms, the cat faced up to the dog and became a hissing arch of porcupine.

By the time I arrived back at the ship I had my rear LED flashing and a Petzel torch strapped to my head. Although I had failed to make it right round the island, my computer had clocked up 48.67 miles and I collapsed on my bunk as a sweaty and tender-of-rear wreck.

**DAY 40**

*Tahiti, 8 December*

Early this morning I was awoken by a CMA CGM container ship sliding into the berth behind us. It was big and French and immaculately painted in blue and white. It was called *Matisse* and made the battered *Speybank* look like a down-and-out drifter. We were supposed to be sailing today, but because of more delay the captain told us we probably wouldn't be off until tonight. I was pleased about this because it gave me more time to ruin bits of my bicycling body. Halfway across the Pacific I had asked Purser David if I could jump ship in Tahiti and then be picked up by the *Speybank*'s sister ship, the *Arunbank*, five weeks later. He said I could if there was room. There wasn't room. So instead I'll have to 'do' Tahiti in two days flat.

As Ian and Ham Man motored off in their nippy little green Europcar, I cycled off to the Quaie des Ferries to catch the boat to the 'Island of the Yellow Lizard', otherwise known as Moorea. Together with Tahiti, Moorea makes up the Windward Islands. When I first arrived in Tahiti I was a bit confused with all these groups of islands (too much sea-staring slows the brain down, you know). But then by concentrating hard (not easy) I learnt that the Windward Islands are all part of the Society Islands, which are all part of French Polynesia. French Polynesia itself consists of some 130 islands which form five groups of archipelagos – the Marquesas, the Society Islands, the Tuamotus, the Tubais (Austral) Islands and the Gambier Islands. The Leeward Islands are all part of the Society Islands too and plop out of the sea 200 kilometres to the northwest. These islands include Huahine, Maupiti, Raiatea and the blue-lagoon famous atoll of Bora Bora, where only the jet-setting super-rich set can afford to stay, thanks to the exclusive resorts that are constantly encroaching upon the beauty of the place. I would like to go to Bora Bora to put up my tent in the overly pedicured grounds of one of these exclusive resorts, preferably one with an immaculate water-wasting sprinkler-system-fed lawn sweeping down to the lapping shores of the dazzling lagoon. And then I would wash my socks in the sumptuous marbled basins of the Ladies. There's something quite nice about cocking a snook at these toffee-nosed places. I did this sort of thing when cycling around Hawaii. And I don't think I've grown out of it since.

I could have flown to Moorea on a marathon flight that takes seven minutes. But as you can't cycle on to a plane like you can cycle on to a boat, and as planes don't offer a good feel of the sea (unless they crash into it), I travelled the 25 km to Moorea across the Sea of the Moon by the *Aremiti 4* ferry. The ferry was modern and fast and bounced across a huge swell of ocean that squeezes itself between the two islands. The boat was empty save for a smattering of locals (who all sat inside watching telly) and a handful of tourists (who all stood on deck to do some touristy prow-standing and scenery-appreciating – very nice it was, too).

Among us tourists, I couldn't believe my eyes, were Llewellyn and Eleanor. Of all the rotten luck! I thought about jumping overboard, but that didn't seem like a very sensible idea, especially when I wanted to prow-stand and scenery-appreciate rather than drown. So instead I went up to Llewellyn and said, 'Haven't I seen you somewhere before?' I thought he might swot me one, but instead he laughed. In fact he was really very nice, totally different from on the *Speybank*. Maybe the *Speybank* is just very good at doing everyone's heads in. Or maybe I'm just very good at turning people potty in confined spaces.

As we neared the serrated silhouette of Moorea, the *Aremiti 4* was piloted into the blue spangly waters of the Baie de Vaiare by a leaping heap of dolphins, their sleek shining bodies dazzling with diamond spray. As soon as I cycled down the ramp of the ferry and on to the jetty in Vaiare (a veritable metropolis consisting of a dusty shop, petrol station and Europcar pick-up point), I knew I had made the right move by leaving the hectic traffic and scurrying streets of Papeete behind. Once the handful of ferry passengers had dispersed (Llewellyn and Eleanor were whisked away in a little blue car with their French-speaking friends, Roger and his wife Mighty – at least that's what her name sounded like, though it could have been Maité), a state of languor pervaded the place. Dogs flopped in the shade at the side of the road too tired and hot to chase me. An old hollow-cheeked man with a bird-boned chest lay gently swinging in a hammock strung between two sun-blocking jungle trees in which a strange bird performed several standard-issue tropical whoops. The bird then decided it was too hot for that kind of caper and shut up. All the time the old man watched me idly while chewing on a mouthful of air, as old men are known to do.

No wonder no one had energy. The climate felt thick and gluey. When I dragged myself across the empty road to a roadside stall sagging under the weight of tropical fruit, it was a tight squeeze to inhale, exhale and speak all at the same time. A young girl in a flowery dress sat in the dust behind the stall playing with a poochy-faced baby doll. Over in the corner sat an old woman with a withered-apple face and potato-sack body. The girl's mother got up to serve me. She had waterfalls of black curls and a pretty smile and refused to accept any money for the mountain of fruit I had amassed.

I followed Moorea's only road, a coastal-clinging and cycling extravaganza that encircles the island for 60 km. There are no towns on Moorea (hoorah!), only the occasional straggling village overshadowed by trees with leaves the size of boats and flowers the size of trombones. The land round here is so flourishingly prolific that the plants grow almost visibly. Behind this overgrown and verdant thicket, the island is on a constant rise, rearing up through dense jungle to rainforest and finally the soaring and sharp pinnacle of Mount Tohiea, shot through with its mythical giant spear hole. Sometimes the occasional car or rattling pick-up trundled past in slow motion. But mostly they didn't. This was my kind of place. The most lively things I could see were birds that looked like Batman with tight black eye masks, and the crabs, scuttling across the road in front of my wheels. The dragon-flies were pretty lively too. They were Bora Bora blue with bodies as long as my bike pump.

Climbing up over a steep hill I had a good snooping view over a resort with thatched pointy-roofed bungalows on stilts, up to their knees in the invitingly come-hither crystal-clear turquoise lagoon. Through my binoculars I homed in on the sort of happy nuclear families with perfect bronzed bodies and chalky-white smiles that

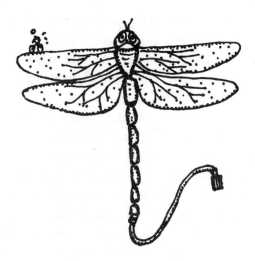

you see adorning the cover of travel brochures. There were also a few doey-eyed couples strolling hand-in-hand along the sun-kissed shore. Maybe they were auditioning for a Thomas Cook advertisement board. Beyond the resort roared the reefs with their large ruffs of breaking water.

I dived back down the hill, bowling along through shady tunnels of mango trees and enormous shrubs – lantanas and pandanus with twisted branched stems, stilt roots and spiral tufts of long, narrow spiny leaves and strange fibrous fruit. There was brightly coloured hibiscus everywhere, too. Just like in Hawaii. I kept hitting wafts of heady pockets that smelt like cycling through a Lush shop.

The most dramatic scenery came when cycling around the fiord-like inlets of Baie de Cook and Baie d'Opunohu. (Incidentally, as well as confusingly, when Captain Cook sailed this way he moored his *Resolution* in Baie d'Opunohu, which comes with a deeper anchorage than the bay named after Cook.) These two parallel bays are part of a sea-flooded caldera, the remains of the crater of a massive volcano which blew to smithereens millions of years ago. Tall, jagged buttresses of mountains stand like sentries, overshadowing the whole area, making you feel about as significant as a pomegranate pip.

Coconut trees and other rattling-leafed palm-like plants leaned into the hot and strong-blowing trade winds – winds that sent the brightly patterned *pareo* (colourful fabrics that make the traditional sarong-like clothing), pegged to lines outside the occasional village boutique, flapping and snapping like carnival bunting.

I stopped at another fruit stall to buy a stack of dwarf bananas from a woman so ancient she looked eroded by a century of sun and wind. A little snippet of a boy played with a circle of shells at her feet. Before I took off up the road, the woman dropped two free-of-charge mangos and a grapefruit the size of a beachball into my pannier. Then she gave me a gap-toothed grin and patted my left thigh with a hand as light and fragile as the skeleton of a bird. Of the 15,000 people who live on Moorea the majority are Polynesian or 'demis' (mixed race), with a hefty current of French culture and savoir-faire never too far away (the Polynesians settled Tahiti in the fourteenth century, but it's been French since 1842). Maybe my mango woman, who looked at least 120, was alive when, at the end of the nineteenth century, Gauguin sailed over this South Sea way to live and paint. Though I hope she kept well out of his way. Having come to despise the materialism of a middle-class Europe, Gauguin had abandoned his wife and children and left France for Tahiti, seeking the inspiration of a 'primitive' society. He had come, he wrote, to paint 'these nymphs. I want to perpetuate them, with their golden skins, their searching animal odour, their tropical savours.' Using bold but simple colour, he wanted to paint scenes of 'natural' men and women living with their fears, faiths, myths and primitive passions, whose traditions he had keenly anticipated to include cannibalism, though he was disappointed to find no one able to remember their ancient customs, least of all this particular one. He was also deeply disappointed to find Paradise despoiled and violated by the progressive influence and rapacious greed of the white man. Even his dream of living in a back-to-nature state went to pot when a policeman fined him for swimming starkers. Instead of finding the primitive savage of his hopes, Gauguin, a sort of end-of-century flower child, discovered more a barbarian in himself, greedy for sensation and ruthless in satisfying his appetite for young girls, turning him into a syphilitic disaster zone. Gauguin's paintings may be brilliantly vivid, but when Van Gogh had a look at them he told Gauguin, 'You've fornicated with the devil, my friend.'

More spools of dolphins somersaulted alongside the *Aremiti 4* as the ferry jounced with the waves, leaving the tall shadowy hulk of Moorea in our wake. Out of all the ferry times I could have chosen to return to Tahiti (well, only three, actually) I found I was on the same boat at the same time as Llewellyn. Again. But things must be improving in our relationship because this time when I saw him I didn't feel like jumping overboard. There again, that could have something to do with the fact that I didn't want to lose my bike, tethered to some pipes on the car deck. Llewellyn sauntered up to me topped in his comical Paddington Bear-type blue sunhat with the rim turned up.

'Have you come back with any souvenirs of Moorea?' he asked.

'Yes,' I said. 'About fifty mangos, seventy-five bananas and a sore arse.' (Forty days and forty nights out of the saddle and I soon know all about it.)

My souvenirs, though, weren't quite in the same spending league as Llewellyn's. He had just bought Eleanor a Moorean pearl necklace costing a shocking £1,700. Or, as I told Llewellyn, about the amount of money I had put aside for New Zealand.

Papeete was just as jostling and noisy and fast as when I'd left it, making me wish I could live for a month with the batbirds and cruisy crabs on slow-moving Moorea. I perched for a while on a wall beside the harbour, gazing out at the near-distant *Speybank* moored on the opposite side. What a magnificent heap! It sat on the water, listing very slightly to starboard as the cargo was worked, splunking out smoke and beggaring belief how it could cross the harbour, let alone half the world. I was just in the middle of counting up the superstructure decks to pinpoint my two cabin portholes when a large smiling woman in a big floaty flower dress swayed past, saying something in French about bicycles and strong legs. Moments later two men meandered alongside. They were both good-looking, black-haired and dark-skinned. Locals. They talked in French, asking me if this bike was mine. I answered in bad French, telling them that it was. They asked me where I had been, so I told them Moorea. For the next little while we talked about Moorea and bikes and strange birds with blindfolds. Then they wished me *bon voyage* and hurried off to catch their ferry.

I continued sitting and thinking. I thought about some notes I'd found in my cabin written by a group of previous passengers who had travelled round the world on the *Speybank*. The notes filled a few sheets of A4 and were their impressions and tips and recommendations of what to see or what not to do in some of the ports en route. This is what George Beard from Barnsley, South Yorkshire, Dave and Carol Foley from San Diego, California, and Walter and Nancy Turner from New Rochelle, New York, jointly had to say about Papeete in September '95: 'Were I to return, I would prominently display the US/Brit flag on my lapel, as it seemed we were immediately accepted by the natives when they found out we were not French.'

What peculiar advice! Advice that is only good for ignoring. No one had yet asked me where I was from, but everyone had seemed very friendly whether they thought I was French or not. But then a bicycle does tend to be a passport to opening people's hearts.

Finally I jumped off my perch and cycled along the harbour front, past the bandstand festooned with incongruous Christmas decorations and a stuffed fat Santa. Tinsel and palm trees. How odd. Further on I stopped to watch a 'native' busker twanging away at *Jingle Bells* on his jangly banjo. He sat on the wall, a big shockheaded person haloed in hair, shrouded in the dying sunlight.

## DAY 41

*Tahiti, 9 December*

We were supposed to be off last night, but instead we are meaning to be off today, unless of course tomorrow becomes today and yesterday becomes the day after.

When it came to Ian, things were a little more certain: after breakfast he was off on his Tahitian parachute for good. I saw no love lost between him and Llewellyn, but I cornered Ian on the stairs and gave his lengthy fathom-and-a-half of frame a hug. Once recovered from this overly close encounter, he handed me a spy thriller called *A Spy by Nature*, written by his son Charles. Inside, he had put: 'Josie, with many thanks for good company and making a strange voyage more enjoyable both by conversation and writing! Love from Ian.' On the page opposite he'd penned a little ditty:

> Some ships sail East: Some ships sail West
> On the selfsame winds that blow
> But 'tis the set of the sails
> And not the gales
> That determines the way they go!

Then, smoothing down his habitually fly-away mad professor hair-wings, which insist on living a life of their own, he climbed into Ham Man's hired car to be chauffeured to his $200-a-night hotel. And that was the last I saw of him – Ian Cumming going.

I spent the morning squeezing in another fifty-miler ride getting my rear-end thoroughly pummelled to pieces, thanks to the road at times being crippled with roughly surfaced roadworks and potholes the size of gunk tanks. On the route out towards the airport, there was a rather nasty traffic-laden overpass to negotiate. The captain told me that when he dined out with the shipping agent man last night (in a restaurant where the bill came to $200 for two – Tahiti is far from cheap, unless you live on pineapples, bananas and coconuts), the agent revealed that this overpass, which is all of 100 metres long, cost US$33 million, when it should have cost US$10 million. All paid for by some foreign grant. He said that a lot of money round here tends to be siphoned from the funds of various grandiose projects only to end up in governmental pockets. Much like at home, then.

I arrived back at our time-ravaged boat base-camp at lunchtime. The latest on the engine-mending process was that it had yet to be mended. The latest on our leaving was said to be later. Probably sometime in the afternoon, I was told. Whether it was the afternoon of this year or next was anybody's guess. More definitely, the spick-and-span CMA CGM ship, which arrived long after us, has already left. For New Zealand. I should have snaffled myself on board. I could be in Auckland by tomorrow. But then, had I flown, I could have been in Auckland forty days ago. Oh well, why spend time getting somewhere efficiently fast when you can get there excruciatingly slowly, with the added delights of possibly sinking on the way?

The captain gave me another three hours to go roaming off alone, so I trotted into town to have a look around. A monstrous cruise ship, the *Tahitian Princess* (registered in Gibraltar), had arrived in the last few hours and tied up in the upmarket dock along the harbour front. Suddenly Papeete was overrun with noisy voiced Aussies and Americans all shouting to each other when talking would have been quite sufficient. The majority looked overblown, overweight and overdressed as they waddled among the tourist-trap boutiques in their neatly pressed and squeaky-clean cruise gear (lots of whites, lots of gold, lots of golfing checks) flashing a small armament of jewellery and credit cards. The women clutched expensive-looking handbags. So did some of the men.

I thought I would test security measures to see if I could smuggle myself on board their costly high-rise to have a snoop around and maybe even to wave to Mr Alex Sasha second officer Nepomnyashchikh from the opulent prow. So I trailed an American woman with a turkey-wattle neck as she toddled back towards her palatial *Princess*. From behind, this woman was a large white triangle, her silvery hair tacked down with bobby pins. As for her hips, well, they were solid and generous, the distance between them wide enough to park a car. But the effort of walking even the short distance back across the boulevard and quay at a pace that even a snail would consider slow appeared too much for her and she collapsed on to a bench to regain her breath. Or die. It was a bit hard to tell quite which. Not wanting a death on my hands (after all, with a boat to catch I was a little pressed for time), I searched around for another cruising victim to trail and soon fell into step behind a slatternly, shapeless woman smoking a cigarette and awash in jewellery.

My chances of getting myself stowed away for an hour or two on board her sumptuous abode the conventional way didn't look promising. A long stripy marquee had been erected on the quayside through which all cruise people were required to pass when either departing or boarding their unship-like ship. This was evidently the security booth, manned by a security-looking man with an insecure haircut (it was threatening to take off in the wind any minute). Beside him stood a leggy whip-thin airhostess-type girl in airhostess-type uniform, her long blonde hair swinging in sheets. Her role was to smile. She smiled ingratiatingly at people coming. She smiled ingratiatingly at people going. But she didn't smile at me. Surely I don't look that uncruise-like a person? I know I might have an abundance of oil stains ingrained upon my person – it's a bit hard not to after spending forty days lolling about on a (un)working ship – but at least I don't have 'PROPERTY OF RUSSIAN RUST-BUCKET' stamped across my forehead.

In short, and in shorts, I was barred from entering the sumptuous stateliness of the *Princess*. The security man as good as picked me up by the scruff of my neck and threw me off the premises. Well, thanks, you snooty lot of toss pots! All I wanted was a quick snoop, and maybe to nick a bog roll or two. Surely not a lot to ask?

I momentarily toyed with the idea of scuttling up the spring lines pirate-style by the cover of darkness, but then I remembered that when darkness came I might well be on the high seas to Nouméa. Or, more like, high seas to Nowhere.

Arriving in Tahiti on board a scruffy urchin ship has its benefits. Wandering around the *Marché Public* (Papeete's magnificent covered market place, a constant ant colony of confusion) I paused at a stall to buy a pineapple. The stall owner was a woman of fantastic size, her substantial thighs undulating under her diaphanous capaciously flowery dress. In *American Caesar*, the author William Manchester found 'the proportions of [Polynesian] women were closer to those of duffel bags'. In Polynesia, big isn't shameful, it's not something to hide and beat down. Which is really very refreshing. The pineapple woman asked me if I was off the cruise ship. I replied that no, I was off the broken-down Russian freighter – the one that looks like scrap metal. The woman threw back her head and roared with a great heaving spasm of laughter that flowed through her body like a tidal wave. I looked at her a little nonplussed. Maybe she thought I was joking. But maybe because I made her laugh, or maybe because she was just generous in spirit as well as body, she filled up a bag of fruit for me and accepted no payment. Outside, a sudden tropical rainstorm poured in crowds from the streets to take shelter in the market. I tried to say, '*Merci beaucoup, madame,*' but my words were washed away by the rushing whirligig of wall-to-wall noise.

**DAY 42**

*The Pacific, 10 December*

Well, here we are again, bobbing about in the middle of the Pacific just like old times. With the same old broken engine, too. I've got one of those déjà vu feelings that I've been here before. And I've got one of those advanced déjà vu feelings that I am going to be here again. In fact I've got a déjà vu feeling that I'm going to be living in a déjà vu moment until my feet touch down on Kiwi soils. Don't ask me why, I can just feel it in my waters.

It may come as no surprise to you that our supposedly top-pro German mechanics (Josef and Hardmut) have not yet revealed anything particularly top-pro about themselves.

Although they were supposed to have pulled out all stops and got us up and running in two Tahitian days flat, before flying home to Deutschland, here they are on board with us for the lop-engined ride to Nouméa. I think the engine room should be renamed Last Chance Saloon. They are down there now, in all that thirst-making heat, fiddling and tinkering. I'm not exactly sure what the problem is – something to do maybe with no one being able to find the right spanner for the right job? I've tried offering them my services by rummaging around in the lesser known nooks and crannies of my tool kit, but unfortunately neither my multi-nozzled spoke nipple key nor handy bottom bracket extractor gadget is quite what they had in mind.

It seems strange not having Ian around. I rather miss his hovering around the ship, GPS in hand, muttering discontentedly to himself that we are seventeen degrees off course. At meals, Ian always sat directly opposite me, but now there is an empty place between Llewellyn and Xavier. No one has filled this place because no one wants to sit directly next to Llewellyn.

Talking of Llewellyn, he is feeling very depressed with the never-ending lateness of this ship. He has gone from saying at the beginning of this voyage that he and Eleanor were considering doing another round-the-world trip on the *Speybank* (I told you he's off his trolley) to announcing today that, owing to the limited time he has left in his life, he doesn't want to be wasting it this way. He must also be having a bit of a brainstorm, because he said at lunch, 'I didn't agree with Ian on most things, but I do agree now that we ought to be told more about what is going on. We may be cargo, but we are fare-paying ones.'

Ham Man, who is feeling equally as dispirited, said, 'I don't agree with you on most things, Llewellyn, but I do agree with you about that! We're like mushrooms – kept in the dark about everything.'

I'm enjoying this lateness. Means that along with having more time to stare at the sea (always a revelation), we also have a month or more of food and accommodation provided to us all for free. You don't get that sort of bargain if you travel by air. There again, if you travel by air, you tend to get to where you're going within the blink of an eye and without the emergency call-out needs of Josefs and Hardmuts. But where's the fun in that?

The other advantage of all this dallying is that we might get to miss Christmas altogether. Since Santa stopped bringing me 5 mm allen keys and multi-adjustable socket sets in my stocking (I felt at home dissecting my bike from an early age), I've never been a great fan of Christmas. A perfect Christmas to me is to spend it as far away from anything Christmassy as possible, ideally with my bike and tent on top of a mountain (don't ask me to your party if you're looking for a livewire). So the fact that the only sign of the fast-approaching festive season on board this rub-a-dub-dub is a Simpson's chocolate advent calendar, which has suddenly appeared beside the chart table on the bridge, is right up my non-festive street. For all I know it could be June. And a good thing, too.

I was talking to Mr Alex Sasha second officer Nepomnyashchikh today and he told me that in Vladivostok they celebrate Christmas on 7 January. I said that was a bit late in the day, and he said something a bit complicated about Russian time differences and people in Vladivostok not wanting to do what everyone does in Moscow. I said, if anything, I would have thought Vladivostokians would celebrate Christmas before Muscovites, as Vladivostok was at least seven hours ahead of Moscow. But Mr Alex Sasha second officer Nepomnyashchikh said something even more complicated about how they do celebrate Christmas earlier, but that Vladivostokians just celebrate for a lot longer (such as weeks instead of days), all of which culminates on 7 January in one huge drunken orgy.

We then got on to the subject of Christmas trees. Whenever Mr Alex Sasha second officer Nepomnyashchikh talks about Christmas trees he calls them merry Christmas trees. (He also has trouble mentioning the word Christmas without prefixing it with 'merry'.) I decided not to spoil things by telling him that they are actually called plain old Christmas trees, because I like the idea of him going into a farm shop in, say, Piddletrenthide, and asking for a five-foot Merry Christmas tree with roots and all the trimmings.

Every now and then I shut my eyes and try to picture the mad rushing Christmas flurry going on at home – the Christmas decorations, the lights, the shops, the crowds, the crackers, the parties, the hats, the holly, the ivy, the money, the drink, the stress, the strain, the suicides. But the picture keeps slipping from focus, leaving only the heat and the light.

**DAY 43**

*The Pacific, 11 December*

At dawn this morning the blue-black sea was mirror-smooth with just the odd little cat's-paw ripple for good measure. By breakfast it had developed a flaccid and sleepy swell with wide glossy rolls. By late morning it bore crimped ruffles with the odd sparkle-ridged flip-over wavelet. By teatime the wind was throwing itself at us from the southwest to form big messy tussled waves. Everything looked confused and lumpy. Tonight the wind is blowing a breezy bellow through my open portholes and I can hear the sea sounding all very slap-happy smacking against the hull with sloshing great splashes. After weeks of sailing across a sea as flat as a plank, we are rolling around again.

**DAY 44**

*The Pacific, 12 December*

In a plane it takes only eleven hours to cross eleven time zones. We are now eleven hours behind home and it's taken six weeks, though it feels more like three months. Three months is the amount of time it used to take for a ship to sail from England to New Zealand in the 1860s. That means if I had been a Scottish pioneer heading for the Tuapeka goldfield to search for my fortune in the gold-rich rivers of Central Otago, I would have reached South Island not that much more slowly than had I waited 140 years to catch a Russian freighter with twin diesel Wartsila Sulzer engines with a shaft power of 15,446 kw and a Kamewa CCP four-blade propeller the size of a windmill. I think this is called development gone round-the-bend bonkers. But whatever it is, I'd rather be on a time-reversing boat trip than on a limbo-land airliner where the only events that feel real are the taking off and landing and being sick (I don't make a good flyer). Everything else is just neither here nor there suspension.

The temperature has dropped ten degrees from the high nineties to the high eighties. I even had to pull a sheet over me last night. This morning I was struck with a dose of shivery goosebumps. Mickael, who is still on board with Xavier until the final French ammo dump in Nouméa, ran a finger over my goosebumped arm (I nearly passed out with excitement) and told me that in France they call goosebumps *chaire de poule* – skin of chicken. I'm now holding my breath wondering what else I can entice Mickael to touch, chicken skinned or not.

**DAY 45**

*The Pacific, 13 December*

Josef and Hardmut are not looking happy. There's a lot of furrowing of brows and scratching of heads going on. They now seem to be spending more time in the bar drinking than in the engine room tinkering. I think it's safe to surmise from this that the engine repairs are not going particularly swimmingly. Or more to the point, they are not going anywhere at all. It seems they have got something jammed. On top of this, a wrong tool has been ordered. This is not the time to go around asking whether my chain-removing tool or small rack-strapped bundle of 4 mm zip ties would be of any use. Frosty faces are much in evidence. The atmosphere around the Germans and captain and chief engineer is like treading on ice. I'm tiptoeing around, doing my best to keep out of their way. All unhelpful comments I'm keeping well under wraps.

I think Gary must have been having a hot flush because on his daily email he was coming over all a bit mechanically minded. 'Sounds like your engineers should be applying some heat to the offending gear wheel. Expansion is an engineer's best friend when moving interference fit components.'

Pardon?

'Or use a zip tie and a couple of packers, perhaps from a packet of cornflakes.'

Ah, this was more like it. He was now alluding to the fact that whenever I've been in a tight squeeze with Gary, he has always managed to mend something (broken bikes, wonked tents, ill-fitting latches, explosively jetting toilet cisterns) with the simple concoction of a zip tie and small piece of cardboard. And it's been causing us much overblown amusement ever since.

Opting to keep all cornflake packet tricks to myself (I couldn't see them going down well with hard-faced Hardmut and Josef) and to try to find out just what the sweet fanny adams is going on with the jammed engine, I cornered Vitali in the gunk tank shortly after he had belly-flopped on top of me again. This is the general gist of what he told me among the slopping sloshes that slapped back and forth as the ship tipped and tilted, though I could have quite a lot of it round the wrong way – it was all rather sloshy down there. Josef and Hardmut are using a special 20 tonne hydraulic press which generates 2000 bar (*not* 2000 psi – very important differentiation, said Vitali; I said, I know, as I am well acquainted with my bars and psi's following frequent encounters with my bicycle pump). The Germans are using this 20 tonne press to try to push a gear ring off a shaft (they have to slide it on to a mandrel) but because there is a slight gap between the shaft and the mandrel, this causes the pressure to drop to 500 bar. They have managed to move the gear wheel ring thing about an inch. And it is now stuck. They can't get it back on, and they can't get it back off. (I've been in a similar position myself with the fixed cup of my bottom bracket – and believe me, it's not an enviable position to be in.) Apparently, there's a high-pressure grease pump which feeds the inside of the gear ring thing that facilitates sliding it off onto the mandrel, preventing something else sliding onto something else which could then slide somewhere else where it shouldn't be sliding. So, in essence, there's quite a lot of sliding to be doing where there currently isn't any sliding being done. Sorry if I'm coming over all a little technical here with my slidings. I think it's a safer bet just to take you back to the more familiar ground of the Manchester tart.

Yes, the now legendary Manchester tart has made yet another appearance at the dinner table. Ham Man was so depressed about the non-working of the engine that he actually tried some. He took one mouthful and declared it tasted like plastic bags. I'm going to preserve a slice in formaldehyde to send to Ian for old times' sake. Who knows, it could make him quite nostalgic for his days at sea in a tub.

## DAY 46

*The Pacific, 14 December*

We're about to enter the confusing state of the International Date Line, that lovely kinked line of 180° longitude that means we're 12 hours different from GMT. As we are crossing the line from east to west I think we're supposed to add 24 hours and omit a day and then walk around in a daze wondering where it's gone. Or there again, maybe we're meant to subtract 24 hours and repeat a day and then wander around thinking: I'm sure I've been here before. Which is what I tend to do most of the time on this boat anyway.

So at dawn this morning I peered over the side looking for Lines of International Dates but all I found was a sea trembling with colour, the messy rifts of waves collapsing in on each other from every direction in a state of heady confusion. The sky was looking as equally shambolic, loaded with great tumblings of clouds that have spent all day banking up from the horizon like airborne glaciers. It's very easy to stare at this for hours. And I do.

Ham Man and the Frenchmen made no appearance at break-fast (rumour has it they are feeling a bit seasick with all the bouncing around) so I just had Llewellyn and Eleanor to myself. Oh joy! Llewellyn was in a bit of a heavy mood, telling me I was at a very deci-sive time in my life. He thinks I have only the rest of the voyage to decide whether I keep doing what I'm doing (i.e. silly things on my bike around the world) or go home to Gary from New Zealand and 'settle down'.

'Your relationship with Gary can't possibly work,' he told me, 'if you spend so much time apart. Eleanor and I have scarcely been out of each other's sight in forty years.'

'Blimey! Poor Eleanor!' I said. Llewellyn gave me one of his glowering looks, whereas Eleanor gave a little smile before quickly dabbing the corners of her mouth back into a semblance of seriousness with her napkin.

Llewellyn said, 'If you're serious about Gary, Josie, you've got to be serious about your relationship.'

'Gary and me are fine, thanks, Llewellyn,' I said. 'We like having room to manoeuvre.'

Llewellyn didn't look very satisfied. 'You've got to really search your soul,' he said, 'for what you want from this life before it's too late.'

'Llewellyn,' I said, 'you're making me feel as if I'm in the psychiatrist's chair when all I want to do is eat my kipper. I don't want to search for anything. I just like letting it happen.'

By lunchtime Ham Man had appeared, looking decidedly bleary eyed. Once he'd regained consciousness he told us that earlier on he had been on his ham radio and learnt some news: Saddam Hussein had been captured hiding in a hole of rubble in his hometown. Although he had a stash of guns with him he surrendered without a fight. Apart from the German cannibal, this is the only bit of news we've heard in weeks, so you'd have thought we would be quite excited to hear something of the outside world. Instead, we were more interested to learn that Chief Phil has managed to get the bit of engine that was jammed on, off. What a breakthrough! Means we're now back at square one, though square two may not be too far behind. As a result of this development I said, 'What a spot of luck!'

Llewellyn, feeling all semantically inclined, pounced on that statement and said, 'There's no such thing as luck, only circumstance.'

I said, 'Well, luck and circumstance go together because circumstances can lead to luck – either good luck or bad luck.'

'Give me an example, then,' said Llewellyn.

'All right,' I said. 'I'd say we've been very lucky that we haven't yet sunk. Especially given the unlucky circumstances of broken engines and uncooperative lifeboats.'

Llewellyn said, 'Can you pass the mustard?'

So I did. And that was that. Because the next thing Llewellyn said was, 'Don't forget I can remember the future.' There's really not a lot you can say to that, because if Llewellyn possesses these powers to do what he thinks he can do, then he knows what I'm about to say, so there's not much point in saying it. Though I did ask him if we were going to come across another Manchester tart before this trip is out. It's always best to be prepared when it comes to shocking puddings.

Around 5 p.m. Tonga passed off our starboard bow. That means that not far away is the Kermadec-Tonga Trench, a precipitous crack in the ocean floor extending from just north of New Zealand to south of Western Samoa. It's here that the westward-drifting Pacific plate folds and crunches beneath and into the Indo-Australian plate, causing the earthquakes and volcanoes that make this area part of the Pacific's tempestuously volatile Ring of Fire. The water off the Tongan island of Tafahi is 'only' about four miles deep (that's like cycling from the centre of London all the way out to the Hanger Lane gyratory system, which, if you've ever done it, feels like quite a hike), though down further south, near the Kermadec islands, the water is almost seven miles to the bottom (that's like cycling from the centre of London all the way out to Roberts Cycles in East Croydon, which, if you've ever done it, feels even further). The deepest part of the ocean yet recorded is in parts of the Mariana trench (off the Philippines) where at 36,161 feet below sea level, the seabed plunges almost twenty-five per cent further towards the bowels of the earth than Mount Everest soars towards the sky. At these depths the water is pitch-black and in the oozes there exist strange creatures that have only occasionally been sighted from deep-sea submersibles, though many still remain unseen and unknown.

Incidentally, Tonga's Tafahi is the closest populated island in the world to the western side of the International Date Line. This means that because Tafahi lies to the west, and the world turns to the east, out of all the roosters in the world Tafahian roosters crowingly greet the world's new day first, whereas the Tafahians themselves are the first people in the world to tune in to the *Today* programme. Or whatever their local equivalent is.

I'd like to call in on Tonga. It's supposed to be a very friendly place. In fact, when Captain Cook came this way in the 1770s, his waterlogged imagination had obviously run dry because he named Tonga the Friendly Islands. You'd have thought he could have been a little more inventive and called them something like, say, the Chummy Islands. Or even the Matey Islands. Anyway, the Tongans seem to be very smiley people. When the coronation of the Queen (that's our rather demure-faced one, not their smiley one) was televised around the world in 1953, one of the guests who emerged as a popular personality was Tonga's Queen Salote, who grinned non-stop from an open carriage in pouring rain. Even if she was thinking, 'Bloody weather – who'd come to bloody England for a bloody holiday?' she certainly didn't show it, which has got to be the ultimate sign of true star celebrity.

Along with being friendly, Tongans are also rather large. According to the World Health Organization, Tonga – along with the South Pacific island of Nauru – has the largest obesity problem in the world. Until recently King Taufa'ahau Tupou IV weighed in at some 31½ stone (194 kg), making him the world's weightiest monarch. What a magnificent lardy achievement! Today though, he is half the man he once was, having shed 15 stone after a diet and exercise plan. Women on one of the islands of Tonga average 5 foot 4 inches tall and weigh around 12 stone. That's a lot of love handles to the pound. If Captain Cook drifted along this way today, he could call Tonga the Tubby Islands, or maybe even the Portly Islands, both of which have a rather nice nautical ring to them.

Early evening, Chief Phil appeared on the monkey deck with several bottles of beer in hand. He was in an uncharacteristically good mood. This meant he was uncharacteristically talkative. (For most of the time, extracting words out of Phil is like squeezing the last of the toothpaste out of the tube – a struggle.)

'It's been a worrying time,' said Phil, draining a beer in about two slurps flat. 'A job that should have taken two hours, has taken all week.'

But now that the jammed bit of engine was unjammed, Phil thought they should be able to get the whole thing going in about a day or two away from Nouméa. In other words, about half-an-hour out from Auckland.

I don't know what's got into Llewellyn but he's behaving even more oddly than usual. Tonight at dinner he said to me, in much the same way as he has said to me before, 'You don't want to see me angry. I can kill people by thought alone.'

Because I couldn't take a comment like that seriously, I suddenly decided to be on my best behaviour. I sat up Eleanor-straight, tucked my elbows in, talked only when spoken to, delicately dabbed the corners of my pursed mouth with my napkin, and when I'd finished said, 'Can I get down now, please?' Even Eleanor smirked.

I got up from the table with Ham Man and as soon as we were out of the room I burst out laughing. Ham Man said, 'What a wanker!'

An announcement was made tonight that the ship's clocks will go forward by 23 hours. Oh no! Time travelling confusion reigns!

**DAY 47**

*The Pacific, 16 December*

I went to sleep last night (Sunday) and woke up this morning and it was Tuesday. If that's the effect a simple 180° has on my sleep, I could do with a few more International Date Lines. Helps to make the days sail by.

I think the Date Line must be doing something strange to stir up the water because, among all the deep bluebottle blue, we keep hitting strange algae-green swathes of ocean. After the first green splodge sighting, and following a planking session with Mr Alex Sasha second officer Nepomnyashchikh, I saw a note on the chart which said that these weird green splodges were first noticed in 1944. How interesting. I think I might get Ham Man to hold my feet so I can lean out over the side and take a sample.

At lunch Llewellyn urged me to watch the video of *The Sixth Sense*. 'But you'll have to concentrate,' he said, 'which I know is hard for you as you've got a butterfly brain.'

'Better that than a thought-killing one,' I retorted, before being struck down dead.

Just in case you're wondering, I am actually very good at concentrating. For the past forty-seven days I've been concentrating very hard on the slop of the sea and what my plan of action would be if I found we were sinking. I haven't quite hit upon a satisfactory answer yet, but bear with me and I'll let you know when I have.

The temperature gauge has shot up again to scorching hot. The Frenchmen have taken to lying sprawled on the monkey deck in the broiling sun. They've told me they want to top up their tans before flying home to a wintry France from Nouméa. I don't know how they do it. It's way too hot for me. But I'm sticking it out in a narrow slice of swaying shade just so that I can gawp over the top of my Russian phrasebook (*Vi gahvahreetyee pah frahntsooskee?* – 'Do you speak French?') at Mickael, who lies with his legs splayed in a pair of shorts rolled up tight to his . . . erm . . . bits, leaving nothing to the imagination. It's a very nice sight.

In fact, it's a bit too nice for comfort.


At dinner Llewellyn told me that when he was young and stupid as a pilot in Africa during the war ('Now I'm old and stupid,' – you said it, mate) he and his fellow pilots would dare each other to do mad things. One time they had a dogfight for fun and nearly ended up killing each other. On another occasion, to fly as slowly as he could, Llewellyn flew into the wind doing about 60 mph, and then flew alongside a galloping giraffe, its head at cockpit level.

I ended up tonight lying on my camping mat on the floor of my cabin, propped up with pillows (I don't like chairs) watching *The Sixth Sense* – as instructed by Llewellyn. It's a long time since I've watched a film through my fingers. Thank goodness I'm safely enclosed on a rusty tub with thirty Russian crewmen and several containers of French high explosives, and not in a big house in Philadelphia with a cellar and a lunatic in the bathroom.

**DAY 48**

*The Pacific, 17 December*

What a relief. It's been cloudy all day. I had a French lesson today with Mickael, which among other things involved learning that a *pilier de bar* is a person who props up the bar (I can think of a few of those around here), and that a *vielle tau* is a gossiping old woman (am not quite sure what he's referring to here). That's the only printable vocab I can say I've learnt. Anything else might shock my mother.

Have got a pounding headache today, not helped by the fact that the ship is a brain-juddering cacophony of drilling, chiselling, beating, sawing, banging, hammering, knocking, filing, grinding, pounding, smashing and sanding. I'm not quite sure what's going on. Maybe we're leaking and everyone's running around like headless chickens plugging the holes.

It's amazing how far sound carries on a floating tub of metal. When Benji Evgrafov, the ship's electrician and general very handy man, was drilling five decks below my porthole, the noise ricocheted up the side of the superstructure to land in a skull-shattering vibration at the back of my eyeballs. That said, I don't begrudge Benji his drilling one drill bit. Specially not if he's preventing us from sinking. Benji is a lovely man. He's quiet, unassuming, big-hearted and has a face that reminds me of Mansour Bahrami, that comedian of an Iranian tennis player I saw once on telly who, to wrong foot his opponent, does things like twirling his racket on his head and juggling balls through his legs. Benji will do anything for anyone, particularly if it involves wire, electrical tape and bits of wood. Whenever Ham Man wants to rectify or modify his ham radio fishing-rod aerial, Benji is always on hand with his hodge-podge of transforming materials. The other night I was up on the monkey deck with Benji and fourth engineer Valeri Ananin (Japanese-truck-driving-across-Russia Vinnie Jones man). Valeri put an arm around Benji and said, 'Here is example of very good hardworking man! He no waste-a money on drink. All money he give to family to help very much.' Benji looked a little abashed but later told me all the money he made was going towards buying his daughter a flat in Archangel and putting his son through university.

Valeri, on the other hand, likes his drink a lot. But he's very funny and whenever I bump into him on the stairs or meet him up at the salad bowl department in the officers' mess we have these nonsensical conversations in Russian that get us nowhere. Mostly because I'm asking him, 'Waiter, may I have the bill, please?' as well as the number of kilometres to the nearest village and whether I can put my tent behind this bush.

Second engineer Vitali belly-flopped on top of me again this afternoon. As we gunk-tanked together, I took the opportunity of asking him directions to the nearest post office, as well as whether this water was drinkable and that I'd like to reserve a double room with a shower (which incidentally is a *dvighnoy* ***no*** *myer* ***s*** *dooshahm* – always a useful phrase to have up an armpit) and whether he had anything to declare (*oo vahs yehst' shtoleebah zahyahveet' diyah* **tahm***ahzhnyee* – an even more useful phrase to have about your person if you're about to share a room with a stranger), just to see whether my Russian sounded even remotely like anything it should sound like. Evidently it didn't because, apart from emitting a watery cackle of laughter, Vitali went on to tell me (in English) that in New Caledonia (or to be properly French about it, Nouvelle Calédonie) they have a tradition whereby if a woman hasn't given birth to a daughter by her fourth child, she will raise the fifth child as a daughter, even if it's a boy. This is because she needs someone around the house to help her do all the dirty work, I mean house-work. So if a boy comes along who happens to be the fifth son in a family with no girls, he'll grow up a little confused. I said to Vitali that I thought this happened in Fiji. Vitali said maybe it happens there too but he knows it also happens in New Caledonia because that's why around the port of Nouméa you see so many transves-tites.

## DAY 49

*The Pacific, 18 December*

Apart from the midnight blue, the sea today is more like the Atlantic – disturbed and chaotic. The rascally waves are all very unsystematic, rushing at each other from every quarter before colliding and collapsing with an untidy sizz of slop. The clouds are just as unruly and varied. Big bloated bottom-heavy ones roll in from the stern, while great warheads boil over in the sky way off the starboard bow. Then, far to the south, a tear in the sky exposes a ragged strip of blue behind a grubby curtain.

Ham Man is not happy with this churning sea at all. He finds it too wild and anarchic. He prefers a sheet of blue calm. But I love it, like I loved the dirty grey waves of the Atlantic piled high. It's exciting to watch a sea all at sixes and sevens with itself.

Down in the stuffy hot bowels of the ship, on my way to the gunk tank, I came across Natasha, the stewardess, in the squashed-in airless laundry room feeding sheets through an antiquated ironing press. She looked as tired and sad as she always does. We had a little chat and she mentioned, like she has mentioned to me many times before, her young brother who died a few years ago. But she has always been crying too hard to tell me what happened to him. This time I put my arm around her before getting her to have a sit down and a rest while I took over her role as a sheet-feeder. I proceeded to make such an expertly cack-handed job of it that she did something that she almost never does: she laughed. I love it when Natasha laughs. She looks so incredibly beautiful.

Did I tell you that almost every night on board I've been tying myself in yogic knots? I want to try to keep all bendy and pliable so that if I get knocked off my bike in New Zealand by a heap of stampeding sheep, I won't snap every bone in my body. In Gary's email he asked me whether I could get my leg over my shoulder yet. Err, not quite, but I'm not bad at getting my leg over other things. Like monkey deck railings and gunk tank steps.

Am getting a bit concerned about Gary's dietary needs. He told me that for tea tonight (or last night, or whatever day he's on that I'm not on) he had ten fish-fingers, four eggs, a tin of baked beans, a loaf of bread to mop it all up, and a hot pie from up the shop. Seems he has eaten exactly the same thing each night this week. More concerning than this is his state of mind. Says he's feeling a bit glum at the moment and thinks all the dark days are taking a toll on his jollity. 'I leave home in the dark, work in the dark (the bloke across the road has complained about the noise so we have to keep the door of the workshop shut) and get home in the dark. Nothing seems good at the mo and next year seems like a very long way away. Am missing your silliness. Yesterday I even had a day of emptiness and despair! What's happening next year, Jose? Are you writing the book out there or are you coming home to scribe your tome? Not sure yet which direction I'm heading for Christmas. Might go to Mum's. Needing you more today than ever.'

# 8

# *Are We There Yet?*

**DAY 50**

*Nouméa, 19 December*

Was up at 2 a.m. last night to watch the shadowy spot-lit shape of the New Caledonian pilot step off his jaunty little pilot boat and clamber about thirty feet up the hull-slung rope ladder. Because of the abundance of reefs lying in wait to rip a gash out of the bottom of the ship, it's a complicated four-hour pilotage to navigate a delicate course into Nouméa, and we needed this man badly.

Slowly, as night dissolved into dawn, revealing a hazardous fretwork of reef-encircled islands to go crashing headlong into, we inched our way towards La Grande Terre, the main island that is also called New Caledonia. La Grande Terre lives up to its French name, seeing as it's the fourth largest South Pacific country after Australia, New Zealand and Papua New Guinea. And from first impressions, as observed from the monkey deck in the early morning sun-rising light, it also seemed to live up to its English name of New Caledonia, looking like a misty and mountainous land of green and purple hills. It was Captain Cook who named the island in memory of his beloved Scotland when he landed here on his way to New Zealand in 1774. But Captain Cook was a long way behind the great voyaging canoes of the Melanesian people who arrived here two or three thousand years before. And Admiral Febvrier-Despointes was even further behind when, in 1853, he claimed New Caledonia as French territory. So I blame this man for us having to sit tentatively on board a ship-load of French ammunition for the past one-and-a-half months. Talking of which, what an amazing relief that we've actually made it here without someone accidentally setting all this ammo off (can't have my bike being blown into oblivion, you know). I can now breathe a little easier at night.

The first shock on docking in the polluted port of Nouméa was not the reception party of transvestites that disappointingly failed to materialise (well, breakfast time was probably a bit early in the day for them). Nor was it the highly toxic-looking and smelling blue flame flaring from the chimney of a waterfront mineral-processing factory across the water (New Caledonia has some of the world's largest known nickel deposits, plus large deposits of iron ore, chrome and other minerals). No, the sight that gave me a jarring jolt occurred when, sliding into our berth, we came to dock directly behind the vastness of the French-run CMA CGM *Matisse*. This was the same container ship that arrived after us in Tahiti, and left before us having unloaded and loaded stacks more tons of cargo. On top of that, this ship had already been all the way to New Zealand from Tahiti (that's about 2,500 miles), unloaded and loaded another titanic amount of containers, *and* sailed all the way up to Nouméa (another 1,500 miles) where it had unloaded and loaded several more sky-scraping towers of containers. We hadn't been docked for long when I saw the *Matisse* reeling in its spring lines and heading off and out again. As if that wasn't quite enough show of Gallic speedy TGV efficiency (yes, I know it's a ship, not a train), the *Matisse* had also spent a whole day in port doing nothing and going nowhere because of a one-day strike called for by the crew. And yet they were *still* steaming ahead of us in schedule. An exasperated Ham Man said,

'How much more of an Anglo-Franco two-fingered salute can ye have than tha'?'

Whereas I found all this really quite amusing, Ham Man went through the roof. Steam streamed from his ears like smoke from a funnel. His face burnt beetroot as veins on his temples bulged blue. Profanities poured from his mouth. It's just as well he didn't have much hair or else he would have pulled the whole lot out in huge angry handfuls. I felt it was best to steer clear of Ham Man in such a simmering state and took to my wheels.

Beneath a skull-burning sun I cycled off into the turgid waves of city traffic – hundreds of cars and trucks moored and congealed in a hot ocean of tarmac – overtaking and undertaking them in that liberating way that only a bicycle affords. Nouméa looks like a much tidier capital than Papeete, with a lot less visible poverty around. Further from the centre, a liquid rush of traffic flooded onto an artery of roads, which before long had dribbled itself into near extinction.

As on Tahiti, I rode my bike like a demon repossessed of its wheels. And as on Tahiti, I wondered how I could have survived so many weeks without riding. The sensational sensation of freedom and free power that cycling affords can work wonders on your endorphins. I don't mind where I'm cycling – snaking mountain roads, windy prairie flats, wet Wales, Hanger Lane gyratory systems. Just so long as I'm spinning along on my bike, I feel normal and I feel happy.

I felt much tempted to cycle the length and breadth of New Caledonia as the snippet I saw looked very becoming: palms, lagoons, reefs, come-hither beaches and hills of bird-whooping jungle. Although La Grande Terre is not particularly *grande* – 250 miles long and thirty miles wide with an enticing splattering of outer islands (the Loyalty Islands and the Isle of Pines) – I couldn't really tackle it if I had to be back on the ship by this evening ready for a possible departure that more possibly than not would not be departing.

In the 1960s the population of New Caledonia was 84,000; today, there are 210,000 inhabitants, of which more than two thirds live

in and around Nouméa. Nouméa is busy. Nouméa is also like Nice.
Or St Tropez. At least, parts of it are, especially around the city
seafront where there is a lot of Riviera-like money splashing
around: big yachts, big cars, big houses, big hotels and big apart-
ment blocks – all dripping in opulence. And all very different from
the days when New Caledonia served as a penal colony. Once it was
a land of punishment. Now it is a land of reward.

Back at the ship I discovered, not unexpectedly, that no one knew
when we would be leaving except that it would not be tonight. The
unloading and loading of containers was taking even longer than
usual because no dock cranes were available, which meant the
crew had to use the creaking slow ship cranes instead.

Another cruise ship was in – this one the P&O *Pacific Sky*, registered in London. But at least this one actually looked like a ship,
with a blunt stern and a pointy prow, and not some palatial extravaganza of a floating hotel. The passengers, as on the *Tahitian
Princess*, were mostly Americans and Aussies. This afternoon I
helped an American woman to find her way out of the port. She
was of an indeterminate vintage with no hips and scratchy hair the
colour of butterscotch Angel Delight. Somehow she had managed
to squeeze her well-upholstered body into a ruffled sundress
revealing her upper arms, which were splotched and doughy. She
told me her name was Lorraine and that her husband had died
earlier this year of a heart attack and that this was her first time
abroad and that she had been worried about doing something so
rash but her kids had said, 'Go for it, Mom!' I also learnt that she
lived in Portsmouth, Ohio. So as we weaved a path among the teetering maze of parked containers, I told her that I lived just up the
road from Portsmouth, England. Lorraine's Portsmouth, though,
differed notably in so far as it was nearly 500 miles from the sea.

## DAY 51

*Nouméa, 20 December*

Early this morning I walked into the emailing machine room, where Llewellyn was sitting stabbing crossly at the keyboard while Eleanor sat beside him, her legs crossed, demurely reading a copy of the *Daily Telegraph* she had picked up in town for about a fiver. Llewellyn turned and scowled at me.

'You don't look very happy, Llewellyn!' I said.

'I'm not!' he replied. 'It's the second day the email's not been working!'

He shoved back his chair and stormed out with a slam of the door. Eleanor and I exchanged an elevated eyebrow. She folded the paper neatly before heading off in pursuit of her volatile husband.

It was anybody's guess what time we would be off today. First it was 08.00 hours. Then 13.00. Then 18.00. In the event it was 20.00 hours. It made going out to get a hundred-mile cycle under my belt all very stop-start and bitty as I had to keep reporting back at boat base-camp to find out the latest happenings on the departure that wasn't happening. But I managed it in the end (very hot, sweaty, windy, tiring, palm tree-flapping fun) with just enough time left over for a quick whip round the Musée Territorial de Nouvelle-Calédonie. I'm not usually a museum person so all the cycle pulsating heat must have affected my head. But I'm glad it did or else I'd have missed a chance to admire a medley of musical instruments made from vegetable matter – dance whistles from coconut leaves, flutes from reeds, trumpets from conch shells, ankle rattles from the dried *Cycas circinalis* fruits that Kanak musicians would pound, tap, knock together or blow.

There were fig-bark beaters, too, and rustling women's dance skirts made of white bourao tree bark and pandanus roots. There were even 'water' stones (stones placed in fields to encourage water to gush from the earth), 'sun' stones (stones with holes that called for good weather for planting yams), 'banana' stones (phallic-type stones put in fields to allow banana plants to bear fruit all year long), and 'phallic' stones (banana-type stones placed in fields to allow a fruitful supply of phalluses for the girls to reap pleasure – sorry, I tell a lie; they were actually used in war rituals: after being passed over grasses and leaves, the phallic stones were rubbed on clubs to make them more powerful to bash people's brains out).

Oh no! In the entrance of the museum whom should I meet but Llewellyn and Eleanor. Was there no escape from the Lewellynors of this world? I braced myself for the impact of an insult but instead I got a raving running commentary relating to the contents of the museum. They both seemed to hold the exhibits in high esteem. But Llewellyn was not so raving about Nouméa. 'In the three years since we were last here,' he said, 'the city seems to have grown three times as busy and three times as big.'

On my way back to the boat I spotted Ham Man emerging from McDonald's. 'Well, I had to get the taste of that Manchester tart out of my mouth somehow,' he later told me.

**DAY 52**

*The Pacific, 21 December*

New Caledonia is a lot closer to Australia than it is to New Zealand. I was rather hoping I could persuade the captain to drop me overboard somewhere in the vicinity of the Great Barrier Reef (Flinder's Passage would do nicely) where I could hitch a lift ashore from a passing shark-scarred surfer before nipping down the coast to Tassie. But before I could say kookaburra, we were cutting a course across the 23.5° S latitude of the Tropic of Capricorn into a sea that sparkled like crinkled foil. Though the sparkling didn't last. Before long a froth of clouds on the horizon had been swept upon us by a knifing southerly wind turning the waves to a chaotic shamble of tatters. Just when I was getting used to the heat, the cold is back with a whack.

Hardmut and Josef abandoned ship (and engine) in Nouméa. As did Mickael and Xavier. It's odd to think that all four are by now back in their European homes, while we're still here bobbing about with a conked-out engine.

I was on the bridge this morning with Young Alex when he pulled out a handful of photographs to show me. They were of a very crunched-up car lying on its roof in a dried riverbed. 'I was driving that!' said Alex, a little too cheerfully for the circumstances. This is how he got the car into that sorry inverted position. On his last voyage around the world on the *Speybank*, Alex got friendly with some cadets on board and told them that he knew of this fantastic beach on Vanuatu and that he would take them there. 'I was going on about it for weeks,' said Alex. So when at last the ship docked in Port Vila (the capital), he hired a car and set off with the cadets (there were five in the car altogether) down a bumpy dirt road in search of this long-awaited South Pacific paradise. 'I was driving along,' said Alex, 'when I hit this bloody great pothole. The front wheels turned one way so I turned the steering wheel the other and away we all flew!' Airborne off a bridge.

Amazingly everyone managed to crawl out of the smashed-up vehicle alive, no one sustaining anything worse than a few cuts and bruises. A small group of locals had seen the whole thing happen and stood by looking bemused. When a busload of locals trundled along the road, Alex and the cadets crammed themselves on board for a lift back to town.

A few moments later, an American tour party arrived at the scene of the incident. Some of the tour party were off the *Speybank*. They climbed out of their bus to take pictures of the crashed car lying upside-down in the riverbed. The small group of locals who had witnessed the whole thing told the Americans that two people had been killed. Back on the *Speybank*, the Americans showed their pictures of the sights they had seen of Vanuatu to Alex. When they got to the photos of the smashed car, Alex said, like he had said to me, 'I was driving that!'

'I had to pay the rental company $800 for the car,' Alex told me, 'and I never did make it to that beach that I had been raving about to the cadets for the whole trip!'

Mealtimes are now even more of a struggle, as Ham Man and Lewellynor are the only ones left on my table. None of them is exactly a bundle of laughs at the moment because, despite New Zealand being only a couple of Cook's petrel flight days away (I think I spotted one of these makes of petrel today – notable for jazzy wing markings), they are all too depressed about the possibility of spending Christmas on board (our day of arrival is still up in the air). A look of glumness prevails and there is much constant fretting about hotel bookings and ferry bookings and car-hire bookings that have gone up the spout. So instead I turn to the Russians, who can always be relied upon for a little light entertainment.

'**Doktahrah**,' I said to fourth engineer Valeri as we rubbed elbows over the cheeseboard on the sideboard, '*vi mnyeh **mozhehtyeh** pahkahbzaht' nah kahrtyeh gdyeh yah? Spahseebah. Yehst' oo vahs soop s kooreetsay?*' ('Doctor, can you show me on the map where I am? Thank you. Have you any chicken soup?')

Valeri replied by giving me his tomato. Which probably means there's a little more room for linguistic improvements.

**DAY 53**

*The Pacific, 22 December*

This morning I found the email machine back in operational order. One of my emails was from Mum. She had sent it two days ago. At first I was excited to hear from her, but then as I read what she had written, my excitement turned to shock. I stared at the words, reading them over and over again, yet I still couldn't believe what she was telling me.

'Dear Jose,' she wrote. 'We've had some terrible news. Jonnie was killed in a car crash yesterday. Dave rang us and said Mel had gone to be with Beverley. It's such a terrible thing to happen, especially before Christmas. I know how you don't like things being kept from you and although in one sense Dad and me didn't want to tell you just now, I know I would not have been able to write to you without saying anything. In case you are tempted, you mustn't alter your cycling plans in any way – there is nothing anyone can do. Beverley and Richard will have many around to try and comfort them, but the whole thing seems truly terrible. More news soon, lots of love Mum.'

Jonnie was the nineteen-year-old son of Beverley and Richard. Beverley is the sister of Mel. Mel is my brother Dave's wife, though Mel and me are like sisters. I'm very close to Beverley, too. A few days before I left for Dunkirk, I cycled up to her and Richard's to say goodbye and have a little party in the back garden. Dave and Mel were there with their three young boys, Fred, Alex and Jake. As was Charmian (Jonnie's sister) and her boyfriend Ben. And of course Jonnie was there.

After I'd read Mum's email, I went up to the monkey deck and slumped in a corner staring out to sea for hours. I didn't want to see anyone or speak to anyone, and I didn't go down to eat because I felt a sick hollowness shaking me to the core. I kept thinking of my last words with Jonnie and my last hug with Jonnie and I couldn't believe he was dead. It didn't seem fair. Beverley is too lovely a person to have this happen to her. I can't imagine how totally devastated she and Richard and Charmian must be feeling. Jonnie was still living at home, driving back and forth to his job as a builder's apprentice, and his bedroom next to Bev and Richard's will be just as he left it on Friday morning. He and Bev were so incredibly close. Whenever he got back from work he would do a little whistle to let her know he was home. I don't know how Beverley is ever going to survive without him.

Finally, I went to see the captain to ask if I could buy a $33 phone card and have permission to use the satellite phone later. He noticed I wasn't my usual self and asked if I was okay. Suddenly I couldn't say anything. He sat me down in a chair and put a hand on my shoulder. I tried to tell him what had happened but no words came out. My eyes filled with tears and the cabin turned blurred. I tried not to blink. I couldn't talk. It felt as if I'd had all the air crushed out of me. I kept trying to catch breath, trying to suppress all emotions. I didn't want to cause a scene.

The captain just waited until I was ready. And then I told him. He listened and then said that this is always one of their fears, of something terrible happening to a relative when they are at sea, because when you're stuck out in the middle of an ocean, nothing can be done.

And it's that feeling of uselessness and hopelessness and inability to do anything to help which is just adding to the awfulness of it all. All I want is to be with Bev and Mel and instead I'm stuck on a lump of slow-moving metal in the middle of the sea on the opposite side of the world.

We are now thirteen hours ahead of home so I had to wait quite a while until I could phone Mum without jolting her awake in the middle of the night. But at last I made a crackly connection. She sounded so relieved to hear from me, but it was a relief soon swamped by the sudden death of Jonnie.

Tonight the cloud that had hung heavy and troubled all day suddenly broke and fractured towards the horizon into a sky-splintering eruption of fire. For a few brief moments the sun appeared as an achingly brilliant ball of crimson flame, tearing a deep rip of cadmium light across the water towards us. The ocean seemed to be coming apart. It was the most mesmerising sunset of the voyage so far and I felt certain Jonnie was up there and part of it. Seconds later the sun slid over the edge of the world and darkness quickly fell.

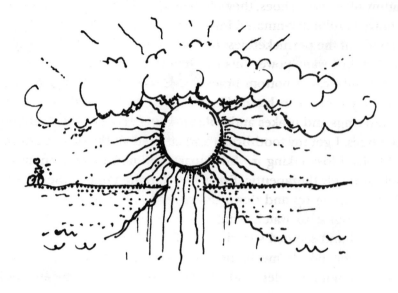

**DAY 54**

*The Pacific, 23 December*

The Christmas decorations are up in the bar and the officers' mess. Everyone is suddenly acting very festively jolly. It looks like we're going to make Auckland by tomorrow morning. So tonight's the last night on board for us four passengers. There's a boozy session planned for this evening (drinks on the ship) with the officers and Russian crew, followed by a Christmassy dinner. Even Llewellyn and Ham Man are smiling. I'm looking at all this going on around me, but walking around in another world. I'm not excited about anything. Not even setting foot and wheel on New Zealand. When someone so young and gorgeous dies, it makes everything else seem pointless.

It was calm and blue and hot all day, with mile-high cumulus battleships floating on the horizon. Purser David gave me a little lecture today about how fastidiously nit-picking New Zealand customs are and that if they find the merest speck of dirt on my tent or my bike or my shoes, they will haul the offending item off to be sprayed and exterminated into all oblivion. I've heard many stories about the pernicketiness of Kiwi customs. So, as I like my bike and didn't want power jets of chemicals being sprayed up my nicely lubricated bottom bracket, I carried my bike up on deck with my tool kit in hand. Here I spent hours dissecting all my chain rings and brakes and polishing every spoke and scrubbing the tyres. I got my toothbrush and cleaned all threads and heads of bolts. I love taking my bike apart, and now more than ever it felt strangely therapeutic. Every now and then one of the Russian crew running up and down the nearby steps would see me and divert course to watch what I was doing. They all joked and laughed and seemed surprised that a girl could take something apart even faintly mechanical and put it back together again. Fourth engineer Valeri said maybe I might like to come and look at the engine next.

I bought another phone card today and in the few minutes it allows I spoke to Dave. Bev was too upset to talk to me at that moment, but she had told Dave to tell me not to come home, to cycle round New Zealand for Jonnie. Mel said Jonnie wouldn't have wanted me to come all the way home from Auckland just for him, 'not after spending two silly months on a boat trying to get there, Jose!' Dave said the same. He said there was nothing anyone can do. 'All Bev wants is to have Jonnie back, and that's not going to happen.' He said Mel was going to stay with Bev, while he took the boys to Mum and Dad's to have as normal a Christmas as possible.

I didn't feel like going to the Christmas drinks or dinner tonight so I stayed by myself up on the monkey deck in the wind. But then the ship's electrician, Benji Evgrafov, came looking for me. He had heard from the captain what had happened. Draping an arm around my shoulders, he said, 'Life has to go on.' Then he said, 'We Russians want you down there!' So I went down to the bar with him and, switching on to automatic pilot, managed to join in half-heartedly with the crew. And I'm glad I did, because that was the last chance I'd have to see most of them.

**DAY 55**

*Auckland, 24 December*

When I climbed up on to the monkey deck at dawn this morning I was soaked within seconds. Sea and sky met and touched in a uniformity of grey as a heavy rain fell. I stood in a stabbing wind, the rain falling slantwise and stinging, as we weaved a path through dark smudgy outcrops of islands. Islands that would have looked green if they hadn't looked so grey. Welcome to New Zealand at the height of summer. Yet I hadn't felt so cold since Dunkirk.

By 6 a.m. the coat-hanger of Auckland Harbour Bridge had ghosted out of the murk and appeared to be bending in the socking wind. As did the giant hypodermic syringe of the Sky Tower. Moments later it seemed as if the *Speybank* had overshot the buffers and invaded the city by docking in the heart of downtown. Suddenly there was a high-rise skyline hanging above my head, and ships, shouts, noise, cranes, cars, coaches, people all around. Heaving spring lines with heavy 'monkey's fists' on the end tightened and creaked like painful knee joints. The gangway was lowered and hit its little slice of New Zealand with a clattering sigh of relief. Shiny-booted customs men with fluorescent yellow coats and no-messing expressions clambered up the greasy wet steps and disappeared into the captain's quarters. So did immigration officials and quarantine officers from the Ministry of Agriculture and Fisheries.

Hours went by. Ham Man was itching with impatience to get off. Llewellyn and Eleanor were still packing their multiple supplies of cruise gear into suitcases the size of Spain. I shook hands with the captain, had a few quick hugs and goodbyes with the crew, and then carted my bike and loaded panniers down a multiple of steps to the poop deck, all poised and ready for the great escape. After a while a young muscular and suntanned official appeared and said, 'Hi, how's it going?'

'Very nicely, thank you,' I said. 'Though it's a bit early days to tell.'

Ham Man laughed. I think he was nervous. We had joked about this moment on lots of occasions, wondering what the immigration men would make of us. There was me with troublesome bikes and muddy tents and porridge oats and self-defence gas sprays, and there was Ham Man with a suitcase-load of suspect radioing and transmitting apparatus and a rucksack containing the weird protuberances of fishing-rod aerials.

'Okay, who's first?' asked the customs man.

'He is,' I said, indicating Ham Man. 'He's probably the easier of the two and he's got a ferry to catch.'

So the customs man asked Ham Man a few questions, what was he carrying and what were his plans, and then let him go, just like that. I ask you! He didn't even look in his bags. I wanted to say, 'Errm, excuse me Mr Official Man. Don't you think you ought to have a little rummage in Ham Man's suitcase? You might find something quite interesting in there.' But in the event, all I had time for before MOM man turned his attention to me was a quick hug. Ham Man then lifted his load of radioing rods out past the crew's messroom and vanished through the door.

Before MOM man started on me I thought I had better declare that I had a couple of suspect substances on board. Better that than a fine of NZ$100,000 or five years in the clink.

'One is a pack of unopened porridge oats,' I said. 'The other is a little self-defence gas-spray canister that I bought in France. It makes me feel better when I'm camping alone in the middle of nowhere.'

MOM man turned over the packet of oats in his hands and declared them fine. But as for my spray he said he was very sorry, but as it was illegal, he would have to confiscate it.

'Oh well, never mind,' I said. 'I'll just clonk anyone unpleasant over the head with my bike pump instead.'

MOM man laughed. 'Good on yer!' he said, which I thought was rather matey of him. He then gave my bike a once over and seemed very impressed at its shininess.

'Awesome!' he said. 'Looks like new!'

I thought 'awesome' sounded like a bit of an overblown adjective for the occasion, but I let the comment pass.

'It does help to have just had fifty-five days to do nothing else but clean it,' I said by way of explanation.

Next my tent was called for. MOM man shook it out and climbed inside, inspecting all the corners for the likes of gypsy moths, piratical stowaways and illegal immigrants. My pegs were touched and sniffed.

'Where did you last use these?' he asked.

'Denmark,' I replied, wondering if he could smell the sterilised taint of Scandinavia, 'in a field outside Esbjerg.'

That seemed a good enough answer for him because he suddenly said, 'Okay, great stuff. You can pack up and leave when you're ready.'

So I did.

Outside, a full-blooded rain was falling from a sky that looked like a morgue. After nearly two months of imprisonment I was suddenly free to find my feet in a foreign land. Here was New Zealand, a country I had been trying to reach on my wheels for years. And now that I was here, all I wanted was Jonnie.

What I got, though, was Mr Alex Sasha second officer Nepomnyashchikh. He had momentarily broken away from his unloading duties to give me a quick hug and say goodbye. 'Keep up the planking!' I said.

Mr Alex Sasha second officer Nepomnyashchikh gave me one of his little raised eyebrow smiles. Then, putting his face very close to my ear, he whispered, 'Merry Christmas trees!'

# Portscript

After a journey like this, I suppose the inevitable question is: would I do it again? The answer? No fear. Not on your nelly.

Actually, I would. I would love to. I would jump (ship?) at the chance, though were I to travel on board the *Speybank* I might just pack my own lifeboat, and check that Llewellyn was not within radar-blipping distance.

Despite the raft of delays and setbacks and breakdowns, not to mention the surplus of Manchester tarts, I can heartily recommend Bank Line to those who are not averse to a little adventurous rough and tumble. Their four cargo ships offer a fascinatingly slow way to travel the world and provide a unique service by calling at many of the islands in the South Pacific.

My advice? A strong stomach helps, but is not essential. As is a body that does not go bananas with lack of exercise. A good working knowledge of hypersensitive vacuum toilets would come in handy, as would a predilection for boobies.

On that note, may a fair wind blow your way – but not too favourable, because you want a little fun. And big waves.

Josie Dew, October 2005

# Ship Details

| | |
|---|---|
| *Name*: | MV *Speybank* |
| *Type of vessel*: | General Cargo with Ro-Ro facilities |
| *Previous life*: | Originally built as Russian icebreaking freighter (*Okha*) for use in the Arctic regions of Russia |
| *Flag*: | British |
| *Registered*: | Douglas, Isle of Man |
| *Built*: | Helsinki, Finland, 1983 |
| *Length*: | 174 metres |
| *Width*: | 24.5 metres |
| *Moulded depth*: | 15.2 metres |
| *Gross tonnage*: | 18,663 tonnes |
| *Net tonnage*: | 10,372 tonnes |
| *Dead weight*: | 19,943 tonnes |
| *Container capacity*: | 576 TEU |
| *Service speed*: | 17.5 knots |
| *Engine*: | 2 × Wartsila Sulzer – 14ZV 40/48 (diesels, 20,999 bhp) |
| *Propeller*: | Kamewa CCP 4 Blade |
| *Cargo oil capacity*: | 6,000 tonnes |
| *Fresh water*: | 785.8 cubic metres |
| *Ballast water*: | 4,069.5 cubic metres |

*For the latest news about Josie's travels and
information on all her books,
please visit her website at:*

www.josiedew.co.uk